AGAINST THRIFT

ALSO BY JAMES LIVINGSTON

*The World Turned Inside Out: American Thought and
Culture at the End of the 20th Century*

*Origins of the Federal Reserve System: Money, Class,
and Corporate Capitalism, 1890–1913*

*Pragmatism and the Political Economy of Cultural
Revolution, 1850–1940*

*Pragmatism, Feminism and Democracy: Rethinking
the Politics of American History*

AGAINST THRIFT

Why CONSUMER CULTURE Is GOOD for the Economy, the Environment, and Your Soul

JAMES LIVINGSTON

BASIC BOOKS

A Member of the Perseus Books Group

New York

Published by Basic Books
A Member of the Perseus Books Group
387 Park Avenue South
New York, NY 10016

Books published by Basic Books are available at special discounts for bulk purchases in the United States by corporations, institutions, and other organizations. For more information, please contact the Special Markets Department at the Perseus Books Group, 2300 Chestnut Street, Suite 200, Philadelphia, PA 19103, or call (800) 255-1514, or e-mail special.markets @perseusbooks.com.

Designed by Pauline Brown
Typeset in 11 point Berling LT by the Perseus Books Group

Library of Congress Cataloging-in-Publication Data
Livingston, James, 1949–
    Against thrift : why consumer culture is good for the economy, the environment, and your soul / James Livingston.
        p.   cm.
    ISBN 978-0-465-02186-4 (hardback)—ISBN 978-0-465-02809-2 (ebook) 1. Consumption (Economics)—United States. 2. Financial crises—United States—History—21st century. 3. Income distribution—United States. I. Title.
    HC110.C6L58 2011
    339.4'70973—dc23

                                                                    2011021759

10 9 8 7 6 5 4 3 2 1

For E. S. and L. K.

Contents

Introduction:
Waiting for Galileo

THE DOWNSIDE OF THRIFT

We're the most affluent people on the planet, us Americans—our choices among foods, ideas, clothes, schools, and destinations are almost without limit—and we love to shop. But we also know that consumer culture is bad for us. How come?

In a word: *excess*. We're afraid that we consume too many resources, that we save too little of our incomes, and that meanwhile we produce almost nothing of real value. We're afraid that we can't observe any limits on our consumption of goods, so that every substance, even food, begins to feel addictive, and every urge, even sex, begins to feel compulsive. When armed with credit cards, it seems, we're unwilling to defer the immediate gratification of our desires, and we're thus unable to "save for a rainy day." We're also afraid that we're mere cattle—herded by corporations and "branded" by their admen. We're especially afraid that consumer culture is making us fat.

So, yes, we love to shop, most avidly between Thanksgiving and Christmas. Still, we know that in the long run, consumer culture is bad for the economy, the environment, and our souls. We sometimes express this split in our personalities by complaining about the "commercialization" of Christmas, typically when we're fighting crowds of last-minute shoppers. More often we apologize to ourselves, among others, for buying things we didn't really need, or for indulging a child's ad-induced desire for a molded plastic toy that will never decompose. Complaining or apologizing, we're divided by very different orders of feeling. On the one hand, we experience the pleasure of buying, using, and giving away the things on the shopping list. On the other, we know without thinking that the same things already contain a barbaric history of exploitation—"Made in China," the label says—and foretell an ugly future of mountainous landfills.

In this book, I make the case for consumer culture: why it's actually good for the economy, the environment, and our souls, among other things. In this sense, I'm trying to heal the split in our personalities by demonstrating that less work, less thrift, more leisure, and more spending are the cures for what ails us.

So I make two basic arguments: one about the economy and the other about the culture, using a strategy that keeps me coming back to the historical record.

First, sustainable economic growth doesn't require more saving by households and more investment by CEOs, bankers, traders, and fund managers. In other words, more consumption is the key to balanced growth in the future. That's right: we need to save less and spend more. Just to begin with, a much larger dose of consumer spending is absolutely necessary to prevent the kind of economic catastrophe that still racks the domestic and international economies. That new dosage requires a redistribution of national income away from profits, which don't always get invested, toward wages, which almost always get spent. This new course of treatment does more than invert the supply-side cure for our economic ailments—cut taxes on profits, let private enterprise prevail!—because it assumes, in view of the historical record, that profits won't be productively invested. That's right: *higher profits almost never lead to more investment, more jobs, and more growth*. In fact, there's no demonstrable link between private investment and economic growth, so cutting taxes on corporate profits is pointless at best and destructive at worst. We might as well stop pretending that there is such a link.

Second, consuming goods is as morally complex and significant as producing goods. Making things—the work that requires tools and skills and time—is no more meaningful than buying and using things. In fact, work as such is *less* important than, say, buying and driving a car, or choosing and wearing that little black dress. (It turns out, in any event, that the kind of work we typically imagine as the obvious alternative to

The Mall is what we do at our leisure, after hours: it's already taken up residence in the neighborhood of consumer culture, where you don't get paid for what you produce.) As part of this polemic against work—against alienated labor—I demonstrate in Chapters 5 and 6 that consumer culture doesn't siphon political energies and fragment social movements by "privatizing" experience: instead it grounds a new politics by animating both new solidarities and new individualities. In the same spirit, I show in Chapters 7 and 8 that advertising—the headquarters of consumer culture—speaks the last utopian idiom of our time because it urges us to create identities unbound by work.

The order of this argument is determined by a simple assumption: I can't explain the downside of thrift—or the morality of spending—unless I first convince you that the Great Depression and the recent economic crisis are comparable events, both of them caused by an excess of profits and a shortage of wages, or too much saving and not enough spending. That's what Part 1 of the book is about. It's where I explain how the available explanations of the catastrophe are inadequate—and why the story we tell about the origins of economic crisis will dictate the practical effects we call public policy (Chapters 1 and 2). It's also here, in Part 1, that I use the historical record to explain why cutting taxes on high-end incomes and corporate profits in the name of increased investment is worse than pointless. And finally, it's where I explain why "saving for a rainy day" is just as destructive (Chapters 3 and 4). My case for the morality of spending in Part 2 doesn't make much sense in the absence of these explanations.

With or without Part 1, it's a hard case to make because everyone knows how and why to defer gratification. All adults—not just parents—have a powerful psychological urge to put their desires on hold, and that urge makes us receptive to the notion that we'd better be saving more and spending less, just like all the mainstream economists and reputable journalists keep telling us to. We know what will happen to our bank accounts, our waistlines, and our marriage vows if we stop listening to their insistent voice of reason.

Even so, we've reached the point where we have to confront our fears about consumer culture, because the renunciation of desire, the deferral of gratification, saving for a rainy day—call it what you want— has become dangerous to our health. To heal ourselves, we need to spend more freely, to live less anxiously, more easily and generously, with ourselves and with Nature. (I, for one, don't believe that there's much left of Nature—merely planting crops changes the chemical composition of the original soil—but I'm willing to entertain the possibility in the name of an inhabitable environmental future, and, as you'll see in Chapter 9, I think consumer culture is a promising path to environmental integrity.)

Let me put it more plainly, and way more polemically, in the terms first offered us by Sigmund Freud (soon I'll be citing Karl Marx and anybody else who can help me make this case). If I'm right about the economics of the case, we could learn to live with a lot less repression of our instincts, drives, and desires—and this learning experience might produce a new human nature that is more at ease in the world. That would be a human nature moved by a "double consciousness," as W. E. B. Du Bois put it, a human being informed by a constant awareness of the needs of others, whether animal, vegetable, or mineral. But I must admit that learning to live with a lot less repression could produce a human nature moved only by compulsive desire for the new experience, the next big thing, whatever it may be. This would be a human being that had replaced civilization and its discontents with hell on earth, where mastery of a video game means intellectual attainment.

The thing is, we just don't know what will happen when the renunciation of desire and the deferral of gratification and the delay of satisfaction are no longer necessary to organize society and build character—let alone when renunciation and deferral and delay have become destructive of both society and character. That's why consumer culture makes us so uneasy, and that's why it's worth treating as a moral universe still in the making.

THINKING WITH COMMODITIES

Throughout the book I assume that the philosopher Friedrich Nietzsche got it right when he observed that economic calculations were the origins of thought, but didn't meanwhile reduce all cognition to the rationalization of material interests: "Setting prices, determining values, contriving equivalences, exchanging—these preoccupied the earliest thinking of man to so great an extent that in a certain sense they constitute thinking *as such*." I extend this Nietzschean insight by suggesting that saving, investment, and thrift are the active, "economic" embodiment of emotional or psychological states. To save is to withhold earned income from what would otherwise be spent in consuming; to invest is to place that income where it will show a profit, produce a surplus: both acts reveal and develop an emotional capacity—or a psychological disposition—to delay the immediate gratification of spending on consumer goods. We praise this emotional capacity as foresight when it balances present desires and future needs; we condemn it as miserliness when it sacrifices the enjoyment of the present to the compound interest of the future. Either way we look at it, the question is how to make the distinction between our real desires and our genuine needs concrete, measurable, and useful. What emotional or psychological armature is required by the choices that follow?

These are the questions that any defense of consumer culture must raise. And they've now become pressing, *practical* questions for Americans as they grapple with the causes and consequences of the Great Recession—as they decide whether more saving/investment or more consumption is the cure for what ails the economy, and as they decide whether emotional frugality or expenditure is the proper structure of their souls. So when I urge Americans to save less and consume more as the solution to the economic problems they face, I'm also urging them to be less thrifty in the broadest sense, to withhold less and desire more, in view of the material abundance at their disposal. I'm urging them to see that saving for a rainy day—treating this life as austere probation for another—is a soul-crushing emotional trap as well as an economic dead end.

As a defense of consumer culture, this book is necessarily about commodities. So I'll be drawing on Karl Marx, the great theorist of "commodity fetishism"—but not because I want to overthrow capitalism. No, Marx is essential to my argument for much less exciting reasons.

To begin with, he showed that all commodities have two properties, a use value and an exchange value—a particular, subjective, mostly material meaning on the one hand, and a placeless, objective, monetary meaning on the other. Every commodity raises, or just is, a question that divides our attention: what is this thing good for, and what is its price? (The exceptions to this rule are of course paper money, the not-thing that's valuable only if you can use it as a medium of exchange, and credit, the future tense of paper money.)

Marx also showed that before the advent of capitalism, the consumption of goods was both the goal and the limit of production. He called that situation "simple commodity circulation," and diagrammed its crucial circuit as C-M-C, where C stands for commodity and M stands for money. At this stage in the development of markets, the point of producing and selling goods was not to accumulate ever more exchange value, more money in the bank, but to acquire just enough use values, just enough material goods, to validate your accustomed way of life.

When capitalism emerged, labor itself became a commodity—now you had to buy the right not to die of starvation by working for wages—and the "formula for capital" reversed the relations of simple commodity circulation. The new formula looked like this: $M\text{-}C\text{-}M^1$, where money, exchange value, wealth in the abstract, became the premise and the purpose of goods production, while use values—particular, material things, even human bodies—became the means to more exchange value, more money in the bank, rather than ends in themselves. The "cash nexus" accordingly became the site of every transaction, and consumption gave way to accumulation as the proper goal of the good life.

Students of Marx have invariably deployed these distinctions—between use and exchange value, or between simple commodity circulation and the formula for capital—to indict consumer culture for the crime of commodity fetishism. By this he meant what follows from our uniquely human ability to treat a chair, say, as both a particular, material thing, right here and now, and a symbolic property that transcends its local function and shape. It's when we endow dead matter with transcendent meanings that objects begin to stand in for sentient beings and the fetishism of commodities becomes the norm. Here's how Walt Whitman explained this weird process: "When the minted gold in the vault smiles like the nightwatchman's daughter, / When warrantee deeds loafe in chairs opposite and are my friendly companions." But unlike almost every student of Marx, Whitman didn't stop there; he went on to announce that he would craft poems from commodities: "I intend to reach them my hand and make as much of them as I do of men and women." I'm going to follow Whitman's example in this book. I'm going to use Marx's distinctions and definitions to defend consumer culture. But I won't be satisfied with mere acquittal. Here's why.

When you buy a car or a jacket or that little black dress, you don't expect to profit from it. In fact you know it becomes less valuable, except to you, the moment you buy it. In this sense, your purchase of consumer goods constantly reinstates the archaic circuit of simple commodity circulation. In the same sense, your purchase has *removed* the object of your desire from the domain of commodities: its significance no longer includes its price, even when others recognize how much it cost you, because everybody knows that if you put it back on the market, you'll get less than you paid for it. Where the commodity once divided your attention between its price and its purpose, between its exchange value and its use value, the thing you've bought now has only a use value: it's been "defetishized" by your purchase.

So consumer culture is a practical limit on the accumulation of wealth in the abstract; it resists the restless, expansive formula for capital, which sacrifices enjoyment in the present to the compound interest of the future, always in the name of growth. It urges us to acquire use values rather than exchange values, to save less and spend more, but it doesn't sacrifice the future in the name of present enjoyment. In fact, it teaches us how to produce and preserve the things our children might want or need—the things they might use.

"A BROADER CHANGE OF MINDSET IS STILL NEEDED"

So far I've referred to the "economics of the case" as if I'm a lawyer entering an implausible appeal. But I'm neither an economist nor a lawyer.

I'm a historian, and I'll be using historical evidence rather than economic theory to make my case.

Why, then, should you take my argument seriously? Because the economists blew it, and we all know they did. There were honorable exceptions like Robert Shiller, Paul Krugman, Dean Baker, Brad DeLong, and Nouriel Roubini. But the *Economist*, the indispensable syllabus for the CEO set, summarized our frustration on July 18, 2009: "Economists misread the economy on the way up, misread it on the way down, and now mistake the right way out."

All true. As it stands, mainstream economic theory obscures, denies, or obliterates reality—mainly because it wrongly assumes that private savings and private investment are the prime movers of robust growth. The historical record shows that this assumption is a mere article of faith with no empirical basis: like a strong religious belief, it can't be proven, but it is nonetheless persuasive. So we need to follow the example of John Maynard Keynes, the renegade economist who revolutionized his discipline in the 1930s by escaping what he called the "habitual modes of thought"—the ones that obscured, denied, or obliterated the reality of the Great Depression. As the *Economist*'s editors put it, citing Keynes, "A broader change of mindset is still needed."

But how to meet this need of a new mindset? The first step in the program I recommend here is to treat economists as Keynes himself proposed in 1930, as "humble, competent people, on a level with dentists." The second step in the program is to treat this necessity, this "broader change of mindset," as a genuine possibility rather than a defiant, radical urge to reject conventional wisdom—as something like a "paradigm shift" that's already in the making because the Great Recession has exploded so many myths about markets, money, and growth.

John Cassidy, a staff writer at the *New Yorker* and the author of an indispensable book, *How Markets Fail* (2009), tells a useful story about how these paradigm shifts take place. In late 2009, in the thick of the economic crisis that started in 2007, he visited several of the University of Chicago professors who long ago invented profoundly unrealistic and yet widely used theories of efficient (self-regulating) markets and "rational expectations"—the theories used by the traders who gave us "securitized investment vehicles" and "collateralized debt obligations." Cassidy's thankless errand into this arid wilderness reminded him of the intellectual upheaval caused by early twentieth-century astronomy:

> The over-all reaction I encountered put me in mind of what happened to cosmology after the astronomer Edwin Hubble, in 1929, discovered that the universe was expanding, and was much larger than scientists had believed. The profession fell into turmoil. Some physicists stuck to the existing theories, which posited a stable universe. Others, Albert Einstein included, tried to adapt the old models to Hubble's data. Still others attempted to come up with a new account of how the galaxies formed; it was this effort that ultimately produced the theory of the big bang.

Cassidy tells the story to remind us of an earlier episode of scientific revolution—the moment in 1610–1611 when Galileo Galilei used his homemade telescope to discover the moons circling Jupiter, then the orbital phases of Venus. Of course the Catholic Church soon accused him of heresy; he wasn't finally convicted, though, until 1632, when he tried to publish a book proving that Nicolaus Copernicus was right: the earth revolved around the sun. Now Einstein called this heretic the "father of modern science," but Galileo wasn't a deep thinker. He was a radical empiricist who wanted data and description rather than high theory. He was more like Hubble than Einstein.

That's what we need just now, empiricists like Galileo and Hubble. We need a paradigm shift, to be sure, but for the time being, we don't need a big bang theory; we need data and description. These won't come from economists, however, because they *can't* come from this source: practically speaking, the facts and figures I will cite to demonstrate my case are invisible to most economists, just as invisible as the moons and phases Galileo measured were to most mathematicians and physicists of his time. They're invisible because *in theory*, they're preposterous, even impossible.

To be sure, Galileo's discoveries galvanized the scientific revolution we take for granted. But most mathematicians and physicists of the seventeenth century "stuck to the existing theories"—the ones Aristotle and Ptolemy had written up—which insisted, on principle, that everything must revolve around the earth. So will most economists of our own time stick to the "existing theories," which insist, on principle, that saving and investment must be the crucial components of growth, despite all the empirical evidence to the contrary.

Don't get me wrong. I have nothing against theories as such. Part of my task here is to work through them (with the help of John Cassidy, Justin Fox, and others), to show where they failed us. Nor do I believe that facts can exist apart from theories. Indeed I'm convinced by Galileo himself that theories *produce* facts. He famously said that the Copernican account of the heavens was "surely false," and he knew his primitive telescope couldn't clinch the deal, but he went ahead and made the case anyway.

Still, I won't be writing here as a theorist with a ready-made alternative to the consensus that unites economists and policy makers on the importance of saving, investment, and capital formation.* As a radical empiricist, my goal is different: I want to raise awkward questions rather than present elegant theorems. I want to ask, for example, Why do we believe, in the absence of evidence, that private investment creates jobs and drives growth, and what would follow if we didn't? As a historian, my methods are different: the telescope at my disposal compresses time rather than space. Unlike the camera obscura that mainstream economists use to project their upside-down theories, this device lets us live forward by understanding backward.

---

* It's worth noting, however, that the rudiments of such a theory are already in place, and have been for a half century. In the 1950s and 1960s, for example, it was almost commonplace for economists to doubt the role of capital formation and net private investment in determining the pattern and the pace of growth—and meanwhile to define "technical change" as the real source of growth. Among the economists who expressed such doubts and developed such definitions were Robert Solow, Moses Abramovitz, Solomon Fabricant, Kenneth Kurihara, Wassily Leontief, Harold Vatter, Edward F. Denison, Edmund Phelps, Simon Kuznets, Anatol Murad, Sydney Coontz, Burton F. Massell, Richard Du Boff, and Harry T. Oshima (Paul Romer is a more recent contributor). Their essays and books were part of a larger theoretical controversy started by Joan Robinson and amplified

by Piero Sraffa, which questioned the explanatory adequacy of "production functions" in measuring the "marginal product" of capital (as against labor or land). The result of this controversy was the kind of professional turmoil Cassidy remarks on above, because it made marginal productivity, the centerpiece of neoclassical economic theory, look like the emperor's new clothes; and yet it has had no long-term effects on the evolution of the discipline: "normal science" still prevails. See the Appendix, coauthored by Steve Roth.

PART ONE: OUR VERY OWN PERESTROIKA

CHAPTER ONE

Understanding Backward

The Past as Imprisonment

Why do we Americans of the early twenty-first century still respond to economic calamity as if we're citizens of the late nineteenth century? Because we still identify with the Populist revolt of the 1890s, when small farmers in the South and West rebelled against their corporate masters, and, having formed an insurgent third party, came close to nationalizing the banks, the railroads, and interstate communication. The distant echoes of this revolt are the most influential explanations of the Great Recession in our own time: from Left to Right, these explanations are reiterations of the antimonopoly tradition that the Populists once used to press their compelling case against corporate power.

They tell us (1) that avoidable *mistakes* were made by private-sector enthusiasts and/or policy makers in government, particularly at the Fed; or (2) that the *monopoly* power of banks "too big to fail" distorted the anonymous market forces that left to themselves would have yielded intelligible and satisfactory results; or (3) that the *money* supply is the source of all business cycles, so a "financial fix" is still the key to everything else; or (4) that when corrupted by lax credit, monetary sleight of hand, and mere fraud, *morality* becomes the backstory of every economic problem we face.

But how is it possible that these influential explanations of the recent economic crisis could be remnants of the nineteenth century? Therein lies a story.

In December 2010, in the drawing room of an Upper East Side townhouse, I was happily eating exquisite appetizers served by white-gloved young men when a well-dressed and thoughtful individual explained his opposition to the federal bailout of the banks by quoting William Jennings Bryan's famous speech of 1896—"we shall not be crucified on a Cross of Gold," he said, meaning to hell with what the bankers wanted—and the other guests, equally well dressed and thoughtful, started nodding their heads, murmuring their assent.

I stopped eating and asked myself, How did that happen? Why do these affluent New Yorkers respond to this reference? Do they know that Bryan called bankers mere predators, parasitic growths on the body politic, and proposed to abolish the banking system by making it the property of the federal government? And regardless of what they know about Bryan, why are we falling back on the political rhetoric of the nineteenth century to express our fear and loathing of finance capital? Yes, *we*: I was nodding my head along with everybody else.

Meanwhile I answered myself. I thought, Yes, we live forward but we understand backward, just like Søren Kierkegaard said. No wonder this well-dressed man is quoting Bryan. And then I thought, We Americans, who are said to lack a sense of history, we actually excel at understanding backward because historical narratives are what constitute us as a people and a nation: to be an American is to argue about what it means to be an American, and the only way to get into the argument is to think historically, to figure out what "original intent," or slavery and civil war, or corporate "persons" entitled to free speech can mean in the present, where we live forward.

And then, finally, I thought, OK, but maybe this historiographical excellence of ours has become a curse. So I asked myself one more question, Does our eagerness to understand backward sometimes make us prisoners of the past?

Well, yes, sometimes it does. Our obsession with the "original intent" of eighteenth-century men who couldn't possibly understand our present-day concerns is a good example of this self-imposed imprisonment, although the sentence is commuted daily by our willingness to reinterpret the Constitution. But there's no better example of the same syndrome than our unwitting faith in the good old cause of Populism, the social movement composed mainly of small farmers that made

William Jennings Bryan its presidential candidate in hopes of thwarting what it defined as a corporate-industrial conspiracy against the liberties of the people.

In their radical Omaha Platform of 1892, the Populists demanded the outright abolition of "the trusts"—the new industrial corporations—as well as government ownership of all banks and interstate communication companies (AT&T was incorporated in 1892), on the grounds that these "unnatural persons" were destroying the material groundwork of equality by acquiring too much market power. The Populists almost won the fight they started: until 1898, they held the balance of political power and cultural authority even outside their core constituencies in the Deep South. And even after they narrowly lost their bid for the presidency in 1896, a majority of the Supreme Court used their logic and took their side in antitrust cases. It wasn't until 1911 that the legal standing of the new corporations was finally confirmed by a changed majority of the court, and its decision dissolved the Standard Oil Company!

In effect, the Populists were trying to abort the birth of corporate capitalism and to restore a smallholder economy—a free, competitive market, a "fair field and no favor." That's why we're still faithful to their good old cause: we're still worried about the social and political power of the large corporations, and we're still impressed by the self-made man who owns enough property to be his own boss. Like the Populists, we hate to think of ourselves as wage slaves of the corporations; we hate to think of ourselves as creatures of faceless bureaucracies, whether public or private; and we like to think of bankers—not to mention lawyers—as paper-pushing middlemen who deduct their incomes from the value produced by others. We're still unwilling to be crucified on a Cross of Gold.

But as a result, we can't move beyond Populist explanations of economic crises or moral problems. Whether we're conversing quietly in an Upper East Side townhouse or cheering noisily for Tea Party candidates in Iowa, we're stuck in the 1890s, as if the restoration of the past is our purpose—as if we're afraid to live forward. There's a good reason for this deep emotional attachment to a past that can't be retrieved: like most Americans then as now, the Populists were promarket *and* anticapitalist, thoroughly bourgeois *and* anticorporate, all at once. But how can that be?

The Populists assumed that when immunized by legislation against the concentrated economic power of monopolies—the power of corporations, "the trusts"—the market would yield intelligible, satisfactory consequences, and they thought of these consequences in terms of both politics and morality. If all producers were subject to the same anonymous forces of the market, for example, equality would reign, and so no demagogue (and no large corporation) could hold sway over the oppressed masses. If all producers were subject to the same anonymous forces of the market, they would be punished or rewarded according to the same objective standard. The market functioned in these ways as an inscrutable external force—a kind of godlike presence—that would balance good and evil, or progress and regress, as long as "big business" (the corporations, "the trusts," the monopolies) didn't become powerful enough to alter its laws.

So the Populists programmatically demanded a self-regulating market, a price system that wasn't corrupted by the conspiracies of big business. That's why their explanations of economic crisis came down to *personifications* of the problem at hand: somebody was to blame (probably the bankers) because something had disturbed the coherent moral universe the free market represented. The Populists needed what we would call "big government"—public ownership of the banks, for example—as a bulwark against the predatory power of big business; but their fundamental loyalties were to the anonymous forces of a free market that, when finally restored by outlawing "the trusts," would equitably allocate economic resources, political possibilities, and moral properties among self-mastering smallholders.

In this fundamental sense, the most influential explanations of the recent economic crisis are distant echoes of the Populist revolt against the rise of corporate capitalism. Again, they tell us that *mistakes* were made, that *monopoly* distorted markets, that *money* was too easy—or too tight—and that *morality* went missing.

My explanation avoids these echoes of the antimonopoly tradition by showing that the Great Recession was the inevitable result of surplus capital—of redundant profits with no productive outlet, which eventually find their way into speculative markets that inflate bubbles. This explanation has intellectual roots in both Marx and Keynes, of course, but it also acknowledges the historical importance of what Ben Bernanke— that great admirer of the archmonetarist Milton Friedman—called the "global savings glut" before he became the chairman of the Fed. Like Bernanke, I explain the recent crisis by comparing it to the Great Depression. Unlike Bernanke, I explain *both* events as results of surplus capital generated by huge shifts in income shares away from labor, wages, and consumption, toward capital, profits, and corporate savings. And I draw the obvious conclusion from the historical comparison: if the New Deal succeeded by enfranchising working people and shifting income shares back toward wages and consumption—not by means of a "financial fix"—then a massive *redistribution* of income away from capital, profits, and corporate savings is our best hope of addressing the causes of the recent crisis and laying the groundwork for balanced growth.

On the way toward this explanation and the future it implies, I have to convince you that the Populists got it wrong. This means I have to convince you that the *mistakes* of policy makers, public and private, are more or less irrelevant; that the large corporation (a.k.a. *monopoly*) is more conducive to growth and innovation than small business; that a "financial fix" changes almost nothing because the *money* supply explains very little; and that *morality* accounts for even less. Otherwise you'll think I'm ignoring the obvious explanations for our sorry condition. But here at the outset, the question will be, How did the Populist understanding of late nineteenth-century economic crisis become the "normal science" of contemporary theory?

CHAPTER TWO

How to Explain a Crisis

The Revenge of the Populists

THEORIES OF CRISIS AND THE ORIGINS OF THE FED

When we set out to explain the recent crisis, we're revisiting the late nineteenth-century moment when systematic theories of the so-called business cycle—the "long waves" of economic growth and development—first emerged from close study of modern-industrial capitalism, and from political conflict over the meanings of markets. That's when the big questions became the ones we still ask: What causes economic crises, and how do we respond to them? Are markets self-regulating mechanisms, or do they require our close attention? How can we manage crises without taking control of every contract—without destroying the free play of plural market forces? Or can we? In sum, can we manage crises in a way that avoids state control of markets?

The first "Great Depression," which plagued the Atlantic economies of the late nineteenth century by deflating prices and driving profits to the point of no return, convinced most interested observers that the distribution of income was the key to the future; insufficient demand for goods now looked much more important than anything that happened on the supply side. Almost overnight, it seemed, the industrial solution to the age-old problem of scarcity had become the modern problem of chronic *surplus*. The question that followed was, How do we sell what we produce at profitable prices, or, how do we create demand for this oversupply of goods? Most observers accordingly set out to revise "classical" economic theory (the founding fathers were Adam Smith, Jean-Baptiste Say, and David Ricardo), which had all but ignored consumer demand in seeking to discover an objective measure of value in the quantities of labor time required to produce goods.

Their efforts led quickly to the creation of economics as a distinct academic discipline: in the United States, it soon became a powerful voice in the new state universities and the older private colleges that were remaking themselves as secular institutions. The academic urge to record every spasm in the price system led the newly credentialed professionals to found the *Journal of Political Economy* in 1892, the American Economic Association (and *Review*) in 1911, and the National Bureau of Economic Research (NBER) in 1919. The NBER—it's not an arm of any government—is still the official referee on where we are in the business cycle, reassuring us in the spring of 2010, for example, that we'd been in recovery since the winter of 2009.

The rise of a new imperialism toward the end of the nineteenth century meanwhile motivated economists to explain it in terms of the larger transatlantic slump. As framed by John A. Hobson in England, Paul Leroy-Beaulieu in France, and Charles Conant in the United States, the driving force in this new stage of Western civilization was surplus capital seeking foreign investment rather than surplus goods seeking foreign markets. In their view, over*saving* was the most important kind of "overproduction": it now appeared as the fundamental cause of both economic crisis at home and colonial conquest abroad (V. I. Lenin agreed with them). Here is how Conant, who served four presidential administrations between 1898 and 1915, and who was the single most important theorist of banking reform in the early twentieth century—it's no stretch to call him the intellectual godfather of the Fed—explained the problem in 1901, while he was reconstructing the Philippines' monetary system on behalf of the State Department: "The benefit to the old countries in the control of the underdeveloped countries does not lie chiefly in the outlet for consumable goods. It is precisely to escape the necessity for the reduplication of the plants which produce the goods, by finding a field elsewhere for the creation of new plants, that the savings of the capitalistic countries are seeking an outlet beyond their own limits." In short, surplus capital was a problem because it caused chronic economic crisis; the export of this surplus via the new imperialism was part of the solution.

Systematic business cycle theories emerged, finally, from the movement for reform that led to the Federal Reserve System, the central banking apparatus designed to manage economic crises so that short-term hoarding by panicked banks wouldn't freeze credit and destroy a system held together by promises to pay. I'll concentrate on this reform movement because it included and built on the other sources of new theorizing. For instance, academic economists were an integral part of the movement for banking reform, and many nonacademic constituents of the movement, Conant included, argued for a central bank on the grounds that it would enable an American Empire. The movement also deserves attention because it took shape as a response to the Populist challenge of the 1890s.

A hundred years ago, the U.S. Congress established the National Monetary Commission (NMC), then a novel, hybrid mix of elected officials and private-sector experts. Its purposes were to produce studies of modern banking systems and, on that basis, to recommend realistic reform of the American system. Almost all observers at the time understood that "reform" meant the creation of a central bank apparatus—the design of a new headquarters for the system—and that the general purpose of such a bank was to manage the kind of crisis that had plagued the Atlantic economies for a generation. Almost all observers, from the Populists to the big bankers, also understood that this new headquarters would be an agent of public policy, an arm of the state, "*under the control of the government*," as the New York Chamber of Commerce put it in 1906, when it proposed a central bank as the key to reform.

The NMC duly produced dozens of volumes that became the empirical basis for the Aldrich Plan, a proposal for a thorough centralization of financial responsibility in the hands of bankers themselves. It quickly died in Congress because most Americans were still suspicious of bankers, none more so than the Southern farmers who, having given up on their

Populist dreams, now voted for Democrats. Yet within three years the theory and practice of central banking were institutionalized in the new Federal Reserve System, a landmark reform urged by Woodrow Wilson, the Democrat in the White House.

But the Fed wasn't Wilson's doing, and it wasn't the result of the financial crisis that threatened to break the banks in 1907, either; that was the crisis managed by J. P. Morgan from New York City, not by officials in Washington. The movement that created a central banking system in the United States began long before, in the 1890s, as an inter-regional, cross-class coalition of businessmen, bankers, journalists, academics, and, yes, farmers and workers as well. By the time the NMC convened, that reform movement was defined, indeed constituted, by three crucial assumptions—assumptions that still inform our debates about the current crisis and its comparable predecessors, but not in the ways you'd expect.

To begin with, the movement's constituents assumed that economic crisis was inevitable, even normal, regardless of how scrupulously and rationally business decisions got made: markets were no longer self-regulating, if ever they had been. Fraud, theft, and earnest chicanery were always prevalent in a modern market society, to be sure, because everybody was looking for the "main chance"; even so, by 1910, just about everyone outside the Populist camp understood that the citation of moral defects couldn't explain the depth and the scope of economic crisis in the late nineteenth century. So the question was not whether but how to regulate markets.

Just about everyone also understood that rational decisions at the microlevel of the firm could contribute to disaster at the macrolevel of the economy as a whole. For example, a firm's decision to expand the production of steel rails because yet another railroad was being built could increase supply past the point of effective demand, to where the selling price of the rails no longer covered the costs of their production. The fall of prices and the disappearance of profits would affect more than the single firm, and would meanwhile signal that perhaps too much capital was sunk in railroad building as such. Then what? Then all steel rail producers, their suppliers, and their customers would face bankruptcy, and all on account of a rational decision by one firm.

But "overproduction"—that is, producing a supply of goods that exceeds effective or profitable demand—in one sector is not the same thing as a general economic crisis. The price of steel rails can fall without triggering a larger disaster. Nonetheless the significant theorists of the business cycle in the late nineteenth century—I call them significant because their ideas profoundly shaped the making of the Federal Reserve and our later thinking about crisis management—defined "overproduction" as the key cause of economic crisis. Among these theorists were David Wells, Jeremiah Jenks, A. Piatt Andrew, Wesley Mitchell, David Kinley, and O. M. W. Sprague. Most of them were university-trained economists, but a few, like Conant and Wells, were financial journalists with some experience in banking. They argued that the production of goods beyond effective demand was no longer a local, sectoral problem; it could be measured across the board, in *every* sector, from agriculture to manufacturing. The second assumption of the movement for banking reform was just this, that "overproduction" as such—not just occasional disproportions here and there—explained more about economic reality and economic crisis than did quantities and kinds of money.

So the argument for the explanatory superiority of overproduction was an argument against the Populists. They had claimed that *monetary* factors were the real cause of all economic crises; they had insisted that the *monopoly* powers of the big banks and the large corporations ("the trusts") distorted market forces that were once decentered, anonymous, competitive, and effective; and they had assumed that legislation to enforce competition by breaking up "the trusts" would restore *self-regulating* markets. The theorists of crisis whose ideas animated the movement for banking reform claimed instead that monetary factors were important but not decisive causes of crisis: panics and bank failures were typically the results, not the origins, of economic disasters.

These same theorists acknowledged that the centralization of economic authority in the hands of the big banks and the large corporations had profoundly *changed* market forces, but insisted that this was a good thing, and proposed to bring the banking system into line with the new contours of social power in the larger economy. On the same grounds, they were dubious of trust-busting across the board: not every "combination in restraint of trade," as the common law named the problem, was an illegal or merely evil conspiracy, and some trusts were "natural monopolies." Above all, these significant theorists of the business cycle in the late nineteenth and early twentieth centuries believed that self-regulating markets were an impossible dream that disabled new thinking about the uses and limits of markets as such.

The third assumption of the movement to install a central bank was that its principal purpose, managing economic crisis, would be realized by following the advice of Walter Bagehot, the editor of the *Economist* and the author of *Lombard Street* (1873)—by "ready lending," that is, by restoring liquidity to the banking system as a whole, so that a credit freeze would not bring all economic activity to an abrupt and catastrophic end. In this sense, the outer limit of the central bank's powers in times of crisis was its ability to increase the money supply, by lowering reserve requirements (reducing the lawful ratio of assets to liabilities), or by cashing out all manner of bank receivables, even the least reputable. At other times, it might deploy what we now think of as fiscal devices—for example, selling government bonds to soak up surplus capital or a savings glut—but in the throes of crisis, the central bank would be conducting a kind of financial triage, deciding between the dead, the dying, and the deserving.

One hundred years later, these three assumptions of the movement to create a central bank are still incorporated in books, manifestoes, legislation, and the operations of the Fed itself. But only the last of them—the need to blunt the effects of the business cycle through ready lending—remains as an uncontested premise of all thinking about the sources and management of crisis. The other two assumptions, that crisis is normal and overproduction is its cause, have been turned into questions by economic, intellectual, and political developments since the 1970s—by "stagflation," monetarism, the Reagan Revolution—so that the recent debates about how to explain the Great Recession have reinstated the Populist voices of opposition once silenced by the movement that gave us the Federal Reserve. The revenge of the Peoples' Party is not complete. But its fervent opposition to corporate capitalism has changed the way we understand and respond to economic crisis: we hear things differently these days.

EXPLAINING THE RECENT CRISIS:
MISTAKES, MONOPOLY, MONEY, MORALITY

To make this difference audible, let me catalog the available explanations of the recent crisis, and notice, meanwhile, how they map onto the debates of a hundred years ago. That way, we can see what was lost in translation and what remains as a fragment of a forgotten tradition. As patriotism is the last refuge of scoundrels, so alliteration is the last refuge of bad writers. Even so, I will now invoke the Four M's, *Mistakes, Monopoly, Money,* and *Morality*, as the content of this tradition. Each of these arguments about the origins of economic crisis contains a degree of truth, but in the end their partial truths lead us away from what we need to understand, and that is the structural, long-term problem of surplus capital. By this I mean the superfluous profits that, when sent in search of the highest return, inevitably find their way into speculative markets, where they eventually fuel bubbles. I call these profits "superfluous" because their reinvestment is unnecessary to increase productivity or output in the industries that generated them in the first place.

I need to emphasize, here at the outset, that the Four M's have no permanent address. These explanations can be found on the Left and on the Right, and everywhere in between, because they're new instances of an old attachment to Populist principles.

Mistakes

"The housing bubble and the subsequent crash were the result of extreme incompetence on the part of the country's top economic policymakers." That's Dean Baker talking, in March 2010. He's the most quoted left-wing economist around, cited even more than Paul Krugman, and in the *New York Times* to boot. The mere fact that Baker predicted the crash, along with Krugman, Robert Shiller, and Nouriel Roubini—not to mention the bond traders who shorted (bet against) the subprime mortgage market, starting in 2005—should make us take his charge of incompetence seriously.

But how? Which policy makers? The public or the private? Michael Lewis, a liberal, levels the charge against the private sector: How could the analysts at the big banks not have seen that the subprime market was about to implode? Why did they keep buying into that market *after* 2005, when default rates were already climbing and nobody—not one person—could figure out the mix of "assets" contained in all those "bonds" (collateralized debt obligations, a.k.a. CDOs) built on mortgages? Many others have asked how the same banks could bet *against* the mortgages they were meanwhile bundling for sale as so-called securities to fund managers. Richard Posner, a conservative, levels the charge of incompetence against the government, claiming that both the Bush and Obama administrations failed the test of economic crisis. In doing so, he joins a huge chorus of critics that insist that the Fed kept interest rates too low after 2001 and that the government's response to the meltdown of 2008 was indecisive at best. These critics have cast Alan Greenspan, the former chairman of the Federal Reserve, as the villain of the piece. His crime was to have enabled the credit binge that let everybody, especially consumers, borrow too much for too long.

In significant variations on the same theme of incompetence, Justin Fox, John Cassidy, and John Lanchester have asked how truly arcane theories about the efficiency of the "rational market" could have become an intellectual virus that contaminated the brains of highly educated individuals, and then caused them to do great damage to the world economy as well as their own fortunes and reputations. How could so many smart, well-trained people buy into such stupidity, and make such colossal mistakes as result? The answers to these questions aren't obvious; they require a certain distance from the event in question, but also a willingness to see the world from the standpoint of the participants. With that doubled vision, let's begin by addressing the incompetence charge against public policy makers.

When the crisis of 1907 struck, most economists and many businessmen accused Leslie Shaw, the secretary of the Treasury, of having kept interest rates artificially low by increasing and then moving government deposits in national banks, usually the biggest banks in New York. He defended his actions by comparing the Treasury to a central bank, and suggesting that major reform of the system was unnecessary in view of the secretary's powers over the money supply (when he moved those government deposits to the National City Bank, for example, this bank was suddenly able to loan far more than it had without them because its cash reserves were increased). Shaw honestly believed that after the huge stock market debacle of 1902, not to mention the extraordinary economic crisis of the 1890s, he had no choice except to keep interest rates low, to encourage price inflation and sustain growth. Alan Greenspan had similar motives in reducing interest rates in the early twenty-first century. He had already presided over the Asian credit disaster of 1997, the collapse of Long Term Capital Management in 1998, and the dot.com boom and bust of the same moment. In the aftermath of these serial crises, he decided that the combination of the Bush administration's tax cuts and lower interest rates—a "fiscal boost" amplified by easy money—was the only available formula for renewed growth.

Greenspan's great fear was price deflation of the kind that has stunted the Japanese economy since the early 1990s. His successor at the Fed, Ben Bernanke, feared it even more because, as an expert on the Great Depression, he understood that the liquidation of "distressed assets" after the Crash of 1929—back then these were securities listed on the stock market—was registered in the massive deflation that *halved* wholesale and retail prices by 1932. These men (and their counterparts at the Treasury, Henry Paulson and then Timothy Geithner) feared deflation more than anything else because they knew it would drive down housing prices, slow residential construction, erode consumer confidence, disrupt consumer borrowing, and reduce consumer demand across the board (pretty much what has happened since 2007). Meanwhile, the market value of the subprime assets undergirding the new credit instruments—those indecipherable CDOs—would have to fall, and the larger edifice of the financial system would then have to shrink as the banks recalculated the "normal" ratio between assets and liabilities. In sum, Greenspan understood that economic growth driven by increasing consumer expenditures—in this instance, increasing consumer debt "secured" by home mortgages—would grind to a halt, and the banking system would be at risk, if he didn't reinflate the housing bubble. So he did, on the assumption that when it burst, the Fed would stand ready to manage the crisis. His remarks on the dubious rationality of market-driven decisions, then and thereafter, were always uttered with this assumption in mind.

These "top policy makers" also feared deflation because they knew its effects on the world economy could prove disastrous. With deflation would come a dollar with greater purchasing power, to be sure, and thus lower trade and current account deficits, perhaps even a more manageable national debt. But so too would come lower U.S. demand for exports from China, India, and developing nations, and thus the real prospect of "decoupling"—that is, a world economy no longer held together by American demand for commodities, capital, and credit. The centrifugal forces unleashed by globalization would then have free rein, and every protectionist urge would be unbound, here and elsewhere—as when the world economy split into competing "spheres of influence" in the 1930s, and world war became the violent means to reunify it. Equally important, American economic leverage against the rising powers of the East would be accordingly diminished, and with it the customary currency of *political* leverage in deciding international disputes.

So Greenspan and his successor at the Fed are not to be blamed for the scope or the scale of the crisis. Under the circumstances, which included the available intellectual or theoretical alternatives, they did pretty much what they had to, hoping all the while that the inevitable "market correction" would not be too severe. They weren't incompetent; they were trying to make the best of a bad situation with the tools at hand. To criticize them for not taking up the alternative policies—by, say, raising interest rates to prick the housing bubble, as the Japanese central bank did in 1990—is something like criticizing the ancient Greeks because they used wheels and understood steam power but didn't build tractors to plow their fields.

Defending their counterparts in the private sector on the same grounds is more difficult. But here, too, the charge of incompetence diverts us from the real issues—from the underlying structural cause of the economic crisis that began in 2007 and overwhelmed markets by 2008, which, again, is surplus capital. There may well be fraud, stupidity, and corruption at work in this mess, but they are much less important than the systemic forces that brought us to the brink of another Great

Depression, as I'll be arguing shortly. In any event, the blame game doesn't get us very far in understanding either what happened in 2007 and 2008, or what still plagues us. There's no theory that can predict exactly what will happen in the future, certainly not in a future determined by unruly and irrational individuals with minds of their own. So why would we criticize anyone for not knowing what will soon happen? In the volatile marketplace of modern capitalism, the future is plural, and crisis is normal, while economic equilibrium is always as tentative as a truce between parliamentary factions in Lebanon, or as uneasy as the outward harmony of a couple on the verge of an ugly divorce. The modern countercyclical practices invented a century ago—more liquidity, ready leading by the central bank—are predicated on the acknowledgment of this simple fact.

Information is never perfect, not even in a planned economy, so prediction is a highly risky business. Indeed one of the benefits of a market economy is that it allows chaotic, unpredictable social forces to inform our behaviors; it teaches us to live with uncertainty, to get by with the available information, knowing all the while that it's not enough to protect us against the next betrayal, the next disaster. So again, why would we criticize anyone for not knowing what will soon happen?

Besides, James Surowiecki and Richard Posner, among others, have explained that the short-term drive for profit by banks and nonfinancial firms makes the so-called irrational exuberance of an economic bubble look like careful calculation. The decentered decisions that determine supply and demand have no predictable result, even while the bandwagon effects of surging markets produce thundering herds of investors on the same narrow trail. As Charles Prince, the former CEO of Citigroup—a bank that has now received close to $40 billion in aid from the Troubled Asset Relief Program—explained in July 2007, "As long as the music is playing, you've got to get up and dance." In other words, if you don't ride the bubble, even *knowing* it's a bubble, your competitors will get the business and reap the profits. So to criticize bankers for investing in (or shorting) the securitized mortgage market is to criticize them for what they're empowered and supposed to do: maximize profits, and thus keep their standing with the shareholders.

By the same token, to criticize model builders like John Cochrane or Robert Lucas because their theories of "rational markets" didn't or couldn't acknowledge the messy details—the ugly realities—of the real world is to criticize them for what they get paid to do as professors of economics at the University of Chicago: abstract from the particulars of the situation and propose universal "laws of motion." The tests and the proofs of their laws were typically mathematical (the preferred idiom of economic theory) and, in their own terms, convincing. Their counterparts in the business schools—Fischer Black, Myron Scholes, Robert C. Merton—were even more convincing because they invented algorithms for "option pricing," which allowed for computerized trading programs that began to pay off in the 1980s and 1990s, first in the stock market and then in the "shadow banking system," where hedge funds became the headquarters.

We should also note, in defense of the model builders' indifference to institutional and historical realities, that faith in self-regulating markets has no predictable political valence. A hundred years ago, Populists on the Left and conservatives on the Right agreed that a trust-busting approach to the new industrial corporations would restore competition; as a result, they believed, all producers would again be *equally* subject to anonymous laws of supply and demand, and economic equilibrium would be the rule rather than the exception. The theory of the "rational market," as Justin Fox and John Cassidy tell the story of its development in twentieth-century departments of economics, is a distant echo of this anticorporate, antimonopoly program—for it posits effective competition between small producers as the ideal state of a market economy, or it falls back on monetary causes to explain business cycles. These aren't "mistakes"; they're assumptions that enable the elegance of theories presented as ever-more-complicated equations.

Monopoly

And that brings us to another explanation of the recent debacle that derives from the original Populist animus against "the trusts"—that is, the *monopoly* power of the big banks and the big corporations. Matt Taibbi, William Greider, Simon Johnson, Thomas Geoghegan, and many, many others have argued that the scope and reach of behemoths like Goldman Sachs or Citigroup have allowed them to distort market forces—to do insider trades that border on fraud as a matter of course, or to pose as essential institutions that are "too big to fail"—and to corrupt politics by paying legislators, literally, for their help in deregulating the financial industry even after the savings and loan debacle of the late 1970s and early 1980s. If these banks weren't so big, the argument goes, they wouldn't have a disproportionate influence on the market or on Congress. Thus their venal decisions wouldn't have warped the entire economy and caused a crisis that has bankrupted Main Street.

There's something to be said for the argument—to begin with, why should the fortunes of so many be determined by the interests of so few?—and Taibbi (the *Rolling Stone* writer who called Goldman Sachs "a giant vampire squid"), at least, deserves our thanks for tracing all the deadly strands that tethered our economic futures to the trading floors on Wall Street. But most of what is to be said in favor of the neo-Populist, antimonopoly tradition he represents so eloquently comes down to three dubious propositions. First, small business is self-evidently more efficient, and more productive of new jobs, than big business (tax breaks for enterprise on this scale thus become a bipartisan budget imperative). Second, a smallholder economy is more conducive to political democracy than one dominated by large corporations. Third, regulation in the name of competition among small producers—antitrust writ large, let's break up the banks!—would give free play to the anonymous market forces we need to promote innovation and keep the bureaucrats at bay.

In order, then, let's have a critical look at these propositions, which are so deeply embedded in American history and culture that they've become political pieties for the Right as well as the Left. Small businesses are *not* all garage bands with great new sounds; they're mostly Mom and Pop enterprises that do things badly but cheaply because some, maybe most, of their costs are carried off the books, in uncompensated hours and familial obligations. They're not more efficient; in short, they're just cheaper. Larger enterprises are almost always more efficient than small businesses because they can impose a division of labor—because they can divide tasks, make people specialize, and so *increase outputs* without increasing inputs of capital or labor. We tend to believe that small business is the source of technological innovation ("genius"), and that large enterprises are a constraint on it, mainly because we know, somehow, that bureaucracy stifles imagination. But in fact, almost all such innovation in the twentieth century was the result of research and development sponsored either by large corporations or by the federal government, usually in tandem. Microsoft, for example, now a very large corporation, is inconceivable in the absence of the R & D that came from IBM and the Pentagon, among other large bureaucratic sources, long before Bill Gates left school for the garage. The Internet as such is another example of the same public/private synergy that typically involves large corporations, big money, government grants, and earnest entrepreneurs.

But wait, don't small businesses, those scrappy little start-ups, create most of the new jobs, somewhere around 60 percent, maybe more? Well, yes, they do. And those jobs disappear within two years—along with the start-ups. That's the average life span of a small business. What's more important here is more obvious: apart from the funky bodegas and the cool bars in your neighborhood, small business exists because big business does (and even here, you want to consider the effect of corporate expense accounts on restaurant revenues, or the marvel of the delivery systems that allow you to buy national brands at the corner store). In commercial and residential construction, for example, the subcontractors make their way by doing what the general contractor tells them to, and this overlord is typically a large corporation from out of state, not a local, small business. The little guys who build "on spec"—who put up a house and hope for the best—are a tiny minority of contractors, they hire as few people as they can, they don't provide benefits, and they're notoriously dishonest. The little guys in *every* line of business are the employers who are most likely to be union-busting fanatics because, unlike large corporations, they can't pass their labor costs on to the final consumer in the prices of their products; so the jobs they create tend toward the minimum wage variety.

But go ahead, take those musty bookstores as your favorite small business threatened by the old chains, like Barnes & Noble, and by the new chains, like Amazon or Alabris. The fact is that those small bookstores can now thrive because they affiliate with the chains—because they serve these large corporations by shipping items directly from their own inventories once the order is placed at the online bookstore. The fact also is that you can find more of what interests you in the online book-stores, because now you're browsing in an impossibly enormous library, walking down virtual aisles on the scale of Alexandria, and because what piques your interest tells the software what other aisles you might want to explore. And go ahead; complain that all the airfreight and the card-board and the UPS trucks delivering the readable goods amount to an environmental disaster. You're wrong. According to Annie Leonard, a most diligent and intelligent environmentalist—her book, *The Story of Stuff*, is a masterpiece of political wit and grace—online shopping for books is "more efficient and sustainable in terms of energy used, con-ventional air pollutants generated, waste generated, and greenhouse gas emissions" than the "traditional model," and that of course is the model that requires you to lug heavy objects from the olfactory hell of the local bookstore.

But what about Silicon Valley, speaking now metaphorically as well as literally, referring to the crowded, dreamlike state where small busi-ness start-ups create loads of good jobs for nerdy intellectual types? Well, since 1999 and the dot.com bust, it's been a slow-growth sector, and since 2007 it's been an employment disaster area, mainly because large corporations have cut back on research and development, or have already realized the economies made available by computer-driven technologies, or have outsourced the high-tech jobs. The proverbial garage bands haven't been looking to hire more players because the recording contracts—the financial affiliations with larger companies—haven't been happening.

So worshipping at the altar of small business doesn't make much *economic* sense. Nor does it make much environmental sense unless the object of our scrutiny is the damage done by corporations that never deal with retail (consumer) realities except as a public relations problem—oil companies, for example, like British Petroleum. But what about the *political* argument in favor of antitrust and renewed competition? Is it true that a smallholder economy is more conducive to democracy than the available alternatives? It all depends on what political theorists you take for granted, which political movements you associate with progress, and who's enfranchised by your preferences. The classical theory of republics invented by Aristotle, updated by Machiavelli, and enacted by the American Revolution held that popular government was grounded in a wide distribution of private property. The great threat to republican liberty was, then, the concentration of property in the hands of a few (oligarchy). The Populists of the late nineteenth century were the last *mass* movement galvanized by this antimonopoly animus—they wanted to abolish "the trusts" because these artificial creatures of the law controlled too much property, made too many decisions about how economic resources would be allocated, and could therefore dictate how political decisions would be reached.

Of course the Populists weren't the only ones worried about the discrepancy between the concentration of economic power in the boardrooms of the large corporations, on the one hand, and the demands of democracy—government of the people, by the people, for the people—on the other. In 1896, Arthur T. Hadley, the conservative president of Yale University, expressed this concern as follows: "A republican government is organized on the assumption that all men are free and equal. If the political power is . . . equally distributed while the industrial power is concentrated in the hands of a few, it creates dangers of class struggles and class legislation which menace both our political and industrial order." Eighty years later, Irving Kristol, the founding father of neoconservatism, said almost exactly the same thing: "There is little doubt that the idea of a 'free market,' in the era of large corporations, is not quite the original capitalist idea. . . . [The] concentration of assets and power—power to make economic decisions affecting the lives of tens of thousands of citizens—seems[s] to create a dangerous disharmony between the economic system and the political."

The nineteenth century looks, on this conservative reading—but then it's also the Left's reading of the same history—like a golden age of democracy, when the economic importance and self-reliance of smallholders made them ideal, omnicompetent citizens. But by any measure, the twentieth century, the age of the giant corporation, was a much more democratic moment, when women and minorities were finally enfranchised in the broadest possible sense of that term—gaining the right to vote, to be sure, but also entering the mainstream of the culture. The twentieth century was also the moment of a dispersal of power from the state to society, when the regulation of markets began to be shared between public agencies like the Federal Trade Commission and private organizations like large corporations and trade unions. This, too, was a democratic promise that couldn't have been made in the nineteenth century; for it taught ordinary people to be aware of their rights, their powers, and their obligations in a new kind of public sphere, where nongovernmental organizations (NGOs), all kinds of associations, became the rule.

Of course most intellectuals in our time complain about the political emptiness of the "public sphere." But they confuse politics as such with state-centered, policy-relevant, electorally oriented activity—and they do so because they think that Aristotle was right, that our true identities as individuals can be discovered only by participation in debates about policy outcomes, in the strenuous public duties of citizenship so conceived. They're wrong. The public sphere is not just a political forum where people make arguments and speeches and laws; it includes most of what we have come to know as civil society, the space between the state and the individual, even that most private sector we call "the" family. It's the place where we imagine and enact new identities, and while we're at it, where we demonstrate new political possibilities—as, for example, those young black men and women did when they refused to leave Woolworth's segregated lunch counter in Greensboro, North Carolina, in 1960.

So a smallholder economy may indeed be beautiful, but it's not the only residence of popular politics. The democratization of American society and culture in the twentieth century coincided with the rise and then the consolidation of corporate capitalism, not the triumph of Populism and the return of the self-made man. Coincidence is not causation, of course, but the fact remains that over the last hundred years, large enterprise has proven itself to be a sponsor of both social mobility and cultural diversity—for example, by building job ladders within corporate bureaucracies that allowed broad access to managerial responsibilities or middle-class incomes, and by taking civil rights and affirmative action seriously. This fact doesn't preclude regulation and reform of corporate behavior, which has never been uniformly progressive (whose has?); it should, however, make us ask whether breaking up the big banks, thus giving free rein to competitive, anonymous market forces (and silencing the special interests?), is an adequate form of either regulation or reform.

Once upon a time, in 1911, the Standard Oil Trust incorporated in New Jersey was broken up by order of the Supreme Court in a landmark decision that restored the "rule of reason"—that is, the common law distinction between lawful and unlawful combinations in restraint of trade, the distinction built into the Sherman Anti-Trust Act of 1890. Within fifteen years, the various components of the former Trust had become giant interstate corporations in their own right, with new reach, new power, and new names (Mobil Oil of New York, for example, and Esso—S. O., get it?—then Exxon of New Jersey), each of them now impervious to another antitrust suit. A similar process resulted from the court-ordered breakup of American Telephone & Telegraph in 1982, following an antitrust suit first brought against it by the Justice Department in 1974. The so-called Baby Bells created by the settlement quickly evolved into companies with more than regional scope, and then began merging with each other, so that by 2010 only four giant telecommunications corporations were still standing (and by 2011, with AT&T's bid to acquire T-Mobile, only three, maybe two).

Breaking up the big banks doesn't come near the real problem, which is that the financial sector has metastasized for a reason unrelated to monopoly power: it became the receptacle, and then the manager, of what Ben Bernanke used to call the "global savings glut," a polite way of saying surplus capital. As a result, investment banks and hedge funds got bloated, and local commercial banks got greedy. Since the 1980s, the system as a whole has been awash in redundant profits, a.k.a. surplus capital—that's why there's been a huge gap between retained earnings and corporate investment for the last decade—so the banks, large and small, have grown by figuring out new interest-bearing places to put this otherwise idle money. And the obvious place to put it was in "retail banking"—in credit cards, for example, in the 1990s, and then in the mortgage market in the early twenty-first century. Even the venture capital that fed the dot.com bubble of the 1990s was animated by the overpowering urge to place bets on retail choices—in other words, consumer preferences—in this case a huge wager on how demand for the personal computer would change the delivery of goods and services.

By all means let's monitor and (re)regulate banking practices, along with every other malfeasant corporate behavior. But let's not assume that small is beautiful and, on this basis, deduce a political program from unexamined propositions that derive, ultimately, from Populist premises. In other words, let's not assume that our self-evident project is to restore competitive, anonymous market forces by means of aggressive antitrust policies—rather than to subject market forces as such to social purposes like, say, better education for everyone, or gender equity in the workplace, or environmental integrity by means of reform and regulation.

The world economy is too big to fail, and so, for that matter, is its indispensable American component. If the financial system had failed in late 2008, as it might have in the absence of massive government intervention, the world economy would have failed, too, and we would all be the poorer, and worse: we would be repairing something that didn't need to break down in the first place.

Money

Explanations of the current crisis that gather under the headings of Mistakes and Monopoly are everywhere you look, but for the most part they flourish at the extreme edges of the political universe—both Left and Right—where mainstream economic theory is just background noise. Meanwhile monetary explanations have become the norm among professional economists, at least those with a purchase on the public imagination. This development is more odd than it might seem, because Milton Friedman, the archmonetarist who claimed that the Great Depression was a result of mistakes at the Fed—they raised real interest rates at precisely the wrong time, he insisted—was once a marginal figure, a voice in the wilderness. How did his innocent update of Populist ideas about economic crisis become the gold standard of analysis?

Winning the Nobel Prize (in 1976) helps, of course, but still, how did it happen that when the crisis struck in 2007, all the middlebrow magazines and reputable newspapers were suddenly crowded with famous economists extolling Friedman's monetary explanations of the business cycle? For example, in a cover story essay for *Time* magazine, Niall Ferguson, the celebrated historian of finance, just took it for granted that Friedman's theories had become the mainstream of thinking about both the big event and the unfolding crisis of 2008: "Yet the underlying cause of the Great Depression—as Milton Friedman and Anna Jacobson Schwartz argued in their seminal book *A Monetary History of the United States 1867–1960*, published in 1963—was not the stock market crash but a 'great contraction' of credit due to an epidemic of bank failures." Ben Bernanke agreed in his apologetic toast to the esteemed authors on the occasion of Friedman's ninetieth birthday. "I would like to say to Milton and Anna: Regarding the Great Depression: You're right, we [the Fed] did it. We're very sorry. But thanks to you, we won't do it again."

This monetarist consensus isn't perfect, of course. It's telling, however, that even Christina Romer, an economist with Keynesian sympathies and—not incidentally—President Obama's first choice to head the Council of Economic Advisers, had already joined the chorus by suggesting, back in 1997, that leaving the gold standard, devaluing the dollar, and promoting price inflation were the keys to recovery between 1933 and 1937. In other words, she argued that the fiscal experiment called the New Deal had nothing to do with the fastest growth rates ever recorded in the twentieth century (yes, in those five years): the supply of money explained everything, just as Friedman and Schwartz had argued. It's also telling that Paul Krugman, a fierce and brilliant critic of Friedman's theories, recently validated the monetarist line on the 1930s: "Standing aside while banks fall like dominoes isn't an option. After all, that's what policymakers did in 1931, and the resulting banking crisis turned a mere recession into the Great Depression." In sum, it's telling that everyone, Left to Right, agrees that a "financial fix" was the indispensable first step in addressing the causes of the crisis, even though there is no evidence whatsoever that the banks made any contribution to real growth after 1933, or that they're contributing anything to recovery today.

In view of the broad agreement on the priority of a "financial fix," this last statement probably sounds a bit extreme. So let me put it another way. If the proximate cause of the Great Depression was a "great contraction of credit," a great *expansion* of credit should explain the recovery of 1933 to 1937, just as it should explain what is called the recovery of 2009–2010. But in the 1930s, the banks folded and never returned to the table. Instead they bought government bonds and parked their assets with the Fed, increasing their loans and discounts a mere 8 percent between 1933 and 1937, from a baseline close to zero—while in the current crisis, the banks are again sitting it out because the value of their "assets" is still in doubt. In the earlier recovery, price inflation was minimal even as industrial output doubled, so currency devaluation accounts for almost nothing there. In the current so-called recovery, both inflation and investment are absent and a 9 percent to 10 percent unemployment rate persists, but the money supply has more than doubled. So it's hard to see why economists believe the money supply or a "financial fix" explains much of anything, either as a cause or a cure for economic crisis. Why then does the monetarist consensus hold?

To begin with, timing is everything, as the ever-perky Friedman himself remarked when asked to explain his overnight success. He won the Nobel at the peak of "stagflation" in the 1970s, when most economists agreed that some kind of shock treatment was necessary to reduce inflation from an annual rate of close to 20 percent and to improve lagging labor productivity. The monetarists stood ready with their remedy, which amplified the effects of the supply-side revolution that was already changing the economic debates taking place in the Republican primaries. Beyond the exquisite timing of Friedman's prize, there was, however, another reason for his newfound authority, and that was the inability of anyone to explain the relation between the price of money (interest rates) and the price of labor (wages) or goods, except to say that the latter—the "real" economy—had nothing to do with the former. The silence was nothing new: there is no account of the Great Depression that convincingly explains this relation, and so far the best book on the big event treats the Crash of 1929 as a "random event" with no legible connection to the real economy, as if the burst of the stock market bubble was like the huge meteor that destroyed life on earth as the dinosaurs knew it.

Finally, the monetarist consensus holds because it's the one place where all sides can meet and agree on a solution to economic crisis—the assumption here being that you have to restore the liquidity of the banks and the confidence of investors by "ready lending," by increasing the money supply. Once you've done that, however, once the financial fix is in place, the so-called real economy is supposed to start working. If it doesn't, some serious government spending is in order, but if you come to rely on a fiscal solution, the rising national debt—the deficit—will sooner or later force you back to monetary policy. In contemporary parlance, to avoid a "sovereign debt crisis," you have to hope that your ability to manipulate the money supply will do the trick. What happens, however, when effective interest rates are at zero, as they have been since 2008, and yet crisis persists, or when you can't induce inflation by devaluing your currency? How, then, does the central bank shape the real economy?

Friedman proposed dropping money from helicopters—I am not making this up—if things got that bad. Of course he was trying to be funny, but his earnest apologist, Ben Bernanke, has, practically speaking, followed his hero's advice, and in doing so has turned the Fed into the lender of last resort for every imaginable kind of institution, from savings banks to hedge funds, even small businesses with commercial paper to discount (that is, to sell at less than face value to replenish their cash flow). The problem with this broadcast approach is not that it makes the Fed a replica of the Reconstruction Finance Corporation, the government agency that *replaced* the banking system in the 1930s (by 1934, it was loaning directly to businesses large and small, but also to cities and states with budget problems). No, the problem with this approach is that it treats every symptom in the same way, as if there's only one cure for whatever ails you. A "financial fix" can't address the causes of the current economic crisis, just as it couldn't address the causes of the Great Depression, because the supply of money can change, and has changed, without any appreciable effect on the "real" economy. Then as now, the banks are just the messengers, the guys who take the pictures and stick them in oversized envelopes, not the guys who read the film, tell you what it means, and give you the painkilling prescription. Then as now, the banks come bearing the bad news, not the cure for what ails us.

Morality

The three previous headings intersect because in every case the banks are the central figure in the narrative on offer—they made mistakes, they're too big and powerful, they need fixing. An explanation of economic crisis in terms of Morality would seem to be of a different kind rather than a different degree. But it secretly functions as the master text of these others; for the fundamental question raised by all of them is, what is to be done, and the answer is always another question: How must we change ourselves and our world to avoid this magnitude of disaster? These have become moral questions, just as they did in the 1930s, and especially as they've been framed by journalists looking for the big picture. The recent, best-selling *Report on the Financial Crisis*, a document sponsored by congressional mandate, similarly frames these same questions, and "Wall Street and the Financial Crisis," a report issued April 13, 2011, by the Senate's Permanent Committee on Investigations, goes further, announcing that Goldman Sachs deceived its clients and the public, exactly as Matt Taibbi of *Rolling Stone* had charged.

The question residing in the explanations of economic crisis I've so far covered is, What went wrong? What follows is, How can we make things right? Again, these are moral questions because they presuppose a certain responsibility or culpability on the part of some party to the bargain, if only we knew which one. Was it the fools, the monopolists, or the bankers, or do they share an address? The great irony here is that we want somehow to *personify* the idiocies of the market economy so as to restore its anonymous, providential force, as if we were trying to deflect the arbitrary effects of fate, hoping to humanize the gods by giving them names. The question never asked is, What if nobody's to blame?

Morality works on several levels, and for good reasons, as an explanation of economic crisis. The rhetoric is familiar, and effective, maybe because the universe it maps is a place no one has ever been. Here are some examples I've culled from books, magazines, talk shows, academic conferences, and conversations, all of them perfect clichés, which are by now so ubiquitous that you'd think there was one big book—some all-purpose moral thesaurus—everybody consults when it's time to pronounce on the real meaning of economic problems.

"Companies and individuals got 'overextended,' they got in over their heads, they started looking for short-term gain rather than long-term profit. They squandered resources rather than harboring them, rather than saving for a rainy day and making provision for an uncertain future. . . . They borrowed against assets they didn't have for frivolous or venal purposes, meanwhile lying to the banks and to themselves."

"At the same time, individuals consumed more goods than they needed—they lived beyond their means—but they never produced anything of value. Indeed their consumption of goods became a constraint on sustainable growth because it replaced saving and crowded out investment. . . . So the 'deleveraging' of debt and the 'liquidation' of doubtful assets—paying it down, going from deficit to surplus—are the necessary virtues imposed by periodic crisis. Equilibrium of both the financial and moral kind is the silver lining in the dark clouds of economic catastrophe."

This rhetoric governs discussion of every major economic crisis since the 1890s. For example, in October 1893, at the beginning of a sharp downturn that would last until 1897, Charles G. Dawes, then a young businessman from Lincoln, Nebraska—he would later be the principal author of the Dawes Plan, which sought to balance payments between the winners and losers of World War I—wrote in his diary as follows: "The panic has had one wholesome effect on business. It has weeded out the rotten concerns. . . . The habit of economy in domestic, business and national expenditures, which has been inculcated by the hard times, will have a good effect after the acute necessity is over." In 1932, at the trough of the worst economic crisis of the twentieth century, Bernard Baruch, the most influential investor of the moment, advocated balanced budgets all around—"Cut government spending, cut it as rations are cut in a siege," he cried—on the grounds that only this retrenchment would restore equilibrium. Meanwhile, Andrew Mellon, the secretary of the Treasury, urged his boss, President Herbert Hoover, to "liquidate labor, liquidate stocks, liquidate real estate," because this would "purge the rottenness out of the system." When the system was cleansed by this economic version of fasting, the body politic would be restored to health, and the good life would again be visible, measurable, attainable: "High costs of living and high living will come down. People will work harder, [and] live a more moral life."

Now you would think that this sort of sermon had gone out of style along with opposition to the New Deal. But you would be wrong. By November 2009 the romance of hard times was a staple of journalism, fed constantly by the exhortations of mainstream economics. And there was no predictable political valence at work here; liberals and conservatives alike were urging everyone to cut back, be virtuous, get real, go green, live sustainably, and above all, stop borrowing. All agreed that the crisis was an opportunity to balance every budget, the kind that fits in your moral calendar as well as the kind that ends with the fiscal year. On the Right, George Will, David Brooks, Tony Blankley, and many others worried about the disturbing economic effects of a decline of household savings after 1990; about an economy galvanized by the reckless hedonism of consumer culture; and about the debilitating moral effects of the entitlements built into the welfare state. These worries culminated in the spring of 2010, when Greece began to look like the end, not the beginning, of Western civilization—when columnists of every persuasion started reading the fate of the United States in the sovereign debt crisis of profligate European states.

On the Left, David Leonhardt, William Galston, Joseph Stiglitz, and many others worried about exactly the same issues, always in the hope of inducing more saving and investment, thus less consumption. So did the environmentalists at *Adbusters*, the glossy, anticapitalist, culture-jamming magazine that parodies famous advertisements and their corporate sources, and *n + 1*, a New York literary magazine, not to mention the new "frugalistas" like Lauren Weber, Laura Miller, and Curtis White, who have urged us to shrug off the trappings of consumer culture and live cheaply, in view of our manifest needs rather than the artificial desires created by advertising. The recent bipartisan drive to cut discretionary spending, undo "entitlements," and reduce the federal deficit is yet another instance of a moral imperative presented as an economic necessity.

The master text of Morality thus organized many strands of thought, like a magnet in the vicinity of those fabled iron filings: it was consistent with the notion that Mistakes were made, that Monopoly was the problem, and that Money was the root of all evil. It allocated blame in a comprehensive way, by suggesting that if only everybody hadn't become so avaricious, so desirous, so loaded up with the material freight of the world, why, that world would be a better place. This master text identifies certain villains, then, but in the end it also announces that we were *all* at fault: we know who the bad guys are, but we know, too, that our excess enabled them. As the cartoon cliché goes, we have met the enemy, and it is us.

The recent indictment entered by Robert Samuelson, the insightful *Newsweek* columnist, is a perfect example of this earnest, prophetic, almost biblical voice. In what follows, notice how the pronouns shift from the third to the first person and back again, so that everybody gets a share of the blame: "People were conditioned by a quarter-century of good economic times to believe that we had moved into a new era of reliable economic growth. . . . Their heady assumptions fostered a get-rich-quick climate in which wishful thinking, exploitation, and illegality flourished. People took shortcuts and thought they would get away with them."

Yes, people did think the future would look better than the disaster of the 1930s or the 1970s. But is that any reason to berate them—us— for a lack of foresight? No, of course not, that was a rhetorical question. Morality explains too little by addressing too much. The weak version of the moral explanation is that greed, self-deception, chicanery, and stupidity were the real causes of the disaster; but these aren't even deviations from the norms of modern life—without them there would be no novels, no movies—so how can we say that they explain anything?

The strong version of the explanatory claim that cites morality is much more compelling. It has two variations. First, several knowledgeable observers, among them Jeff Madrick, have suggested that the entire edifice of trading in derivatives—those securitized bonds known as CDOs—was founded on *fraud*: the banks, particularly the big ones like Deutsche Bank, Citigroup, Lehman Brothers, and Bear Stearns, knew they were selling toxic assets, and they knew well enough to bet against them, at least late in the game (ca. 2007, when the mortgage market was mysteriously buoyed by demand for more collateralized debt obligations). The ratings agencies like Moody's went along with this charade by giving triple-A designations to assets that barely deserved a double-B.

But Michael Lewis's careful research shows that *ignorance*, not fraud, accounts for almost all of the damage. The handful of fund managers who bet against the mortgage-backed CDO market—according to Lewis, these were seven or eight individuals at most, involving no more than five firms—*lost* money for years because they were betting on a sharp increase of mortgage default rates that didn't materialize until 2007. Moreover, for all their diligence and foresight, these lonely Cassandras never figured out what was actually contained in the various levels (or "tranches") of the mortgages bundled by the banks for sale to traditional pension funds and 401(k)s. Everybody was guessing.

The second variation on morality's strong claim to explanatory adequacy is a less exact but more important science, because its declared enemy is consumer culture. Almost all knowledgeable observers have suggested that an economy driven by consumption—to the extent that it accounts for 70 percent of GDP—is simply unsustainable. We need, then, to consume less, and save more, but public policy cannot force the change of habits and sensibilities that a less hedonistic culture would cultivate; a change of moral season, perhaps even a new culture war, is then needed to deliver these goods. The defect in this version of the strong claim is that, since 1990, consumer expenditures have indeed increased at the expense of saving and investment, but *not* because the latter were crowded out by the former, and *not* because the moral fabric of American life has unraveled. Investment has atrophied even as corporate profits have risen because these profits are, for the most part, redundant revenues with no place to go except into speculative markets where so-called securities like CDOs congregate; household savings have declined and consumer borrowing has increased because wages and salaries have stagnated even as executive compensation has multiplied many times over.

Our problem is not morality; it's surplus capital—a "global savings glut" that can't be fixed without redistribution of income from capital to labor, from profits to wages, from savings to consumption, an economic repair that's urgently needed both locally and globally.

THE MISSING M-WORD

So the Four M's do better as accusations than as explanations. My accounting of the available explanations for economic crisis would be incomplete, however, if another M-word were left off the list. That word is Marxism. Hasn't the academic Left offered a more or less Marxist analysis of the current crisis, which avoids accusation by asking the questions that the mainstream can't? Questions like: What if nobody's to blame? What if the deep structure of capitalism is the culprit? Then what?

The specter of Marx has, in fact, haunted debates about causes and cures of the current crisis, and not just at the invisible margins of classroom discussion, where the ghosts of theories past gather to scare unwitting students and irritate their parents. When mainstream economists and journalists turn back to Keynes, for example, you know that Marx is already waiting in the wings, because, as any number of qualified observers can tell you, the theory of business cycles to be derived from a study of Keynes—it's called the Harrod-Domar model—was first sketched in Marx's so-called reproduction schemes, in Volume 2 of *Das Kapital*, where the changing relation between capitalists' investment and workers' consumption became the cause of economic growth or crisis. And when cutting-edge literary magazines like *n + 1* start interviewing or celebrating Marxist icons like David Harvey and Eric Hobsbawm as part of an effort to understand the unfolding crisis, you know that old-fashioned political economy has returned from the grave; you know that, like Freddy Krueger, these world-weary Leftists are talented apparitions with sequels to film.

Younger Marxists have contributed to the debates, of course, most notably and brilliantly Robert Brenner, but they often proceed as if the point is to prove that Marx was right about the trajectory of modern capitalism. In this sense, theory becomes the end rather than the means of understanding the evidence at hand: it's as if the paradigm itself is the issue. Still, that reflexive bias, that self-searching theoretical agenda, is exactly what we should expect when the dominant paradigm—"normal science"—can't account for the available evidence.

But here's the rub: a resolute Marxist analysis of our present predicament is not a marginal event without consequence outside of academia. Instead, it's already entered the mainstream of thinking about this predicament—or so we might surmise from the ecstatic reviews of Brenner and Harvey in reputable, indeed genteel publications like the *Financial Times*, the *Los Angeles Times*, the *New York Times*, the *London Review of Books*, and the *Atlantic*, where both were hailed as prophets. In a political culture famous for its paranoid style, how did the overtly Marxist analysis on offer from Brenner and Harvey attain this intellectual dignity and policy-relevant status? In short, both assume precisely what mainstream economists do—that private investment out of profits in manufacturing fuels growth as such by increasing the (fixed) capital stock per worker and improving labor productivity as a result.

Brenner thus explains the secular trend toward stagnation in the post-1973 period as the result of a falling rate of profit in manufacturing, which in turn reduced investment and productivity, ultimately forcing nonfinancial firms to find higher returns in speculative markets outside of goods production. This process is what Harvey calls "investment in asset values," as against reinvestment of profits in the industry that produced them, and what Giovanni Arrighi called the "financialization" of assets as such in *The Long Twentieth Century* (1994), a book that serves as the backstory of most Marxist theorizing about contemporary issues.

The argument is plausible, to be sure, but it can't address two obvious questions. First, why does the shriveled sector of manufacturing qualify as the benchmark of a postindustrial economy? What historical criteria give it this odd privilege? Competition from what were once less-developed countries has certainly squeezed domestic manufacturers;

but the industrial labor force in the United States hasn't grown since 1905, and the profits from this beleaguered sector have long represented a small and declining share of nonagricultural revenues. Second, if profits are in such short supply, how do we explain the "global savings glut"— the surplus capital that fueled the hostile takeovers and merger movements of the 1980s, the dot.com craze of the 1990s, and then the housing bubble of the early twenty-first century? And here's a harder fact: the huge discrepancy between investment and retained earnings that characterized both the 1920s and the period since 1983 had no measurable effect on labor productivity; in fact, productivity increases in these decades were phenomenal, just as they were in the immediate postwar moment, ca. 1946–1955, when the capital stock per production worker declined and yet output of goods and services increased rapidly in line with productivity. In any event, the rate of profit is too gross a number to tell us anything about capital invested in this sector or that, and, at least as presented, it ignores the most salient feature of the post-1973 period—the systematic redistribution of national income away from labor, toward capital, away from wages, toward profits.

Harvey draws more directly on Arrighi in explaining the current crisis, or rather the "laws of motion" that govern and limit the accumulation of capital: he has a great deal more to say about the history of capitalism than the causes of the contemporary debacle. Here surplus capital looks to be the culprit but it is entirely "fictitious," something specious created by the new rules of debt leverage permitted by the deregulation of banking in the late 1990s. Crisis happens, it seems, when the "space-time configurations" required by orderly accumulation fracture, and the physical, brick-and-mortar limits of capital's mobility suddenly intrude on the instantaneous exchanges allowed by computer programs and financial derivatives. But Harvey hedges his bets when it comes to natural limits on capital accumulation—"the category 'nature' is so broad and complicated that it can encompass virtually everything that materially exists"—and, as a result, he never has to explain how the current crisis exemplifies a radical disjuncture of normal "space-time configurations."

So we have a rich, painstaking Marxist analysis of recent U.S. economic development, but it serves only as deep background on the story of our time. It doesn't really attempt to explain the contemporary catastrophe except as yet another ugly instance of what capitalism makes inevitable. Even so, I must agree with Benjamin Kunkel of *n + 1* when he declares that "it is only from a Marxian standpoint that the recent credit bubble can be understood." How else do we grasp the long waves of economic development that made for this disaster? Who else are we secretly citing when we turn, in desperation for answers, to Keynes? Still, the question is, Which Marxian standpoint? "There is always more than one of them," as Jacques Derrida insists in his most compelling work of mourning, *Specters of Marx* (1993). To my knowledge, there's no Marxist account of the Great Depression, or of our own Great Recession—except for my own ecumenical rendition, presented in Chapter 3—that specifies a legible relation between the mysteries of the financial sector and the fortunes of the "real" economy, then and now.

But there is a Keynesian account of this relation that will inform my occasional borrowings from Marx, and will also determine the interest rate on these short-term loans. It's not in *The General Theory of Employment, Interest, and Money* (1936), the great divide in twentieth-century economic theory. Instead, it's in *The Treatise on Money* (1930), the sprawling two-volume study written before, during, and after the Crash. Here Keynes reported on "the great expansion of corporate saving" in the 1920s, by which he meant the remarkably increased volume of retained earnings that was *neither* reinvested *nor* returned to shareholders (as dividends). In other words, he meant what I have called redundant profits, surplus capital, and he meant what the *Financial Times* columnist Martin Wolf has more recently called "the persistent surplus in the financial sector."

Keynes deftly used the American scene as his leading example: "In the case of the United States these internal resources of Joint Stock Corporations have been accumulating at a time when, owing to changes in methods of doing business, the amount of working capital has been decreasing rather than increasing, whilst expansion in fixed plant has been proceeding at a moderate rate. Thus industry had large liquid reserves which were available to be placed at the disposal of other developments, for example, building and instalment buying, either direct or through the banking system."

Translation: Industrial corporations were awash in profits that had no remunerative outlet, so they placed them with the banks, as time deposits, or loaned them directly "on call" in the stock market and to consumers at interest. Either way, these superfluous profits inflated whatever bubbles were available, because they weren't needed to expand output or productivity: the financial sector, mainly but not only the stock market, metastasized because it became the receptacle, and then the manager, of surplus capital generated elsewhere. As Keynes himself observed, a "profit inflation" coincided with a "deficiency of investment." This insight into the 1920s and its consequence in the form of the Great Depression is, in my view, still useful, and is perhaps the single most useful insight to be drawn from the Marxian tradition that Keynes unintentionally reinvigorated. At any rate I'll be using it in the next chapter to explain the Great Recession of our time.

My goal in appropriating Marx and Keynes, however, is to make them useful, not to prove them right. More to the point, my goal in noting the limits of extant explanations for the recent crisis is to show how each of them contains a certain truth, not to prove them wrong. Here I'm trying to follow the advice G. L. S. Shackle gave us in *The Years of High Theory, 1926–1939* (1967), a book that traced the origins and echoes of the Keynesian Revolution. He duly noted that "the innovating theoretician needs a ruthless self-belief" because he or she is tearing up the roots of tradition, razing the old "intellectual dwelling places." Even so, it's Shackle's concluding admonition that has stayed with me: "Yet reconstruction must inevitably use much of the old material. Piety is not only honourable, it is indispensable. Invention is helpless without tradition."

CHAPTER THREE

Their Great Depression and Ours

The economic crisis that started in 2007 has lived up to its early billing as the worst since the Great Depression—five years after their peak, the real estate markets hadn't yet hit bottom (the commercial real estate market made the residential version look rosy), long-term unemployment remained a serious problem, and consumers were still saving, not spending. At any rate they weren't using credit cards. So in 2011 we're still talking about how to fix the mess made by the so-called housing bubble. But for at least four years now we've been discussing the economy as if we want to return to "normalcy."

Meanwhile the Republicans and the Democrats have squared off several times on the federal budget, but everybody agrees that we need to reduce the deficit by promoting growth—or is it vice versa? And both sides insist that to promote growth, they have to help the so-called job creators in the private sector by balancing the budget and lowering corporate taxes, thus giving investors more incentives and making the United States "more competitive" in world markets.

This is the common sense of our times. It's pathetic, because it has nothing to do with the real causes of the recent economic crisis, and it diverts us from the discussion we need to shape the future we want.

This unfortunate common sense is the product of innocent but highly effective collaboration between influential economists, journalists, politicians, and citizens. That collaboration is animated by four assumptions. First, robust and balanced growth happens as a result of increasing private investment that seeks the highest return in free markets. Second, the money available for this increasing private investment derives from household savings and corporate profits. Third, growth driven by increased private investment in free markets is the best way to (a) underwrite *social mobility* by creating more and better jobs, (b) encourage personal *initiative* and self-discipline by promoting saving for a rainy day, and (c) guarantee individual *freedom* of choice by excluding the state from the most basic decisions on resource allocation. Fourth, tax cuts to induce higher savings and allow higher profits at the *expense* of consumption are the price we pay to maintain both economic growth and moral equilibrium. In other words, we redistribute income as a matter of course, but we reward rich people and large corporations in the hope that their investments will benefit the rest of us.

These assumptions have measurable consequences in the form of budget proposals, tax codes and tax cuts, interest rates, investment subsidies, enterprise zones, and other policy prescriptions. The budget confrontation between the Republicans and the Democrats in the spring and summer of 2011, which threatened to shut the federal government down, is a good example of these consequences. The Republicans proposed to cut corporate taxes as an incentive to investment, thus job creation, and the Democrats never bothered to object: both sides agreed that the path to prosperity is paved with private investment. But the assumptions that inform this bipartisan consensus don't produce an accurate description of the real world because robust and balanced growth under capitalism does not require—and since 1919 has not required—increasing private investment financed out of rising profits. In theory, then, the unfortunate common sense of our time is perfectly coherent. In practice, it produces economic disasters on the order of the Great Depression and the Great Recession.

The historical record shows that redistributing income upward by cutting corporate taxes—on the assumption that higher profits will mean more investment and faster growth—has merely enlarged the sum of surplus capital that is no longer needed to increase industrial capacity, to improve labor productivity, or to expand output by means of investment in new plant and equipment. Since this excess cannot find and has not found productive outlets, it has inevitably flowed into more risky, more speculative channels, creating bubbles wherever it goes. The two best examples of the process and its ruinous results are the Great Depression of the 1930s and the Great Recession of our own time.

The bottom line is this: Once upon a time, from roughly 1840 to 1920, increasing private investment in new plant and equipment made capital formation the engine of rapid growth. That increase of investment was funded from business profits—income withheld from consumption. Since 1919, however, growth has happened under capitalism because more and more of the national income has gone toward consumption, *not* because private investment in pursuit of profit has increased. As a result, the profit motive no longer serves the purpose of growth; tax breaks to enlarge business profits and encourage private investment are, then, pointless at best. By the same token, "saving for a rainy day" serves neither the economic purpose of underwriting growth nor the moral purpose of building character. So income redistribution in the name of more consumption and greater equity has become both the condition of renewed economic growth and the start of a new moral calendar.

That much seems obvious. But if the profit motive is an anachronism because private investment doesn't drive growth, what are the alternatives? What other motives will galvanize and organize the rational allocation of resources? Is there a market-based solution to the market-driven problem we measure by the scale of the recent economic disaster—a solution that isn't a quick fix for the wrong problem? In short, can we fix capitalism without making the market the adjunct of the state?

Well, yes, we can fix it, but to do so we must start with four new assumptions about how growth happens and why it matters. First, consumer spending is the key to robust and balanced growth. So we need to empower consumers by making their demand for goods and services *effective*; we need to make sure that good jobs and good wages are available to anyone willing to work. But beyond that, we need to make sure that no one has to buy the right *not* to die. In other words, we'll have to improve and increase the delivery of transfer payments or "entitlements," for the empowerment of consumers will require that we rethink the meaning and the consequences of work as such. We still tend to treat it as the proper index of both income and character: we think that your income should be proportionate to your effort, and that your character is both formed and improved by the kind of work you do for money (whether a profit or a wage).

Getting something for nothing—income without work—is a scandal in these terms unless it's the lottery that delivered your windfall. But now, with the export of so many good jobs and the more general "de-industrialization" of the American economy—the persistent problem of unemployment exemplifies these trends—we have to decide whether to (a) re-create "full employment" by the repatriation of manufacturing or (b) detach the receipt of income from the production of value through work. The former program puts us back to work in line with the modern criterion of *productivity* (from each according to his ability, to each according to his effort); the latter says enough already with socially necessary labor—to hell with work as we know it—and leads us back toward the ancient criterion of *need* (from each according to her ability, to each according to her needs). These aren't either/or choices, of course. But the criterion of need is more consistent with our historical commitments and our historical circumstances, and now I'm speaking in the first person in the name of the American people.

Meanwhile we need to understand that consumer *preferences* could serve as a qualitative limit on growth in two senses. On the one hand, consumers don't expect to profit from their spending except as future enjoyment of what they buy. They want local, particular, mostly material use values that are literally priceless, *not* exchange values, wealth in the abstract, mere money. They know that what they buy won't last forever, and they know that they can't own the future: their needs and desires are finite. On the other hand, consumer preferences can serve as a reliable guide to the measurable contours of market demand—a better guide, at any rate, than the pursuit of profit by Masters of the Universe who are unacquainted with retail realities.

Second, household savings, like corporate profits, are unnecessary to finance growth via private investment. We need, then, to map a new moral universe, where the deferral of gratification—postponing our desires, withholding our income from immediate consumption—serves neither the public good of fostering economic growth nor the private purpose of building individual character. To put it another way, we have to learn how to inhabit a social reality that is unfamiliar and uncomfortable.

Third, growth is neither endless nor an end in itself. It can of course be a means to the goals of (a) social mobility, (b) personal initiative and self-discipline, and (c) freedom of choice. But growth under capitalism has not always accomplished these worthy goals, and in recent years has even betrayed them. So we need to understand them as *social* goals—as public goods or use values that don't have market prices. Only then can we put them to the test of pubic, political debate, all the while looking for a way to limit the state's power in deciding how they are met. This procedure may sound schizophrenic—how can you make economic growth serve social purposes by means of political debate without creating a "nanny state" that supervises every transaction?—but in fact it's deeply etched in the history of American politics, from the 1790s to the present. The question we've always asked is, What kind of individual and what sort of society are validated by this version of economic development as opposed to that?

Fourth, and this follows from the foregoing, the "socialization" of investment becomes inevitable in view of the requirements of growth. I mean that we ought to treat investment as the Supreme Court treated private property in the very late nineteenth century, as something that acquires a public purpose and a public responsibility "when used in a manner to make it of public consequence." This "ought" is not a mere pious wish that things should be better—a moral imperative with no legible relation to the real world, to what "is." Soon after the court's decision in 1877, the new industrial corporations actually did socialize private property by separating ownership and control of each company's assets, tangible and otherwise. So, too, in this case. As soon as we start debating the social purposes of economic growth in public, political settings, we've acknowledged that investment can't be a strictly private matter. We might as well get on with the debate.

Here's a place to start: Investment should be grasped as the effect, not the cause, of consumer preferences—as something *induced*, from the bottom up, by the changing patterns of consumer demand and spending, not something decided from on high, by "the best and the brightest" on the trading floors. In other words, investment decisions should here-after be determined by a *qualitative* notion of profitability that closely measures the social consequences of such decisions—for example, by treating the occupational composition of the labor force (what kind of jobs does this investment permit?) as a key factor in assessing their costs and benefits. So growth requires a more equitable distribution of income—a redistribution away from profits and toward consumption. If the "socialization" of investment follows as a matter of course, as I have now suggested, growth also requires more, and perhaps better, po-litical democracy in deciding our economic futures; for to socialize in-vestment is ask what common good can come of growth, and to answer as majorities in both public and private venues.

These new assumptions describe an evident yet unknown economic reality and an uncharted moral universe. They invite thinking and imply policies that violate the common sense of our time. But they orient us toward the real world by allowing us to understand how growth actually happens under capitalism. If we want to fix it—it is surely broke—this understanding is indispensable.

THE COMMON SENSE OF OUR TIME:
HOW AND WHY WE BELIEVE THE MYTH OF INVESTMENT

A poll conducted by the *New York Times* and CBS News, published April 7, 2009, tells us exactly what is wrong with the debate on how to deal with the recent economic crisis—and how to imagine the future of growth. When asked about President Obama's plan to increase taxes on personal incomes over $250,000, 74 percent of respondents approved. And then they were "presented with the possibility that taxing those in the higher income brackets might hurt the economy." Only 39 percent of those polled still backed the plan. These results were reproduced al-most exactly in another poll published by the *Times* on May 2, 2011.

Now where did this dreadful possibility of hurting the economy come from? You might say it's just common sense; you can't raise taxes in a recession because, well, because Kennedy cut them and ended that nasty little downturn in his first year as president. And because everybody knows you have to provide incentives to the wealthy in the form of lower taxes on their incomes if you expect them to invest properly and create the jobs we need. And because everybody knows that if you redistribute income by taxing the wealthy, why, their incentives disappear, they stop investing, unemployment goes up, and there you go, you've made a bad situation worse.

This common sense tells us that growth requires private investment, that such investment requires incentives, and that higher incomes for the already wealthy are the best available incentive. Everybody knows that an unequal distribution of income is a requirement of comfortable existence for the masses. As John Lanchester recently explained, when the "jet engine of capitalism was harnessed to the oxcart of social justice" after World War II, the lives of ordinary people got better, and the "most admirable societies that the world has ever seen" were born. Everybody knows that "the prosperity of the few is to the ultimate benefit of the many," as columnists at the *Financial Times* and the *Wall Street Journal* constantly remind us.

To which I say, bullshit.

To put it more politely, our commonsense notion of how growth happens is completely mistaken. From Left to Right, we assume that private investment drives growth by building plant and equipment, creating jobs, raising labor productivity and per capita incomes—and thus underwriting social mobility. So we also assume that the public sector should be providing incentives to private investment, and that the party of growth and the party of redistribution must be at odds. We assume that the jet engine (growth) and the oxcart (social justice) are technologies that pull us in opposite directions.

We're wrong—these fundamental assumptions are false. Acting as if they remain true, regardless of the historical evidence, is what caused the economic crisis that began in 2007 with the meltdown of the subprime mortgage market. Acting as if they remain true, regardless of the historical evidence, will only prolong the crisis and foreclose fresh thinking about how growth actually happens—and why it matters.

Paying attention to the historical evidence lets us debunk the myth of private investment and explain why the redistribution of income has become the condition of renewed, balanced growth. Doing so lets us see that public-sector incentives to private investment—say, tax cuts on capital gains or corporate profits—are not only unnecessary to drive economic growth; they are also destructive. They don't lead to productive investment; instead they create tidal waves of surplus capital with no place to go except speculative bubbles that cause crises on the scale of the Great Depression and the recent catastrophe. Paying attention to the historical evidence lets us see, finally, that robust, balanced growth requires a more equitable distribution of income that favors consumers over investors, with all that implies for public policy, social theory, and, yes, moral philosophy; but to see this last requirement clearly, we have to rid ourselves of the conventional wisdom on the heedless extravagance of consumer culture.

You might well ask, If the historical evidence is so convincing, why do we accept the commonsense notion of how growth happens? The short answer is that the mainstream theories of prominent economists and the conventional wisdom of serious journalists constantly reinforce the myth of private investment. But the culprits are not just the supply-side insurgents who stormed the Keynesian citadel in the 1970s, then planted their flag inside the Beltway. By now the Democratic Party that reinvented itself in the 1990s shares the same assumptions that still guide the Republican Party—the same assumptions that let the liberal *New York Times* scare its poll respondents off taxing the wealthy.

This collaboration of mainstream economic theory, conventional journalistic wisdom, and political expedience has installed a common sense that bypasses reality. Good examples of how the three converge are on display every day in the media, from the manic talking heads at CNBC to the dignified pollsters at the *Times*. Here are two examples, one from the op-ed page of the *Times*, the other from the editorial page of the *Wall Street Journal*.

On May 4, 2009, Alan Meltzer, the influential economist and indefatigable Fed watcher, wrote a longer-than-normal op-ed for the *Times* in which he warned of the impending dangers of inflation—inflation induced, of course, by government spending under the rubric of "economic stimulus," a mantra since taken up by hundreds of "deficit hawks" who assume that the supply of U.S. Treasury bills must soon exceed demand, followed by an inevitable rise in interest rates, and perhaps even default on the national debt (the Republican Party has now staked its future on that assumption). The moral of Meltzer's story goes like this: "It doesn't help that the administration's stimulus program is an obstacle to sound policy. It will create jobs at the cost of an enormous increase in the government debt that has to be financed. And it does very little to increase productivity, which is the main engine of economic growth." Well, OK, there is that bigger deficit, but what fuels the fabled engine of increased productivity?

Meltzer explains as follows: "Indeed, big, heavily subsidized [government] programs are rarely good for productivity. Better health care adds to the public's sense of well-being, but it adds little to productivity. Subsidizing cleaner energy projects can produce jobs, but it doesn't add much to national productivity. Meanwhile, higher carbon tax rates increase production costs and prices but do not increase productivity." All right already, what *does* increase productivity?

Why, private investment, of course! "All these actions can slow productive investment and the economy's underlying growth rate, which, in turn, increases the inflation rate." To reach this conclusion, Meltzer must assume that private investment drives growth by increasing productivity, and that government spending slows growth by crowding out private investment and reducing productivity. The party of growth and the party of redistribution are, as always, at odds.

Here is the other example of the collaboration between economists, journalists, and politicians that produces the common sense of our time—the common sense that bypasses economic reality. On October 23, 2008, the editorial board of the *Wall Street Journal* forewarned its readers against the policies of an Obama administration by touting the results of George W. Bush's tax cuts: "After the dot.com bust, President Bush compromised with Senate democrats and delayed his marginal-rate tax cuts in return for immediate tax rebates. The rebates goosed spending for a while, but provided no increase in *incentives to invest*. Only after October 2003, when the marginal-rate cuts took effect immediately, combined with cuts in dividend and capital gains rates, did robust growth return. The expansion was healthy until it was overtaken by the housing bubble and even resisted recession into this year."

So only increased private investment induced by tax cuts can cause healthy, robust growth—just as Meltzer would argue six months later. *Except that it didn't.*

Leading advocates of capitalism such as Martin Wolf and Alan Greenspan have shown, much to their own dismay, that rising corporate profits and higher incomes for the wealthy did *not* flow into the sacred precinct of "productive investment" after 2001. Instead they flowed into the speculative channels offered by the housing bubble. Wolf noted in August 2007 that a "household deficit" of consumer debt "more than offset the persistent financial surplus in the business sector," where, *for six years*, corporations "invested less than their retained earnings." Greenspan concurred the same year in his autobiography, *The Age of Turbulence*: "Intended investment in the United States has been lagging in recent years, judging from the larger share of internal cash flow that has been returned to shareholders, presumably for lack of new investment opportunities."

In February 2010, Wolf followed up his pathbreaking analysis by citing an Organization for Economic Cooperation and Development report that measured a capital strike. He didn't call it that, of course, but he did note that "the private sector is now spending far less than its aggregate income," and that the idle surplus of profits held by corporations (banks included) amounted to 7.3 percent of gross domestic product in the United States. That figure, by the way, is almost certainly understated, but even as it stands, as a percentage of GDP, it's almost as much as the federal deficit (the so-called national debt), a sum that receives much more anxious attention.

Now Wolf and Greenspan, two advocates of free markets, free trade, and vigorous growth, treated this absence of investment as a deviation from an unstated norm—as something to be repaired as well as remarked. Both have urged less consumer debt, more personal saving, and increased private investment as the cures for what ails us. In this respect, they, too, are peddling the common sense that bypasses economic reality and tells us, regardless of the historical evidence, that growth somehow depends on getting a greater volume of investment out of the private sector.

But you don't have to be an eager advocate of free markets and free trade to peddle this same product. Take, for example, Joseph Stiglitz, a proud liberal, a brilliant critic of both the financial sector and globalization, and—not incidentally—a Nobel Prize–winning economist. On September 29, 2009, he told National Public Radio that while higher savings rates, and thus less consumer spending, are "good for the average American's security, the fact is that if people aren't spending there will be a lack of aggregate demand." This is of course bad news: "The economy will be weak. The question is what's going to fill in that hole [of less consumer spending]?"

And then, having just told us that we need more consumer spending to increase aggregate demand and cause a proper economic recovery— either that or the government keeps spending big time—Stiglitz reiterated the received wisdom by saying that in the long run we need a fundamental shift in priorities, away from consumption, toward saving and investment: "Our growth [after 2000] was based on debt, and it was the kind of borrowing not for investment, but for consumption, and that's just not sustainable."

David Brooks, a moderate conservative, exactly echoed Stiglitz on the following day in his regular op-ed column for the *New York Times*. Here he wrote that "indulgence and decline," the disappearance of "the country's financial values," and a "slide in economic morality" are all attributable to an eclipse of "personal restraint." According to Brooks, that eclipse was plainly visible in the explosion of "personal consumption" sustained by debt: since 1980, he noted, it has "shot upward" from 62 percent to 70 percent of GDP. Like the source he cited for these scary figures—it was the liberal political theorist William Galston, a former Clinton adviser—Brooks called for a new era of "public restraint," maybe even a new culture war on behalf of less spending, more saving, in a word: austerity.

But Stiglitz and Brooks were merely restating concerns about consumer culture that liberals and conservatives alike—from David Leonhardt at the *Times* to George Will at *Newsweek*—have been expressing since November 2009, when the romance of hard times became a journalistic staple. Meanwhile, President Obama and his advisers have kept saying that they want to "rebalance" the world economy—to begin, they want to reduce our trade deficit with China—by making growth in the United States "less dependent on domestic consumption," which presumably means more dependent on domestic investment.

So the unfortunate common sense of our time is not a right-wing ideology inflamed by supply-side firebrands. Not even strongly left-wing economists are immune to its explanatory spell. For example, Robert Brenner, the stalwart of *New Left Review*, explains the economics of global turbulence and the recent crisis in the classical Marxist terms of a falling rate of profit—productivity and growth lag, by this accounting, because lower profits (in manufacturing, and only in manufacturing) mean less investment, thus less capital stock per worker. No one would mistake the moral of Brenner's story for the one drawn by supply-side economists from the very same data, but their story is the same; perhaps that is why his books get praised by reviewers in the *Financial Times* as well as the *Nation*. David Harvey, the eminent Marxist geographer, meanwhile bemoans "investment in asset values" as against *reinvestment* of profits in the goods-producing industries that generated them in the first place, as if this business decision is both possible and necessary—as if investment must drive growth. And Dean Baker defends higher taxes on the wealthy by citing "the need to raise more revenue to run the government" when projected deficits get "larger than desirable," as they must when economic crisis becomes acute. He rightly claims a "powerful element of justice" for his plan to tax stock issues and trades, published in the *Economist* on April 19, 2009, because it would reduce the "gambling in financial markets" that caused the meltdown. But in taking this moral high ground, Baker as much as admits that taxing the wealthy won't promote economic growth; he as much as admits that enterprise and equality don't mix. The party of growth and the party of redistribution remain, therefore, at odds: the jet engine and the oxcart still pull us in opposite directions.

THE HISTORICAL EVIDENCE: CRISIS AND GROWTH SINCE 1919

The only way to free ourselves of the common sense that perpetuates the myth of investment, and to understand how growth actually happens, is to consult the historical record. The evident yet still unknown lesson to be drawn from this record is that the party of growth and the party of redistribution have merged in practice if not in theory: the oxcart is an essential component of the jet engine. Or, to put it more plainly, social justice is a vital source of economic growth. To put it in the terms required by the argument of this chapter, growth has happened precisely because net private investment has been declining since 1919, and because consumer expenditures have meanwhile been increasing.

To illustrate the lesson, let's have a look at the causes and consequences of growth and crisis since 1919. We can then return to our current condition with some comparative perspective in place. We begin with the origins and effects of the Great Depression.

1919–1933

Most contemporary economists now agree in explaining the Great Depression as a normal business cycle that was exacerbated by government policy. The founding father here is Milton Friedman, the archconservative who argued that the Fed unknowingly raised real interest rates between 1929 and 1932, thus freezing the credit markets and destroying investor confidence. But the argument has no predictable political valence. The liberal version of the monetarist line holds that if government does its minimal duty and restores liquidity to the credit markets, an economic crisis is unlikely to devolve into a debacle on the scale of the Great Depression—hence the bipartisan focus on a "financial fix" since the summer of 2008.

We've already seen how Niall Ferguson summarized this mainstream consensus for *Time* magazine: "Yet the underlying cause of the Great Depression—as Milton Friedman and Anna Jacobson Schwartz argued in their seminal book *A Monetary History of the United States 1867–1960*, published in 1963—was not the stock market crash but a 'great contraction' of credit due to an epidemic of bank failures." Ben Bernanke's rationale for the Fed's unprecedented initiatives, which have armed the central bank with the lending powers of a reborn Reconstruction Finance Corporation, derives, of course, from the same source. Here again is his toast at Friedman's ninetieth birthday party in 2002: "I would like to say to Milton and Anna: Regarding the Great Depression: You're right, we did it. We're very sorry. But thanks to you, we won't do it again."

In theory, then, the Great Depression was a financial meltdown first caused and then cured by central bankers. In fact, the "underlying cause" of this disaster was *not* a short-term credit contraction engineered by bankers who, unlike Ferguson and Bernanke, had not yet had the privilege of reading Milton Friedman's big book. The underlying cause of the Great Depression was a fundamental shift of income shares away from wages and consumption to corporate profits, which produced a tidal wave of surplus capital that could not be profitably invested in goods production—and was *not* invested in goods production. In terms of classical, neoclassical, and supply-side theory, this shift should have produced more investment and more jobs, but it didn't. Why not?

Look at the new trends of the 1920s. This was the first decade in which consumer demand for the new durables—autos, radios, refrigerators, vacuums, washing machines—became the driving force of economic growth as such. It was also the first decade in which inherited habits of household saving disappeared and borrowing to buy what you needed became normal; at least 80 percent of those durables were bought on time, using the new resource of installment credit. And it was the first decade in which a measurable decline of net investment coincided with spectacular increases in nonfarm labor productivity (roughly 40 percent) and industrial output (roughly 60 percent).

There are many ways to express this atrophy of net investment (or net capital formation). In his landmark study *Capital in the American Economy* (1961), Simon Kuznets noted that when measured as a component of national income or net national product, net investment fell by 20 percent from 1900 to 1930, declined "catastrophically" in the 1930s, and, in the "prosperous decade" of 1946–1955, was still 50 percent less than it had been in the 1920s (he also took note of "military capital formation," a polite way of saying that in the 1950s, Cold War defense spending by the federal government stood in for private investment). John Latourette has noted that capital-output ratios—capital inputs per unit of measurable output—began a steep descent in 1919. Alvin Hansen, Harry T. Oshima, Wassily Leontief, and others have noted the "capital-saving" technical innovation that characterizes the corporate age of scientific management that commenced around 1910 (capital saving in the sense that in 1925 you could build an oil refinery that tripled output at a fourth of what the same physical plant cost you in 1915). Moses Abramovitz, Robert Solow, Harold Vatter, and others have similarly noted that capital formation accounts for a small—and apparently declining—fraction of growth in the twentieth century.

These economists point us toward the awkward but verifiable conclusion that economic growth since the 1920s does not require net private investment or net capital formation—because the mere replacement and maintenance of the existing capital stock, which is financed out of retained earnings and depreciation funds, increases the productivity of capital and labor. In other words, net additions to the capital stock—private investments in new plant and equipment financed out of profits—are unnecessary to drive growth.

This new trend of the 1920s was the key ingredient in a recipe for disaster. At the very moment that higher private-sector wages and thus increased consumer expenditures became the only available means to enforce the new pattern of economic growth—at the very moment that net investment out of profits became unnecessary to enforce increased productivity and output—income shares shifted decisively away from wages, toward profits. For example, 90 percent of taxpayers had less disposable income in 1929 than in 1922; meanwhile corporate profits rose 63 percent, dividends doubled, and the top 1 percent of taxpayers increased their disposable income by 63 percent. Over the same years, there was a *net loss* of about 1 million manufacturing jobs due to instrumentation, automation, and electrification; the share of wages in the revenue of industrial corporations declined accordingly, by almost 20 percent.

What could be done with the resulting surpluses piling up in corporate coffers? If you can increase labor productivity *and* industrial output without making net additions to the capital stock, what do you do with your rising profits? If you can't (re)invest those profits in goods production because there's not enough demand for the exponential increase in output that would result, where do you place them in the hope of a reasonable return?

The answer is simple: you place your growing surpluses with bankers who, in turn, find the most promising markets, in new securities listed on the stock exchange, say, or in a Florida real estate boom (there's always one waiting), or in German municipal bonds, or maybe even in Peruvian consuls. You could also establish time deposits in commercial banks because you know you won't be needing those profits to invest in more productive plant and equipment. Or you could get ambitious and start issuing paper in the call loan market that feeds the trading frenzy in new securities.

At any rate, that is what corporate CEOs *outside* the financial sector did between 1926 and 1929. They opened time deposits worth $8.7 billion, and meanwhile they loaned directly on call in the stock market to the tune of $6.6 billion. They had no place else to put their increased profits. They could not, and did not, invest those profits in expanded productive capacity, because merely maintaining and replacing the existing capital stock was enough to enlarge capacity, productivity, and output. For example, the value of fixed capital *declined* at the cutting edge of manufacturing, in steel, oil refining, and automobiles, even as productivity soared (by 400 percent in automobiles), because capital-saving innovations reduced both capital-output ratios and the industrial labor force.

No wonder the stock market boomed, or rather, no wonder a speculative bubble developed there. It was the single most important receptacle of the surplus capital generated by a decisive shift of income shares away from wages, toward profits—and that surplus enforced rising demand for new issues of securities even after 1926. By 1929, according to Moody's Investors Service, almost two-thirds of the proceeds from such IPOs were spent "unproductively," presumably on something other than new plant and equipment or labor.

The stock market crashed in October 1929 when nonfinancial firms abruptly pulled their money out of the call loan market. Demand for stocks, whether new issues or old, disappeared accordingly, and the banks were left holding the proverbial bag—the bag full of "distressed assets" called securities listed on the stock exchange, where they had *doubled* their investments in the 1920s. That is why they failed so spectacularly in the early 1930s: again, not because of a "credit contraction" engineered by a clueless Fed, but because the assets they were banking on and lending against were suddenly worthless.

The financial shock of the crash froze credit—particularly the novel instrument of installment credit for consumers—and thus amplified the income effects of the shift to profits that dominated the 1920s. Consumer durables, the new driving force of economic growth as such, suffered most in the first four years after the crash. By 1932, demand for and output of autos were half the levels of 1929; industrial output and national income were similarly halved, while unemployment soared to 20 percent and even more.

1933–1973

And yet genuine recovery was on the way. Increased private investment was not.

No wonder, you might say, the banks remained paralyzed through the 1930s, and so could not transfer the public's savings into "productive investment." The banks were, in fact, more or less inert in the 1930s—according to the Comptroller of the Currency, they doubled their idle reserves parked at the Fed, and they more than doubled their holdings of federal securities (they bought government bonds, what we now call Treasury bills), but they increased their loans and discounts to business by only 8 percent between 1933 and 1937, even though Hoover's Reconstruction Finance Corporation stood ready to recapitalize them in much the same way Bernanke's Federal Reserve does today.

Nonetheless, growth happened without a financial fix. By 1937, industrial output and national income had doubled from the trough of 1932, regaining the levels of 1929 (at a lower price index, so growth was even more rapid than this multiple suggests). Meanwhile, however, net investment continued to decline, so that by 1939, the capital stock per worker was lower than in 1929 (and in 1955, it was even lower!).

How did this unprecedented recovery happen? It's not a rhetorical question. In view of classical, neoclassical, and supply-side theory—not to mention neo-Marxist models—*it couldn't have happened*. In their terms, investment out of increased profits must lead the way to growth by creating new jobs, improving productivity, and providing higher incomes, thus increasing consumer expenditures and causing their feedback effects on profits and future investment. But again, new investment was never forthcoming in the 1930s. H. W. Arndt, the British economist, puzzled over this anomaly in 1944. "Whereas in the past cyclical recoveries had generally been initiated by a rising demand for capital goods in response to renewed business confidence and new investment opportunities," he wrote, "and had only consequentially led to increased consumers' income and demand for consumption goods, the recovery of 1933–37 seems to have been based and fed on rising demand for consumer's goods."

But where did that rising demand come from if unemployment stayed stuck at 14 percent and more? We know it wasn't the result of a financial fix that restored the banking system to its proper place; nor was it the result of money supply expansion and price inflation caused by the abandonment of the gold standard in 1933. That rising demand was instead the effect of net contributions to consumer spending out of federal deficits—and, at another remove, of new collective bargaining agreements that empowered unions and raised real wages.

In other words, a shift of income shares away from profits, toward wages, permitted recovery, and that shift was determined by government spending and enforced by labor movements. Thus fiscal policy under the New Deal accidentally reanimated the new growth pattern that had first appeared in the 1920s: it restored the consumer-led growth that was eventually disrupted by the shift of income shares to profits, away from wages and consumption, between 1924 and 1929.

That consumer-led pattern of growth was the hallmark of the fabled postwar boom—the heyday, by all accounts, of "consumer culture." It lasted until 1973, when steady gains in median family income and non-farm real wages slowed, and even ended. So the same trends that emerged in the 1920s were still clearly etched in the economic development of this period. Certainly net private investment continued its secular decline. That is probably why the period from the 1950s to the early 1960s was when economists wrestled most energetically with the cause-effect relation between capital formation and economic growth. But the business cycles that punctuated the postwar boom never approached the social and statistical severity of the Great Depression. Why not? What offset the atrophy of net investment and sustained a consumer-led pattern of robust growth?

The short answer is what Herbert Stein called the fiscal revolution of the late twentieth century—also known as the rise of the welfare state, the advent of the "padded society," the "welfare shift," the "American Century," and/or "guns and butter." Each of these various designations conveys the essence of the matter: by 1970, public spending on health, social security, and education at home, combined with public spending on national security and economic development abroad, had made government at all levels the residual source of income for the majority of American citizens. In 1930, for example, private investment was still 50 percent greater than all public spending; in 1970 public spending was 50 percent greater than all private investment. Between 1959 and 1999, transfer payments provided by the federal government were the fastest-growing component of all household income, rising by 10 percent per year; by 1999, these payments amounted to a fifth of all labor income.

Meanwhile state and local governments were the fastest-growing sources of employment in the country, so that as early as the 1960s, between 18 and 20 percent of the entire labor force was directly employed by some branch of government. In sum, net contributions to consumer expenditures out of federal and state budgets—not always out of deficits—remained the single most important determinant of economic growth long after the New Deal; they provided the margin of consumer demand that smoothed the business cycles of the postwar boom.

At the same time, organized labor in the cutting-edge industries of steel and autos was enfranchised by law (the Wagner Act and its attendant, the National Labor Relations Board), and by collective bargaining agreements that committed the unions' corporate partners to paying wages consistent with productivity gains. In this sense, the new postwar power of the labor movement prevented any decisive shift of national income shares away from wages, toward profits; by the same token, that power set a limit on both corporate profits and the volume of surplus capital available for speculative purposes, say, in the stock market. The real estate boom on the crabgrass frontier of the postwar period was funded by commercial and savings banks—these were as closely regulated as public utilities until the 1970s—not by New York investment banks awash in profits from industries with bulging bottom lines.

1973–2008

Everything changed in the mid-1970s. This was the moment of "stagflation"—a bizarre new combination of stagnant productivity and price inflation. It sent economists, journalists, and politicians on a search for explanations of lower growth and higher prices. The immediate result was the end of the accidental consensus that had made consumer spending, public investment, and government regulation of markets the crucial ingredients in a proven recipe for growth. Hereafter those ingredients would be found on the supply side of the economic grocery rather than on the crowded shelves of Keynesian demand management.

But in the beginning, until the 1980s, the search for the new ingredients of growth was politically ambivalent. From Left to Right, from Felix Rohatyn and Lester Thurow to Ronald Reagan and David Stockman, everybody agreed that the civilizing effects of market forces had been blunted or softened by a "padded society" in which initiative, character, and risk couldn't count for much. From Left to Right, from Lloyd Cutler and Jimmy Carter to Peter G. Peterson and George Gilder, everybody agreed that a hedonistic consumer culture—a "welfare shift"—had contaminated the body politic, and that the market had in turn been distorted by the politics of economic entitlement. From Left to Right, everybody, even Teddy Kennedy, agreed that more saving, more private investment, and less market regulation were urgently needed. Since 2008 there has been renewed debate on regulation, of course, but on the questions of saving and investment, this bipartisan consensus holds.

Neoliberals and neoconservatives had together written a new recipe for growth, in other words, long before the supply-side revolutionaries penetrated the Beltway and took over the supermarket of ideas. Better incentives for investors—higher incomes for the wealthy—were the crucial ingredients of that bipartisan recipe. And those incentives would of course take the form of tax cuts designed to shift income shares away from wages and consumption, toward profits and dividends.

This shift of income shares was not the hidden agenda of the so-called Reagan Revolution, which carried the supply-side banner to victory in 1980. It was the centerpiece of economic policy for the candidate as well as the president. And it worked—*only not as it was supposed to*. The tax cuts sponsored by Reagan caused growth not by promoting saving and investment, as they were intended and advertised, but by doubling the federal budget deficit and increasing aggregate demand accordingly.

For example, the fifty corporations with the largest benefits from the tax cuts of 1981 reduced their investments over the next two years. Meanwhile, the share of national income from wages and salaries declined 5 percent from 1978 to 1986, while the share from investment (profits, dividends, rents) rose 27 percent, in keeping with the imperatives of supply-side theory—but net investment kept falling through the 1980s. In 1987, Peter G. Peterson, the Blackstone founder who was then chairman of the Council on Foreign Relations, called this performance "by far the weakest net investment effort in our postwar history." And yet economic growth resumed in the aftermath of recession, in 1982, and continued steadily until the sharp but brief downturn of 1992.

The boom of the 1990s similarly coincided with a weak net investment "effort." What changed in that decade was the resumption of labor productivity gains, not the return of economic growth driven by private investment. But unlike in the immediate postwar decades, the greater national income generated by those productivity gains was not shared equitably between labor and capital in the 1990s. Instead, profits, dividends, rents, and executive compensation increased at the expense of wages and salaries. In 1980, for example, CEOs at Fortune 500 companies were paid roughly 42 times the average worker's salary; by 2007, that multiple was 364. Between 2002 and 2006, 75 percent of all income growth accrued to the top 1 percent of taxpayers, presumably as a result of the tax cuts sponsored by the Bush administration.

But why didn't this shift of income shares reproduce the disaster we call the Great Depression? Three factors offset it in the 1990s, and postponed the day of reckoning until the next century. First, transfer payments and so-called entitlements kept growing at the same pace as in earlier decades. Second, household savings began to decline—thus

placing in circulation income hitherto withheld from aggregate consumer demand—as household spending began to increase faster than
household income. Third, and most important, a deregulated financial
industry grew exponentially by extending consumer credit in every de-
mographic direction, most emphatically and effectively by sending a
credit card to almost every adult. In sum, consumer demand kept the
party of growth alive by compensating for the continued atrophy of net
private investment.

In the early twenty-first century, these patterns held. Once again
real growth coincided with surplus capital provided by tax cuts, on the
one hand, and investment failure—or capital strike—on the other. From
2001 to 2007, American consumers went deeper and deeper into debt
to finance the nation's current account deficit, so that by 2007, household
debt was 4 percent of GDP and over 100 percent of household wealth;
this growing "household deficit" offset the idle surpluses that were meanwhile piling up in the business sector, where, for six years, corporations
invested less than their retained earnings (the same pattern still holds
in 2011).

So the Bush tax cuts, which the *Wall Street Journal* touted as the
cause of healthy, robust growth, merely inflated the housing bubble,
the last remunerative receptacle of redundant profits and bloated high-
end incomes. Those cuts did not, and could not, lead to increased productive investment. And that is the consistent lesson to be drawn from
any fiscal policy that corroborates, or creates, a shift of income shares to
profits, away from wages and consumption. A fiscal policy that cuts taxes
on the wealthy and/or lowers the capital gains levy cannot and will not
work to restore growth because, as the historical evidence repeatedly
demonstrates, increased private investment doesn't automatically flow
from increased savings induced by tax cuts—and, much more important,
because the conversion of increased savings to increased private investment is simply unnecessary to fuel growth.

The common sense of our time stands convicted, therefore, of imbe-
cility. The historical evidence shows that there is *no positive correlation
whatsoever* between lower taxes on personal income or corporate profits,
increased private investment, and economic growth. The strong correlation

we *can* demonstrate, in view of this evidence, is between lower taxes on corporate or personal income, declining net private investment, and speculative bubbles that led to economic crises, as, for example, in the periods from 1919 to 1939 and 1981 to 2009.

Put it another way. The financial collapse and the credit freeze that characterize both the 1930s and our own time are symptoms, not causes, of a broader economic crisis determined by our mistaken belief that to foster growth, we must provide capitalists and corporations with incentives to invest. In fact, these incentives are merely invitations to inflate speculative bubbles. So if we want to create the conditions of robust, balanced growth rather than suffer through serial crises on the order of the Great Depression and the Great Recession, we need to empower consumers, and, by the same token, embrace consumer culture.

CHAPTER FOUR

Living Forward

Economic History as Moral Philosophy,
Social Theory, and Political Science

"GREAT CHANGES IN THE CODE OF MORALS"?

What is at stake in empowering consumers and embracing consumer culture? To put the same question more expansively, What is growth for, anyway? Who benefits from it, and who doesn't? Are there any limits on it? Should there be? To address such questions, we'll have to follow the lead of Adam Smith, the founding father, who thought of political economy as a new kind of moral philosophy. For the way we think about the economics of investment and consumption will determine our approach to moral issues, social problems, and political programs. As John Maynard Keynes put it in 1930, "When the accumulation of wealth is no longer of high social importance, there will be great changes in the code of morals."

But we don't have to reach into the history of economic theory if we want to understand the intimate relation between political economy and moral philosophy. The budget battles over so-called entitlements that deadlocked Washington in 2011 are, at bottom, debates about the proper alignment of effort and reward, work and income, production and consumption. The Republican argument for cutting or capping entitlements like Medicare, Medicaid, and Supplemental Nutrition Assistance (food stamps), for example, goes like this: "A government that buries the next generation under an avalanche of debt cannot claim the moral high ground in the world. . . . From a moral perspective, these programs are failing the very people they are intended to help. . . . The safety net should never become a hammock, lulling able-bodied citizens into lives of complacency and dependency."

Moral Philosophy

So let's see what happens when we speak this language. If we go along with the Republicans who wrote the report I just quoted and assume that private investment drives growth, we'll tend to believe that the redistribution of income in the name of more consumption and greater equity is a disincentive to save—that is, to accumulate wealth. As such, it is also a death sentence on individual initiative, personal ambition, and economic growth. It is a *moral* disaster because it teaches us that hard work and the deferment of gratification (saving for a rainy day) are pointless; by the same token, it is an *economic* disaster because it deprives the banks of the deposits they need to loan to businesses that want to invest in new plant and equipment. Taxing the wealthy at higher rates thus becomes a very hard sell even for left-wing economists like Dean Baker, because, just like their opponents on the supply side, they assume that enterprise and equality don't mix; the either/or choice they offer is, as always, between growth and redistribution, between the jet engine and the oxcart.

If we drop the assumption that private investment drives growth—in other words, if we acknowledge the measurable fact that, since 1919, real growth has happened in the absence of increasing net private investment—then we can easily justify taxing the wealthy and redistributing income on both moral and economic grounds. And we don't have to cite the emergency of recession-induced deficits. All we need do is consult the historical record.

The short version of the argument goes like this. Private-sector profits and high-end incomes have not found, and cannot find, remunerative outlets in productive venues because both laborsaving and capital-saving innovations have made them more or less redundant since the 1920s—

because net private investment has been unnecessary to drive growth. They have flowed, therefore, into speculative channels like the stock market bubble before the Great Depression and the housing bubble before the recent crisis. To increase corporate profits and high-end incomes by cutting taxes on them is then to invite more speculation, more "gambling in financial markets."

Incentives to invest in the form of tax cuts can only augment the supply of redundant profits and surplus capital; so they must corrupt the morals of both Wall Street and Main Street by inflating every available bubble. And by inflating those bubbles, such incentives become causes of economic crisis, not conditions of economic growth. By reducing the volume of surplus capital, the redistribution of income in the name of equity reduces both the temptation to gamble with other people's money—a "moral hazard" if ever there was one—and the risk of bubbles and crises. In sum, the redistribution of income in the name of equality changes the moral season for the better, but it also improves the chances of balanced growth.

So conceived, economic analysis unbound by the assumption that private investment drives growth reopens pressing moral questions. For example, most economists, journalists, and talking heads agree that the real causes of the economic crisis that finally struck in 2008 were financial excesses fueled, in turn, by an unsustainable model of growth favoring consumption at the expense of saving and investment. By their accounting, greed, fraud, corruption, and crime on Wall Street were matched—maybe even exceeded—by greed, fraud, chicanery, and debt on Main Street.

From this standpoint, the explosion of household debt in the last two decades is a *moral* problem that stems from the erosion of prohibitions against borrowing and spending beyond one's means. The orgy of excess that resulted was clearly a function of a hedonistic consumer culture, where everybody's "branded" and happily sunk deeper in debt. So the crisis that still besets us is a reminder that the market is a godlike presence, a universal moral calendar: it will finally exact its price; it will eventually reassert a proper, proportionate relation between effort and reward, work and income, assets and liabilities, self-discipline and saving, or crime and punishment—not to mention supply and demand.

With all due respect to God, this idea is at best a faith-based initiative. In fact, the astonishing increase in household debt after 1990 *sustained* growth by balancing the nation's current account deficit in two ways. First, it absorbed the "global savings glut," as Ben Bernanke called it before he became chairman of the Fed. Second, it offset the atrophy of net investment from the private sector. This debt also allowed for consumer spending in line with improvements in labor productivity enabled by computer technology over the last twenty years; in doing so, it temporarily rectified an increasingly unequal distribution of income that couldn't support growth because it rewarded management at the expense of labor, and thus magnified the volume of surplus capital that already saturated the system.

The astonishing increase of household debt is not, then, a moral problem. It was instead a *makeshift* market solution to real economic problems—balancing the current account deficit and sustaining consumer demand. The better solution would, of course, have been empowering consumers through higher wages; but this adjustment of income shares was unlikely in the absence of a strong labor movement and public policies conducive to union organizing, collective bargaining, and wage rates pegged, as in the 1940s, 1950s, and 1960s, to productivity gains.

Social Theory and Political Science

Economic analysis unbound by the assumption that private investment drives growth raises social and political questions as well. Here is how. We know that the social structure and the paths of social mobility are determined by the occupational composition of the labor market—by the quantity and the quality of jobs created from year to year. We have assumed, along with the economists and the journalists and the politicians, that these jobs were created by private investment, and have provided tax incentives accordingly, to maintain an appropriately "American" standard of living. But when we drop this assumption, in view of the historical evidence, our thinking about growth gets complicated.

For then we have to ask, What role does private investment actually play in creating jobs, improving productivity, increasing per capita incomes, and underwriting social mobility? If it does not and cannot play the role written for it in economic theory, how do we choose an understudy that will determine a social structure in which the public goods of mobility and opportunity are realities? The historical evidence suggests that private investment can't play the part as written, so we have to somehow recast the function of investment—we have to redefine this function, hitherto monopolized by capitalists and managers in the private sector, of allocating resources in the most productive ways. We have to schedule new auditions. But where do we post the appropriate announcement? Who'll show up?

As soon as we ask these questions, others appear. If we know that incentives to private investment which increase after-tax profits are invitations to speculation rather than means to the end of growth, the profit motive loses its regulative purpose in allocating resources; it begins to look like a vestigial urge, something like a prehensile tail or an intestinal appendix, maybe even an anal fixation. When we see it that way, as a mere vestige of a past we can't reclaim, we know what Keynes was getting at because we're no longer hostages of what Henry James called the "grope of wealth" and "the reiterated sacrifice to pecuniary profit." But what alternative purposes would be effective in allocating resources properly? If we know that private investment can't create the jobs that will underwrite the public goods—the use values—of mobility and opportunity, we will probably have to use *political* means to define alternatives to the profit motive, and to generate a social structure in keeping with the American Dream.

But if the politics of growth takes on this new meaning, where do we draw the line between the state and the market—or have we already crossed that line in bailing out the banks and turning the Fed into an extralegal equivalent of the Reconstruction Finance Corporation? The questions before us boil down to these: How do we *socialize* the investment function without making the economy the mere adjunct of the state apparatus? How do we preserve the central principle of American politics—the supremacy of society over the state, the sovereignty of we, the people?

To drop the assumption that private investment drives growth, is, then, to ask social questions that carry political connotations. This is especially true when our discussion turns to the relation between private investment, jobs, work, and wages. For example, what has offset declining net private investment in sustaining job growth and rising per capita incomes? If the key offset has been the redistribution of income enabled by progressive income taxes, transfer payments, entitlements, and public spending—if a more equitable distribution of income has *already* proved to be the condition of growth—then we should welcome higher taxes on the wealthy and more federal spending. If the key offset has been the explosion of consumer debt rather than better jobs and higher wages, then we should ask how we can treat it as a macroeconomic problem— a problem of income distribution, not of moral standards—to be solved by public policy, perhaps more federal spending to create better jobs and higher wages.

Either way we answer, more questions arise, because to let public spending stand in for private investment is to start, not settle, an argument about the meanings of work and the distribution of income. We know that the largest and the fastest-growing components of the federal budget are so-called entitlements and transfer payments such as Medicare, Medicaid, Aid to Dependent Children, Supplemental Nutrition, and Social Security; as we have already noted, transfer payments have grown 10 percent per year since 1959, amounting to 20 percent of all labor income by 1999. Income derived from these sources is received by individuals who have made no commensurable contribution to the supply of goods and services; they're receiving income but not working for it. A new analysis of Medicare payments and distributions suggests, for example, that a retired couple's combined lifetime contribution of $140,000 in taxes yields about $430,000 in current dollar benefits from Medicare.

David Brooks, among many others, calls this situation "immoral." They mean that Medicare beneficiaries (or welfare recipients as such) are challenging the premise of the Protestant ethic and the American

Dream, because they inhabit a world in which a legible relation between effort and reward, between work performed and income received— between production and consumption—has been erased. Brooks and his strange bedfellows are too quick to enter moral indictments against what they call an "unaffordable" welfare state. But they're raising the right questions.

They make us ask, What is work for if it is not the basis of a legitimate claim to a share of society's goods? If the receipt of income (wages, salaries, compensation as such) is now detached from the production of things with value, how can work serve as a source of self-discipline or an index of real effort? In other words, what's the proper relation between effort and reward? Should we begin to think of work as an end in itself, as if higher education had somehow become our basic industry? Or should we begin to think of work as *merely necessary*, something we have to get done—not as the proper measure of our meaningful exertions, but as time diverted from what we want to do? In view of increasing incomes without work, are we now to believe that the criterion of need is the principle that should regulate the allocation of resources, as in "from each according to her abilities, to each according to her needs"? If so, what follows for the conduct of American politics? More to the point, what follows for the possibilities of economic growth?

THE POSSIBILITIES OF ECONOMIC GROWTH

Once we drop the assumption that private investment drives growth, we're already in search of alternatives to the profit motive as the purpose that regulates the allocation of resources. And so we're already asking central questions: What is growth for, anyway? Who benefits from it, and who doesn't? Are there limits on it? Should there be?

I've suggested that if we want balanced economic growth rather than serial crises fed by redundant profits and high-end incomes, we should be empowering consumers and embracing consumer culture; we should be decentering decisions about resource allocation by giving priority to consumers' preferences (use values) as against investors' imperatives (exchange values). I'd like to think that decentering these decisions could *democratize* the market economy.

The premise of my optimistic view is that the long-term atrophy of net private investment and the unmistakable rise of consumer spending have made a more equitable distribution of national income the condition of growth. Instead of accumulating surplus capital and inflating bubbles by cutting taxes on profits, dividends, and capital gains, we should now be empowering consumers by ensuring that they can earn, or rather *receive*, incomes sufficient to make their demand for goods and services *effective*; we should be embracing consumer culture rather than bemoaning the excesses of the recent past and imposing austerity on ourselves among others. One way to spell out the morality of spending rather than saving is, then, to say that balanced growth requires a more perfect union based on a closer approximation of equality.

Another way to spell out the morality of spending rather than saving is to say that a model of growth based on consumer culture would have to *socialize* the economic function of investment in two related senses. First, the criteria of productive investment must be complicated by making the occupational composition of the future labor market a public good, a social goal—a use value—which requires political discussion; where shortages of private investment are obvious, public spending can make the difference. The Congress, the electorate, and the media already engage in this kind of discussion by debating tariff and immigration policy, so the politics of growth are, at this level of discourse, nothing new.

But the *quality* of investment is just as important as the quantity of investment. We already know from long experience that the kinds of industry favored by investors, not to mention the employment practices typical of those industries, will shape the racial and the gender and the age composition of the workforce as well as wage levels. So the relevant political discussions must feed into macroeconomic "indicative planning"—not the central plan of Soviet-style development—which uses interest rates, federal subsidies, matching grants, and tax incentives, and meanwhile enlists trade associations, consumer cooperatives, environmental movements, and labor unions to guide productive investment, both public and private. Senator John Kerry's recent proposal for a bank to fund infrastructure renewal and development is a good example of socialized investment in this sense: it's a mix of public and private enterprise, neither a government program nor corporate welfare. It would use matching federal loans and grants to encourage private enterprise in what has long been the province of public spending.

Second, investment as such, whether public or private, should hereafter be understood as the *effect*, not the cause, of consumer incomes and expenditures—as something *induced* by consumer preferences registered in market choices and money values, not produced by the superior wisdom of "the best and the brightest," the insiders who know where to place their bets on the future. Treating investment in this way not only reinstates but also *redefines profitability* as an incentive from the demand side of the economic equation. To my mind, it offers a better market-based solution to the problem of private investment than tax cuts on profits, dividends, and capital gains, because it provides a decentered, bottom-up set of signals in the form of prices rather than a consensus imposed from the supply side by financial planners who are removed from the retail realities of consumer demand. Treating investment in this way is certainly consistent with recent research suggesting that it's the effect, not the cause, of growth: it *follows* the demand curve. More importantly, however, treating investment in this way gives priority to the use values consumers know they want rather than the exchange values investors think they need.

In sum, then, to socialize investment is not to expropriate and collectivize the means of production on behalf of the working class—whatever that may be—but to assert only as much public control of the investment process as necessary to make broadly social goals, rather than the private profit of the very few, its central purpose. The tax system is a good place to start thinking along these lines, especially since discussion about its social functions has already begun in earnest. For decades now, we've thought of taxing corporate profits as a constraint on private enterprise and investment (thus productivity), and so we've lowered them in the hope of growth induced by more enterprise and more private investment. The revenue side of the question has rarely come up, because faster growth is supposed to increase the volume of taxes the government can collect: the social goal of growth has trumped the fiscal requirements of the state. In this sense, investment has already been socialized, since elected officials have reshaped the tax code in the name of a social goal most Americans still agree on. So I'm proposing to take the socialization of investment a step or two further, to broaden, maybe even redefine, the social ends that economic means can meet. A radical redistribution of income has been happening for a generation because the tax code, among other political artifacts, has allowed and enforced it. But to merely reverse this redistribution is not enough to protect us from the effects of private investment driven by profit alone. We now have to discuss and decide on the goals that a socialized rendition of investment could realize.

But notice that to treat investment in this way is also to export *consent* from the public sector to the private sector, and meanwhile to turn a principle of political obligation into a *social norm* that could enlarge the domain of democracy by including the market economy. Here is how. We're politically obligated to abide by the decisions of the state—by the laws—because we've participated in their making, mainly but not only by electing our representatives. Our *prior consent* as citizens and voters of the republic gives legitimacy to the ongoing exercise of power—the enforcement of the laws—by the state. Now public opinion is the *practical* embodiment of consent. The politician who claims to ignore it in the name of a higher truth, or just because he knows better than his constituents, is therefore betraying the very possibility of democracy because he's acting as if consent is irrelevant to legitimate governance.

So, when I suggest that we need to socialize investment because consumer spending has become the condition of growth, I'm also insisting that the investors among us learn to treat consumer preferences as politicians have learned to treat public opinion, as the practical embodiment of consent—something to be consulted, not controlled or ignored. With that lesson learned, consumers would finally be given a voice, and a choice, in answering those central questions about growth. When they are thus enfranchised, the future of public goods—use values like equal opportunity and social mobility in the labor market—would no longer appear as "externalities" that are irrelevant to the decisions made in private by investors in search of higher profits, more exchange value.

By the same token, the public good or use value of *environmental* integrity would no longer appear as another one of those "externalities." So the limits to growth could become a real, practical question to be decided democratically, in public, using both market devices and political measures—but only if we understand consumer preferences as a vital, measurable form of public opinion. We will probably decide that growth must go on because it serves our social purposes; the point is that we will have the choice to speak as a majority, and to debate the means to our common ends.

The possibilities of growth are not endless. By this I mean that there are limits to growth, and that we can no longer treat it as an end in itself. But we now have the opportunity and the obligation to ask what we want from it. In the past, growth was a way of avoiding class formation and then pacifying class conflict. Herman Melville got it right in *Clarel*, his epic poem of 1874: "The vast reserves, the untried fields / These shall long keep off and delay / The class war, the rich and poor man fray." Economic growth had an overriding political purpose—to preserve popular government by allowing social mobility, thus avoiding the rigidities and resentments of class society. Growth still has political purposes, of course, as every piece of American foreign policy and every defense of globalization will attest. But now we can see that the economics and the politics of democracy converge on the meanings and the scope of consent—on what we, the people, can choose. And this range of choice is where consumer preferences can become a form of public opinion as well as an economic option.

Once upon a time, before capitalism changed everything, consumption was, in fact, the end—both the goal and the limit—of goods production. Money and credit were widespread, but they were merely means of exchange, what people needed to acquire the use values they wanted. The point of goods production was not, then, to expand wealth in the abstract, to enlarge monetary claims on the future by seeking the highest return on investment in the present; instead, the point of goods production was to re-create the material foundation of a self-determining individual, a priceless use value if ever there was one.

But when I propose to empower consumers by socializing investment, I don't mean to point us toward a precapitalist arcadia in which
easy money and instant credit were economic encroachments on a moral
equilibrium. Instead I mean to improve the market efficiencies of capitalism by redistributing income, so that balanced growth rather than another speculative bubble is the likely result of consumer preferences as
well as public policy; consumer credit will be a key component of growth
so conceived. Unlike the politically correct talking heads on both the
Left and the Right, I can't blame the wretched excess of consumer culture for either the degradation of the environment or the current financial debacle. I can't because I assume that when consumption is the end
of goods production, then exchange value can be *contained*—in both the
inclusive and the exclusive sense—by use values, and the proper limit
of growth comes into view.

But in saying this, I don't mean that we already know what we
need, so that bearing coupons, buying locally, and bargaining aggres-
sively will suddenly align us in a self-evident program of moral improvement with all the right economic results. The new Puritans, those
"frugalistas" who believe that a sustainable model of growth requires
a "return to thrift"—less consumer debt, more saving and investment,
and so on, in keeping with the common sense of our time—are peddling nineteenth-century news.

I mean instead that we can't know what we need until we ask the
following questions. What kinds of individuals do we want to be, and to
cultivate in the future? And what is the material foundation of that
individuality—what kind of economic development, and what kind of
consumption, would sustain it? Does consumer culture undermine political engagement by "privatizing" personal experience, or does it permit
a new politics? Does the sex of things determine their meanings? Does
advertising deceive you, or teach you where true freedom lies? And what
kind of work do we want to do? Or are we finally in a position to ask
not how but *whether* the production of value through work determines
your character and measures your moral capacity? My answers follow
in Part Two: The Morality of Spending.

PART TWO: THE MORALITY OF SPENDING

CHAPTER FIVE

The Politics of "More"

From Gompers to Du Bois

WORKERS AS CONSUMERS: WHAT GOMPERS MEANT BY "MORE"

My aim here is to counter your intuition and convince you that consumer culture is not the enemy of social movements and political agendas that matter—it's not the place where important solidarities and commitments to social justice go to die. I want to persuade you that a new kind of politics, "the politics of 'more,'" is enabled by consumer culture, *and* that it takes on revolutionary meanings in the late twentieth century. So I start with Sam Gompers in North America and end up with Vaclev Havel in Eastern Europe, passing, meanwhile, through the neighborhoods occupied by W. E. B. Du Bois and the civil rights movement, where consumer preferences and boycotts became political weapons.

You've probably read about Sam Gompers in a history textbook, high school or college, maybe even earlier. If you remember anything about him, it's probably his woeful lack of "militancy" with respect to wage labor and the large corporations; he wasn't much interested in overthrowing anything. He was the founding father of the American Federation of Labor (AFL), along with many other Marxists, Socialists, and trade unionists. The Federation got started in 1882, and consolidated its leadership of the larger labor movement in the early twentieth century (although "renegade" unions flourished then, as now), becoming, by 1918, the poster boy for civilized class struggle.

Gompers's approach to the labor question has always been known as "business unionism" or "pure and simple" trade unionism. These labels still carry a lot of political weight on the Left—they remind us of the radical alternatives offered by the Knights of Labor and the Populists— because the AFL did relinquish any urge to abolish wage labor, the essential component of capitalism. Unlike the Knights, Gompers and his compatriots accepted the permanence of their propertyless status—they knew they'd never be their own boss, so they gave up on the ideal of the self-made man—and, unlike the Populists, they treated "the trusts" (the new corporations) as a given, a mere fact, not something to be legislated out of existence.

When asked what the labor movement wanted, Gompers always said, "More." This answer got him in trouble with the radicals of his day, who, like their distant cousins among the contemporary critics of consumer culture, wanted broader and deeper change—maybe even the overthrow of capitalism—and who distrusted the gross materialism of the AFL's refrain. Then as now, these critics assumed that our material and spiritual ends must be at odds, that our bodily desires and mindful needs are always in conflict. Then as now, they asked, What's the point of piling up more stuff if you impoverish your soul in doing so? What's the point of compromising with the values the market imposes on you? Why not reject or escape the market system as such, become a radical like, say, Eugene Debs or Big Bill Haywood or Emma Goldman, Socialists or anarchists all, and all of them disgusted by the pragmatic, programmatic plodding of Gompers and his Federation?

The strange fact is that Gompers was a lifelong Socialist who read Marx quite carefully—more carefully, it's pretty clear, than Debs, who's supposed to have read *Das Kapital* while imprisoned for his part in the Chicago railway strikes (or rather boycotts) of 1894. At any rate, Gompers always thought of the Federation as the embryo of a cooperative society—a kind of "parallel social structure"—that would eventually supersede capitalism. One of his fondest hopes was that organized workers' loyalty to this society in the making would wean them from their attachment to electoral politics, their eager exercise of the right to vote. In this sense, he was one of the first vulgar Marxists, someone who believed that "in the final instance," economic change (the "base") would determine political change (the "superstructure")—that material realities were more fundamental and causative than ideological exhortation. In the same sense, however, his agenda of "more" sounded politically impoverished because in the American vernacular, excess has always appeared as the enemy of dutiful citizenship.

But by "more," Gompers meant a great deal more than the material goods procured by the higher wages trade unions would negotiate. He meant what philosophers, economists, social theorists, and literary critics were, at the very same moment, calling the promise of American life: they called this moment an "age of surplus," and sometimes they actually used the word "abundance" to explain what they were getting at. By all accounts, it was a new phase in the development of civilization (what isn't?). But they wrote about it as if it were also unprecedented, because for the first time in the history of the human species, everyday life wouldn't be defined by the pressing demands of necessary labor—the work that gets you by—or be confined by the cruel limits of economic scarcity. This new phase of civilization would be more democratic, they argued, simply because easier access to material goods—to a larger share of society's growing surplus—emboldened and empowered people as individuals and as citizens. "In the midst of plenty," Walter Lippmann (a cofounder of the *New Republic* in 1914) explained in *Drift and Mastery*, the book Theodore Roosevelt wished he had written, "the imagination becomes ambitious, rebellion against misery is at last justified, and dreams have a basis in fact."

Gompers said almost the same thing on dozens of occasions, although he believed that "plenty" was a state of things the labor movement would provide by raising wages and improving working conditions; it wasn't something the capitalists could produce, because they were too interested in the bottom line, too keen on cutting wages to protect short-term profits. For example, in an impromptu speech of 1899, he explained that American workers—all workers—wanted "more *leisure*, more *rest*, more *opportunity* . . . for going to the parks, of having better homes, of reading books, of *creating more desires*." These new desires would someday translate, as higher wages, into increased consumer spending for goods, and would thus solve the problem of "overproduction" from the demand side.

But as this utterance implies, Gompers wasn't a blockheaded materialist—"more" meant something other than tangible goods, the things themselves. So the new margin of meaning he mapped had symbolic properties that were nonetheless concrete use values; they carried prices, but they were real possibilities. "I am in entire accord with [the romantic poet Heinrich] Heine," he once said. "Freedom is bread. Bread is freedom. . . . [Heine] did not mean simply the pieces of bread . . . which one may eat, but all that term implies." He clarified by saying that "liberty can be neither exercised nor enjoyed by those who are in poverty." So workers wanted more; they wanted "higher education, higher aspirations, nobler thoughts, more human feelings."

THE INTELLECTUAL BLUEPRINT OF A "PLEASURE ECONOMY"

According to the leading economists, philosophers, literary critics, and social theorists of the time, these desires for more of what the world could mean were already within reach of the majority—and their realization would have political consequences. All of these intellectuals drew on the work of University of Pennsylvania economist Simon Patten, who suggested in 1907 that a "pleasure-economy" had replaced a "pain-economy," that an "age of deficit" had given way to an "age of surplus." They followed his lead, even copied his language, in claiming that material abundance and more leisure for everyone were measurable trends, not utopian urges. Walter Lippmann did, for example, in *Drift and Mastery*, as did his colleague Walter Weyl, another founding editor of the *New Republic*. So did Wesley Mitchell, the founder of the National Bureau of Economic Research who also pioneered the theory of business cycles, and Van Wyck Brooks, the man of letters who invented the American literary canon. And so, too, did William James, the philosopher who had, by all accounts, the most ecumenical and influential mind of the early twentieth century.

Weyl was a student of Patten at Penn, so he was especially attuned to the economics of the professor's argument. But he went well beyond his teacher in *The New Democracy* (1912), the book that brought him to the attention of Lippmann and Herbert Croly, the third founding editor of the *New Republic* (who also had interesting things to say about the "age of surplus" in *The Promise of American Life* [1912] and *Progressive Democracy* [1914]). Here Weyl insisted on the validity of three fundamental claims, always arguing on historical rather than theoretical grounds. First, the quantitative increase in the "social surplus" of goods and income available for redistribution (via taxation) had created a qualitative change in the prospects for democracy. "Our excess of social product over social effort," he declared, "renders ignorance, poverty, and minority rule anachronistic, and gives to our democratic strivings a moral impulse and a moral sanction." This excess was unprecedented: "It is a new factor in man's career."

Second, the scale of the increase in the "social surplus" made the class struggle program of "absolute socialism" seem quaint, because this surplus allowed for the kind of "conditional socialism" that would socialize goods production and distribution rather than expropriate private property as such: "What the democracy desires, however, is not government ownership for itself, but merely enough government ownership, regulation, or control as may be necessary to a true socialization of industry."

Third, the economic change denoted by an increase in the social surplus had psychological as well as political connotations: "We—all of us alike—have drifted into a new economic, and therefore into a new psychological world." That was the new world in which the moral imperatives of saving and accumulation could no longer build character by containing and organizing the individual's emotions. Expenditure, redistribution, and consumption of a large and growing social surplus were the important events on the new moral calendar framed by a "pleasure economy."

Wesley Mitchell was a student of Thorstein Veblen at the University of Chicago in the 1890s, so, unlike Weyl, he was prepared to be disgusted by the early warning signs of consumer culture in the new millennium. In 1899, Veblen, already the delinquent stepchild of an immature academe, published *The Theory of the Leisure Class*, a droll critique of "conspicuous consumption" and the obvious origin of every subsequent sermon on what the author called the "invidious distinctions" afforded by the display of goods (among these dour sermons is Pierre Bourdieu's *Distinction* [1984], a gloss on *The Theory of the Leisure Class* that earnestly renounces Veblen's irony and yet achieves the same hilarious results). It's a book that has caused thousands of innocent readers to feel guilty about shopping for cool jeans, to believe that their money can't buy them power or love—*hello*, what are they thinking?—and to assume that their consumption of goods is illegitimate, maybe even parasitic, if they aren't meanwhile producing something worthwhile. But the diligent student wasn't convinced by the flamboyant professor.

In fact, Mitchell spent most of his long and distinguished career (at Columbia) worried about what he called "the backward art of spending money," the title of an article he published in the *American Economic Review* in 1912. Here he dutifully cited his mentor, but went on to define the family as the key constraint on the spending that would create enough consumer demand for the "gigantic increase in the volume of goods" produced by the new industrial corporations. Or rather he defined marriage as the real problem: "Our race-old instincts of love between the sexes and parental affection, long since standardized in the institution of monogamy, are a part of experience at once so precious and so respectable that we have looked askance at any relaxation of the family bond, whatever material advantage it has promised." He also proposed a solution, the "socialized spending of money" on public nurseries, among other things, which meant "reorganizing family expenditure on the basis of large groups"; in making this proposal, we should note, he followed the lead of Charlotte Perkins Gilman, the radical feminist who made her reputation with *Women and Economics* (1899).

As early as 1912, then, Wesley Mitchell understood that marriage and the family stood as limits on the intrusions of the larger political economy—"we have jealously insisted upon maintaining the privacy of family life, its freedom from outside control"—but, unlike later critics of consumer-driven economic growth, he also understood that these limits were already giving way. To put it another, more provocative way, he understood that what we call consumer culture was a threat to both the sanctity of monogamous marriage and the private sector of the family, and still he treated the threat as a promise, trying, in his own way, to turn tragedy into comedy.

For this economist, the socialized spending of money that could increase consumer demand for goods to where it would be effective required a profound transformation of the family, so profound that it would change, maybe even erase, the boundary between the public and the private sectors. But that boundary is where "civil society" takes shape—it's the site of modern politics as such, where different kinds and sources of power square off. In this sense, Mitchell's early thinking about the ramifications of consumer culture already allowed for a new kind of political discourse: it was a way of *re*thinking the modern liberal opposition between the state (the public sector) and society (the private sector). By his accounting, an "age of surplus" wouldn't drain off the political energies of the majority: the politics of "more" would instead involve serious debates about the proper scope of political power, the legitimate role of the state, and the future of the family—debates that would surely frame ideological differences and party programs but probably not supply the specific content of electoral campaigns and public policy.

Van Wyck Brooks published his *America's Coming of Age*, the first installment in his successful attempt to convene an American literary canon, a few years after Lippmann's *Drift and Mastery*. It was in some ways a rebuke to his friend at the *New Republic* because it was animated by the idea that "to patch up politics" was of the "least importance" as long as nobody understood that Americans were now "faced with the problem not of making money but of spending it." Still, he sounded just like Patten, Lippmann, Weyl, and Mitchell: "A familiar distinction between the 19th and the 20th centuries is that the problem of civilization is no longer the problem of want but the problem of surplus." The question Brooks kept asking—he found answers in nineteenth-century American writers, especially in Whitman—was, If scarcity, hunger, and need can no longer motivate us to do the right thing, the productive thing, what will? Now that we have the time away from work to get what we always imagined, what we really want, who will we become? Will we regress to "economic self-assertion" because that's what we know best as Americans, or will we move toward an ideal of "self-fulfillment" that resides some-where "between vaporous idealism and self-interested practicality"?

For all his cynicism about Lippmann's obsessive interest in public policy, these were questions Brooks asked with *political* possibilities in mind. For the time being, he said, American culture was split between highbrow and lowbrow, between "the cultivated public and the business public, the public of theory and the public of activity," one largely fem-inine and the other largely masculine. He wanted to forge ahead and find the middle ground, where Whitman had camped out and cooked up a fresh democratic ideal, based on the whole personality rather than its scattered parts. But this search for a political future was now necessary because the age of surplus had made the economic self-assertion of the profit-motivated man pointless, or worse. So for Brooks, the politics of "more" meant pretty much what Gompers meant, even though they spoke different languages to different constituencies—it meant the de-velopment of a personality liberated, on the one hand, from the rigors of necessary labor and accustomed, on the other, to the pleasures of leisure. The personal was already political. This, too, was already a kind of cultural politics along the lines Mitchell had glimpsed in 1912.

William James drew even more directly on Patten than on Lippmann, Weyl, or Brooks in contemplating the moral universe made inhabitable by an age of surplus. He did so by sketching the prospects of the human personality with an essay called "The Moral Equivalent of War" (1910), his most influential contribution to the political discourse of his time (and ours). Here James wondered if the "masculine virtues" could be preserved when they could no longer be performed in the theaters of war and work, where boys had always learned how to be men. War was out of the question because it would mobilize the new machinery of mass slaughter—tanks, Maxim guns, battleships—on a global scale. But work wasn't an alternative because the transition from a "pain economy" to a "pleasure economy" (Patten's idiom) was already under way: the strenuous production of goods was already a lot less important than the passive consumption of goods. In other words, "pacific cosmopolitan industrialism"—what we'd call corporate capitalism—had shrunk the social scope of necessary labor, and thus had created a world ruled by women: "a world of clerks and teachers, of co-education and zoophily [sic]," as James put it, "of 'consumers' leagues' and 'associated charities,' of industrialism unlimited, and feminism unabashed."

What then? How to reinstate those "masculine virtues"? James proposed to put all the teenagers to work, to teach them something about "the military ideals of hardihood and discipline" hitherto bred in war—but instead of military conscription, the "whole youthful population" would be drafted into an "army enlisted against Nature." In these ranks, in "coal and iron mines, to freight trains, to fishing fleets in December, to dish-washing, clothes-washing, and window-washing, to road-building and tunnel-making, to foundries and stoke-holes," they'd learn the lesson of necessary labor. It was a rare utopian moment for William James, the most worldly of the original pragmatists.

His real worry in designing this moral equivalent of war was that personalities held together by the economic and thus *emotional* imperatives of saving and accumulation—by the imperatives of necessary labor—would fall apart when exposed to the excessive, pleasurable possibilities of an age of surplus. The reintegration of these personalities, the restoration of these vulnerable psychic structures, might then become pathologically regressive, and make the "romance of war" its preferred medium: "The transition to a 'pleasure-economy' may be fatal to a being wielding no powers of defence against its disintegrative influences. If we speak of the *fear of emancipation from the fear-regime*, we put the whole situation into a single phrase: fear regarding ourselves now taking the place of the ancient fear of the enemy."

Twenty years later, John Maynard Keynes, who, like every other literate person on the planet, had read a slice of James, voiced very similar concerns: "Thus for the first time since his creation man will be faced with his real, his permanent problem—how to use his freedom from pressing economic cares, how to occupy the leisure, which science and compound interest will have won for him, to live wisely and agreeably and well." Keynes was writing in the immediate aftermath of the Great Crash of 1929, but somehow he saw architectural promise and moral progress in these ruins: "The strenuous purposeful money-makers may carry all of us along with them into the lap of economic abundance. But it will be those peoples, who can keep alive, and cultivate into fuller perfection, the art of life itself and do not sell themselves for the means of life, who will be able to enjoy the abundance when it comes." Still, Keynes, like James, did worry where these artists of life would come from: "Yet there is no country and no people, I think, who can look forward to the age of leisure and of abundance without a dread. For we have been trained too long to strive and not to enjoy."

Late in their lives, then, both William James and John Maynard Keynes were as worried as we are about the psychological—and thus moral—effects of this new stage of civilization, a "pleasure economy" where the deferment of gratification looks impossible and saving for a rainy day seems silly. But, like Patten, Lippmann, Weyl, Mitchell, and Brooks, they clung to a principle of hope, which might be summarized as follows. In the transition to an "age of surplus," an era of abundance— a consumer culture—we can glimpse, for the first time in human history, the possibilities of true freedom.

To put that principle in terms Gompers could endorse, the politics of "more" comes down to the redefinition of what we mean by politics— mainly because "more" is that margin of meaning where your "higher aspirations," what you haven't yet attained, already tells me who you are, and where your "nobler thoughts," what you haven't yet become, already designates the real dimensions of your freedom. Again, the personal is political. To put the same principle in terms Weyl would endorse, the age of the politics of "more" arrives when the social surplus—what we don't need to increase our output of goods in the future—becomes large enough to treat taxation as "an instrument of the socialization of production and wealth." As he framed it, this is the point where "the *social*, as well as the merely *fiscal*, ends of taxation are held in view."

To put that principle of hope in terms we, us citizens of the twenty-first century, could accept—but not on faith, not as a utopian urge to escape the real world's measurable limits—the politics of "more" means a "war of position" in the name of leisure as against labor, consumption as against investment, expenditure as against saving, excess as against austerity. It means that we treat the domain of socially necessary labor as just that, something we have to get done rather than the source of character and the seat of freedom; it's work, not life. The politics of "more" means that we learn to live less anxiously with our desires and our needs.

THE "SOCIALIZATION" OF POLITICS

But this formula—less work, more leisure, less thrift, more spending—sounds a little too abstract or academic, maybe even anemic, like philosophy on a low-fat diet. So let me try another approach to the idea of the politics of "more," by first accrediting its opposition. For a hundred years, the reflexive response of most intellectuals to consumer culture—and this response comes from both the Left and the Right—has been more or less revulsion. Until public defenders appeared in the guise of the "new social history" and cultural studies in the very late twentieth century, the intellectual majority's three-count indictment carried the day in the court of public opinion. It still does, because the public defenders are, as always, underpaid and unconvincing.

The indictment reads as follows. First, the culture of consumption is commodified, or "reified," as Frankfurt School theorists put it—in this setting, everything is for sale, including expressions of affection for loved ones, which we buy as Hallmark greeting cards. So it homogenizes individuals by turning people inside out, by making their inner selves, unique talents, and learned skills *marketable*, along with cosmetic products that change only outward appearances. It may even destroy individuality, because it turns everyone into an echo of the latest advertising campaign or the bearer of the most banal sentiments, mouthing slogans—*Whassup?*—concocted at corporate headquarters.

Second, the culture of consumption *privatizes* experience, as Benjamin Barber and many other critics have claimed: it encloses and isolates us in silent fantasies of unearned mastery, even when advertising is offstage, because the consumption of goods requires only payment and delivery; there's nothing public or cooperative or durable about it, particularly when we're watching TV or surfing the Internet in the privacy of our own homes. So consumer culture disables community and solidarity, the necessary ingredients in any social movement that matters.

The apparent exception to this rule would be the physical, largely vocal gestures of the rabid sports fan—the spectator par excellence—emboldened by the collective sounds of the home team's stadium. But this man's identifications with others in real time are either pathetic, because he's nowhere near a professional athlete, or fleeting, because the fans in his row will always be strangers; again, there's nothing public or cooperative or durable about his experience. Certainly there's nothing even remotely political in it.

Third, and this follows from the first two counts, the culture of consumption enforces an infantile passivity, a kind of universal spectatorship that makes for inertia in both the workplace and the larger polity. On the one hand, whether we're hands-on in the factory or pushing paper in the cubicle, we're mere recipients of orders from on high rather than self-mastering producers of goods (material and otherwise) in our own right. On the other, whether we vote or not, we're abject creatures of distant political decisions rather than active citizens who think globally and act locally. We can't make things, not even the things we need—we just buy stuff that we'll soon throw away—and we treat political choices as if we're reading a *Zagat* guide, casting our votes as informed consumers looking for the best dollar value at the right restaurant. Marx once said that men rather than abstract social forces make history, but not under circumstances of their own choosing. As the hapless inhabitants of consumer culture, we choose our circumstances—we eat at the cool restaurants and shop at the right stores—but we make no history.

Now change the pronouns and experience this third indictment from a different position in the class structure, where the accusations might feel more pointed. You eat at the worst restaurants (McDonald's), you shop at the wrong stores (Wal-Mart), and you vote for well-educated fools (Bush) because you're the helpless creature of the admen and the demagogues who sell you double-bacon cheeseburgers, crappy China-made clothes, and faith-based politics. As a passive consumer of cheap and shoddy goods, you understand neither your social standing (you stupidly think you're middle class) nor your economic interests (you suffer from false consciousness because you're an addict of what passes for public life at The Mall). You will make no history except as the last hurrah of political reaction; meanwhile, you're so addled by the drug of consumer choice peddled by corporate power that you don't even know what's good for you. What *is* the matter with Kansas, anyway?

My response to the indictment can't be completed in this chapter; my summation for the jury comes later. But let me make a beginning, as a way of introducing a different version of the politics of "more," the one that goes by the name of the civil rights movement. Notice that each count of the indictment expresses a concern about the kind of individual enfranchised by consumer culture. It does so by confident though unstated reference to a past in which the individual must have been different—this earlier species of individuality was apparently less marketable, and as a result was more autonomous, more sociable, and more active, in the workplace and in the larger public sphere of politics. So the critique of consumer culture is a *metapolitical* discourse of its own, where the question always asked is, What kind of individual do we want to cultivate in the name of democracy? In other words, how do we make the personal political, and vice versa?

The politics of "more" as Gompers and his intellectual counterparts understood it—as a way of dealing with an age of surplus—was an answer to the same questions. It acknowledged the differences between the old individualism and the new, but it didn't assume that the new individualism was a deviation from the old. Instead, it redefined autonomy, sociability, and politics. The earlier species of individuality was based on the idea that an individual's independence from others was a function of his property ownership: if he owned productive property, he "owned himself" in the sense that he didn't have to work for someone else. He was his own boss. The politics of "more" defined autonomy differently, as a *collective* result of association with others—fellow workers, to be sure, but also people gathered with purposes or interests reaching beyond any workplace. Patten, Lippmann, Weyl, James, and many others called the individual convened by these associations the "social self"; by their accounting, this new individual's identity was anything but private. It wasn't an enduring inner self you discovered by retreating from the outer world; it was instead a social construction, the result of interaction with others.

Defenders of the old individualism, then and now, typically insisted that the site of self-discovery and self-determination—the address of autonomy—was *work*, where productive labor taught the moral lessons of punctuality, frugality, and honest effort, and meanwhile imposed external, objective, material limits on the imagination of the producer. Defenders of the new individualism moved this location, or rather scattered it, so that the site of self-discovery and self-determination could be *leisure*, the pleasurable scene of goods consumption, as well as work, the strenuous scene of goods production. Thus necessity and freedom, occupation and identity, even males and females, were now aligned at different angles.

But this "social self," the exemplar of the new individualism, did have a new relation to the circulation of commodities and the "reification" of social life. Gompers and his constituents looked at wage labor as a given, for example. To that extent they understood their labor time as a commodity to be sold to the highest bidder; to the same extent they accepted the simple fact that everything now had a price. Even so, the point of joining a trade union was to be treated as something more than a variable *cost*, a quantifiable "factor of production"—the negotiation of the wage rate (the price of labor) made workers something more than an accountant's abstraction to be flayed in pencil, especially since the union often had enough real leverage to get wages for workers that exceeded the bare economic cost of their reproduction or replacement. Everything now had a price, but the market wasn't an external, godlike force to be endured in the name of freedom; it was an economic means to deliberately chosen social ends, and one of those ends was justice.

The intellectuals' rendition of the "social self" was equally ambiguous about the proper role of the commodity in the conduct of both private life and public life. That's why they asked odd questions like: Can we increase consumer demand for goods by reorganizing the family without letting the market reach into the most private spheres of modern life? Or, is everything for sale in a world of clerks and teachers and consumers, where industrialism is unlimited and feminism is unabashed? But if these intellectuals knew of an ideal zone of use value—if they longed to sail for that coast of utopia where labor is *not* a commodity and everybody works for himself—they never let on. In their view, the point was not to abolish the commodity form and its market habitats, thereby freeing all workers from alienated labor; it was instead to *socialize* the production and consumption of commodities by means of "industrial democracy," a kind of local government that Eastern European reformers would later come to call "workers' self-management." These intellectuals assumed that open markets and pluralistic politics—government of the people, by the people, for the people—were symbiotic cultural creations. That point has been lost on the contemporary critics of consumer culture.

It may be that the emphasis on the *socialization* of politics has obscured the meanings of "more." As we know, Gompers was skeptical about the advantages of universal suffrage and the attachments of workers to the major parties. He didn't think voting mattered very much in organizing his long-term project of replacing capitalism with the embryonic cooperative society—the parallel social structure—residing in the labor movement. But then neither Lippmann nor Weyl thought that the "new democracy" they championed would be the result of electoral politics as conducted by the two-party system. Lippmann ridiculed the "omni-competent citizen" who, according to political legend, voted constantly as well as knowledgeably in the nineteenth century, the age of "popular politics"; in his view, election results had always reflected irrational preferences (public opinion) determined by the partisan press and the major parties. Weyl proposed to bypass politics as usual by making the referendum the standard form of the ballot. Their idea of democracy was more social than political: it was less about whose votes were cast than whose voices were heard in narrating the future.

All three assumed that policy-relevant, state-centered, programmatically specific politics organized around electoral campaigns were, for the time being, beside the point. All three assumed that the very nature of political representation was the real question of their time. So they asked, Who could speak for the future, for "the people," for the nation? Who had the credentials to do so? Their answers were determined by what they understood as the *dispersal of power* from the state to society—a result of the new organizational structures and associations forming outside of electoral politics, without any obvious orientation to a party or to the state. These new associations had already made interest groups rather than individuals the atomic particles of politics.

Workers, women, and black folk still lacked the proper standing as credentialed groups, but once recognized as legitimate, their new associations—trade unions, women's clubs, consumers' leagues, so-called interest groups like the NAACP—would quickly change the composition of the body politic. So the politics of "more" was, again, a kind of cultural politics; it was a way of inquiring into the sources of citizenship rather than assuming these were the self-evident properties or dividends of white manhood; it was a way of asking how *groups* hitherto denied the rights of citizenship could assert identities once used against them as legitimate claims on power. Now the basic meanings of citizenship and power were in play, in motion.

DUSK OF DAWN: THE BLACK AESTHETIC FROM DU BOIS TO SNCC

The 1920s were the years when these questions, these meanings, were addressed and charged with a "terrible honesty," to borrow Ann Douglas's bracing description of what animated that remarkable decade—when the New Woman came of age, when the Agrarians took their stand with T. S. Eliot and Ezra Pound against modernity, when the Young Intellectuals exiled themselves from Main Street, and when the New Negro fulfilled the promise of American life by staging the Harlem Renaissance.

The weird diversity of these identifications and events might be read as an index of the decline of the labor movement. What happened to the class struggle, either as the AFL had sublimated it through collective bargaining, or as it had erupted so flamboyantly in the great strikes of 1919? What happened to the class-determined politics of "more" in the 1920s? The answer lies, of all places, in the unprecedented economic trends of the decade—the same economic trends I cited in Chapter 3 as the causes of the Great Depression.

The class struggle didn't disappear from the American scene just because the organized labor movement lost its standing and momentum after the Great War, having been momentarily defeated by a strident new coalition of small and big business. But the salience of class in everyday experience *did* recede, because the size of the industrial workforce actually declined after 1919: the number of workers in manufacturing, transportation, construction, and mining—where job growth had been concentrated for a century—fell between 1919 and 1929, while output in these sectors increased by 40 to 60 percent, as the electrification, automation, and instrumentation of the production process translated into spectacular improvements in labor productivity (400 percent for the decade in automobile production). This "technological displacement" of industrial workers in the 1920s meant that, for the first time in human history, neither more labor nor more capital was necessary to increase the amount of goods available to any buyer.

In the late 1920s, Wesley Mitchell and many other economists measured this sharp decline of what Marx called "socially necessary labor," by which he meant simply the labor time required to reproduce the material groundwork of civilization as known by its inhabitants. Their measurements indicated that the direct confrontation of labor and capital on the site of goods production—the confrontation that had fueled class consciousness and class struggle for at least two generations—now contained or described a shrinking proportion of social relations as such, simply because fewer and fewer people did the work of producing goods. Alternative identifications (gender and race, to start) could then flourish, and begin competing with the solidarities of workers once created on the factory floor: you could now think of yourself as a consumer, for example, instead of a producer. As Walter Lippmann suggested as early as 1914, "We hear a great deal about the class-consciousness of labor; my own observation is that in America to-day consumers' consciousness is growing very much faster."

W. E. B. Du Bois, a founding father of the NAACP, stood at the heart of these changes. He was born to play the part of the New Negro, the "race man" who realized that by the mid-1920s African Americans were no longer a backward peasantry confined to the benighted South. They had now become a cross-class, inter-regional social mass that included every economic function of modern industrial society: every function from backbreaking manual labor on the farms and in the factories to mind-bending mental labor at all the new journals and "little magazines"—the *Chicago Defender*, the *Whip*, *Poetry*, the *New Republic*, the *Crisis*, the *Dial*, the *Freeman*, the *Seven Arts*, the *Masses*, *Fire!*, and so on—that reorganized intellectual life in the early twentieth century. "There is almost no need that a modern group has which Negro workers already trained and at work are not able to satisfy," as Du Bois awkwardly put it.

W. E. B. Du Bois, Alain Locke, Jesse Fauset, Jean Toomer, Countee Cullen, Nella Larsen, Langston Hughes, Zora Neale Hurston, Sterling Brown—these are the names we typically associate with the Harlem Renaissance, especially when we treat it as a literary event defined by authorship of poetry, novels, and plays. But the participants themselves, these and many others, thought of the event in the making—they knew they were on to something big—as a great deal more than literary, even as they stressed the huge importance of culture in the liberation of the people they newly depicted in words and images.

They thought of their renaissance, in other words, as a redistribution of *representational* authority that had immediate political implications: they knew that merely speaking for themselves, as themselves, was already a radical departure from the past, when the white majority had monopolized depictions of the black minority. Framed in this way, from the standpoint of the participants themselves, trade union activists and journalists like A. Philip Randolph, Chandler Owen, and George Schuyler, or musicians like Louis Armstrong, Ma Rainey, and Bessie Smith, were as much a part of the Harlem Renaissance as, say, Wallace Thurman, who mapped the barrier island of his brilliant uptown acquaintance in a novel, *Infants of the Spring* (1932).

All of them were fighting what Antonio Gramsci, the renegade Italian Marxist, famously called a "war of position." This was not a class struggle, where the goal is to seize state power by force of arms; it was not a Leninist "war of maneuver" animated by what Walter Weyl had called "absolute socialism." It was, instead, a cultural revolution, where the goal is to change the premises of political debate by asking difficult questions about the *sources* of intellectual authority. Charles S. Johnson, the editor of *Opportunity* who hired Locke as his "cultural attaché," explained the project as follows: "If these [racist] beliefs, prejudices, and faulty deductions can be made accessible for examination, many of them will be corrected." American culture was the "soft spot" in the armature of white supremacy, he insisted, and so he would probe there as deeply as possible.

Du Bois thought of Johnson as a competitor, but he understood his own situation and purpose in exactly these terms until 1934. It's no stretch to call him the Gramsci of the American Century, although their affiliations with the Communist Party came at opposite ends of their careers. In deciding how his people could free themselves from the deadly constraints of a merciless white majority, Du Bois always emphasized the importance of a black aesthetic—what it meant, what it could contribute to American culture—rather than the nuts-and-bolts economic strategies of his early nemesis, Booker T. Washington, and his later critics among the "absolute" socialists of the 1920s and 1930s. In this crucial sense, he defined true freedom as release from the imperatives of economic necessity, as what happens *after* work, at our leisure, in what he called the "kingdom of culture." He defined the real struggle against oppression as an artistic and intellectual enterprise, as the production and consumption of immaterial goods—as a different politics of "more."

In "The Criteria of Negro Art," for example, a speech at the Chicago convention of the NAACP in 1926, Du Bois began defensively, by asking, "How is it that an organization of this kind ["a group of radicals trying to bring new things into the world"] can turn aside [from economic issues and material realities] to talk about art?" He was elaborating on a theme he had introduced much earlier, in *The Souls of Black Folk* (1903), where the color line, the "problem of the 20th century," still barred the Negro from the promised land, that kingdom of culture. But on this occasion, twenty-odd years later, he was more emphatic in suggesting that even in the "land of dollars," the things "you really want" aren't faster cars, bigger estates, fancier clothes, or "perfect happiness." No, what you want is "a beautiful world" that includes (indeed requires) hard work, sadness, and suffering, a world that allows for *knowledge, creation*, and *enjoyment*—"higher aspirations," "nobler thoughts," as Gompers had put it—precisely because it demands these sacrifices of you. As his critics on the Left kept saying, the logical result of Du Bois's position was an inversion of the typical socialist's emphasis on economic arrangements and imperatives: he was always more interested in what the vulgar Marxists called the "superstructure" of ideas, law, music, and art than in the material foundation of society they called the "base."

The Great Depression changed Du Bois's tune, but not in the ways you'd expect from someone who was meanwhile reading deeply in Marx and writing a book, *Black Reconstruction, 1860–1880* (1935), that recast the Civil War as a monumental class struggle. In fact, the cultural bent of Du Bois's politics got more pronounced in the 1930s, even though he gave up on Charles S. Johnson's agenda of "correcting" the white majority's ignorance by means of ideological agitation or intellectual exhortation. Here is how he expressed his disillusionment in 1934: "For many years it was the theory of most Negro leaders that this [generally racist] attitude was the insensibility of ignorance and inexperience, that white America did not know or realize the continuing plight of the Negro. . . . Today there can be no doubt that Americans know the facts; and yet they remain for the most part indifferent and unmoved."

But this ideological impasse didn't convince Du Bois that a "war of position" was pointless. Instead, it made him rethink the question of racial separation, and eventually, it led him toward acceptance—or rather eager embrace—of a *cultural* segregation between white and black folks. In 1934, this public rethinking in the pages of the *Crisis* got him in trouble with his superiors at the NAACP, who believed, with good reason, that Du Bois's ideas could compromise its ongoing legal battles against the doctrine of separate but equal. They fired him over it. But he persisted.

When he started down this road in 1934, he argued that the "main weakness of the Negro's position is that since emancipation he has not had an adequate *economic* foundation." Yet he already recognized that the "technological displacement" of workers in the 1920s and after— the result of "new techniques, new enterprises, mass production, [and] impersonal ownership and control"—made it unlikely that black folk could gain an economic foothold in American life by moving to cities and getting jobs in factories. How then would the Negro lay this foundation of liberation? In 1934, Du Bois answered with ritual incantations, solemnly announcing, for example, that the black man "must prove his necessity to the labor movement," and meanwhile, through race solidarity and "inner cooperation," develop "an economic nation within a nation." He never got around to explaining how these happy events would occur.

By 1939, however, he had more specific answers. These derived from a fresh analysis of the extraordinary crisis we call the Great Depression, and were published as a chapter in *Dusk of Dawn*, the quirky book of 1940 whose enigmatic subtitle is worth a thousand dissertations: *An Essay Toward an Autobiography of a Race Concept*. His premise was simple, and startling (and it sounds like it could have been written in the spring of 2009): "We have reached the end of an economic era, which seemed but a few years ago omnipotent and eternal. We have lived to see the collapse of capitalism."

So now the problem—or the promise—of segregation was complicated by this question: where would the Negro fit in a postcapitalist social order? Du Bois was still convinced that racial segregation could be a method of progress rather than a sign of regress or weakness, rather than a mere obstacle to be overcome by legalized integration: "Instead of letting this segregation remain largely a matter of chance and unplanned development, and allowing its objects and results to rest in the hands of the white majority or in the accidents of the situation, it would make the segregation a matter of careful thought and intelligent planning on the part of Negroes."

So the "*planned and deliberate self-segregation* on the part of colored people" was a given for Du Bois, but its success or failure would depend on the way they understood and addressed the "profound economic change" the Great Depression had created. And there could be no uniformity of opinion among colored people—they were just as divided along class lines as the white population. For the time being, the "well-to-do with fair education" were stuck in the nineteenth century along with Andrew Mellon and Booker T. Washington: "They are thinking in terms of *work, thrift, investment and profit*." Meanwhile "the younger and more intelligent Negroes" were exploring two new possibilities, one offered by the Communist Party USA, another by the newly awakened labor movement (which was itself shaped by union organizers and leaders with Communist Party affiliations or sympathies). But neither was adequate to the scale and the scope of economic change as Du Bois understood it, the change he summarized as follows: "Gradually *economic revolution is substituting the consumer* as the decisive voice in industry rather than the all-powerful producer of the past."

His alternative plan of liberation via self-segregation was, then, "a racial attempt to use the power of the Negro *as a consumer*." This alternative would build on two strengths. First, "as a consumer the Negro approaches economic equality [with whites] much more nearly than he ever has as a producer." Second, "in the Negro group the consumer interest is dominant" outside of agriculture; its "social institutions, therefore, are almost entirely the institutions of consumers."

The history of the very near future is written in Du Bois's program, for its politics of "more" combined racial solidarity with an economic agenda that moved beyond the African focus of Marcus Garvey's Universal Negro Improvement Association (founded in 1916, it was by far the most popular organization among black folk until the 1940s). Du Bois's program acknowledged the new political circumstances determined by the apparent success of revolutionary movements in Russia and China, but it emphasized the revolutionary economic changes residing in the Great Depression. The civil rights movement that came of age between 1955 and 1960—between the bus boycott in Montgomery, Alabama, and the student sit-ins at the Woolworth's lunch counter in Greensboro, North Carolina—would combine these same intellectual ingredients in an incendiary recipe of direct action carried out by what Du Bois called the "key man" in the impending "reorganization of industry": the consumer.

CHAPTER SIX

Exporting the Black Aesthetic

From Du Bois to Havel

THE BLACK AESTHETIC AS A CONSUMER GOOD

The 1955 Montgomery bus boycott, which made Martin Luther King Jr. a leader of the civil rights movement, and the 1960 sit-ins at Woolworth's, which made silent, nonviolent "witnessing" an effective political tactic, were local attempts to desegregate the dollar. They were radical renditions of the politics of "more," new instances of consumer culture. Neither Dr. King nor the students from North Carolina A & T cited W. E. B. Du Bois's *Dusk of Dawn* when they deployed black consumers as the shock troops in the war against white supremacy (nor did César Chávez celebrate consumer culture as he meanwhile used boycotts of nonunion produce to enfranchise the United Farm Workers). Even so, Du Bois read the future right.

Voting rights remained a crucial issue in the 1960s and beyond, becoming a vital form of leverage against white supremacy, but, in a brilliant reprise of the Harlem Renaissance, the civil rights movement succeeded because it aimed to redistribute *representational* power by using, not ignoring, the corporate-controlled media of mass communication. The movement worked, in other words, as a "war of position," a form of cultural politics, by urging the kinds of changes that come before and after elections. The original spokesmen for Black Power, for example, acknowledged measurable electoral gains, but also said, "No one should think that the mere election of a few black people to local or national office will solve the problem of political representation."

The civil rights revolution was, in fact, televised. It succeeded because its constituents—leaders and local people alike—exploited photos and moving pictures to show us how brutal racial segregation could be in Birmingham and Selma, Alabama. But the soundtrack was more important. The civil rights movement succeeded because a national audience exploited the technologies of music to listen in on the revolution—the technologies that made the difference between black and white audible, first as a color line worth hearing, then as a borderline worth crossing.

This is a way of saying that the black aesthetic became the mainstream of American culture, and thus the principal challenge to institutionalized racism, insofar as it became a consumer good. And that sounds almost grotesquely demeaning of the revolutionary struggle for black equality. Do I really mean to claim that the civil rights movement was the furthest outpost of the politics of "more"? Well, yes, I do, but I want to modulate—and maybe even amplify—the claim by saying that African American music was the crucial medium in the redistribution of representational power accomplished by the movement, and by saying that the technologies of twentieth-century music are extreme instances of the "reification" or commodification of social life we (rightly) associate with consumer culture. Here I follow the lead of Harold Cruse, who suggested long ago that the intellectual promise of the Harlem Renaissance was based on the new possibilities of "mass communication" (in the 1920s, that meant the phonograph and the radio)—based, in other words, on what both C. Wright Mills and Daniel Bell identified in the 1950s as the new significance of the "cultural apparatus." I also follow Cruse's lead in assuming that the black aesthetic is not the property of any racial group, but rather the place where Americans of all kinds imagine, depict, record, and renegotiate the color line.

Let me work backward in this list of claims. To begin with, I'm suggesting that the music that matters in the twentieth-century United States is African American in origin. It's a hybrid music born of a confrontation between European forms and African styles, so it's a music that always lets us hear the color line dividing the Americas as a boundary in question, in motion. This music came of age in ragtime, blues, and jazz in the miraculously compressed moment of innovation between the late 1890s and the early 1920s, from Scott Joplin and W. C. Handy to Bessie Smith and Louis Armstrong. Thereafter it shaped all other musical composition in the Americas, even as its origins were muted in the late 1920s and after by the ascendance of Broadway and Tin Pan Alley— muted, I mean, by the white composers who superimposed European harmonic modes on the blues idiom. It resurfaced in the explosive form of rock 'n' roll in the 1950s, and since then it's radically changed the way the world listens.

I'm also suggesting that the reification or commercialization of this music is precisely what made it successful in redistributing representational power, particularly in the 1920s and 1930s, and then again in the 1960s. On the one hand, its status as a commodity with mass-market appeal allowed it to be sold to an entire continent, so that it finally crossed the color line of so-called race records and became a consumer good available to every audience, white as well as black, North as well as South (meanwhile, of course, it conquered the world). On the other hand, the expensive recording technologies that made the music *reproducible* were not incidental, disposable vehicles of delivery—these machines actually infused, even determined, the nature of the sounds the nation and then the world could hear. As Andrew Ross has pointed out, popular American music discovers and conveys "'black' meanings, precisely because of, and not in spite of, its industrial forms of production, distribution, and consumption."

I'm suggesting, moreover, that this reified music—blues, then rhythm and blues, then rock 'n' roll—was the crucial medium in the twentieth-century redistribution of representational power that made the black aesthetic the mainstream of American culture. I don't mean that the boycotts, the sit-ins, the marches, the demonstrations, and the voter-registration drives were unimportant or secondary in representing African Americans as active citizens willing to assert their rights. I mean instead that the wide distribution of this new music in the 1950s and 1960s, from the gospel choirs to Motown and everything in between, suddenly allowed for white middle-class identifications with black styles of being in the world, including the style of "departure" or "dissent"—and thus allowed for (they didn't guarantee) political majorities in favor of racial equality, not to mention cultural revolutions in Eastern Europe.

To my mind, it's not a particularly controversial claim, but the retort is by now familiar: these weren't *authentically* black or dissenting styles because they'd already been diluted or distorted by white producers looking to turn a buck by selling records to a mass audience. The assumption at work here is that authenticity in African American music, as in anything else, is a result of abstention from the corrupting demands of the market and the profit motive—abstention from the commercialized forms of entertainment we associate with consumer culture. This assumption informs even the most serious and insightful analysis of popular music, just as it informs the most serious and insightful criticism of consumer culture as such. For example, in *Music of the Common Tongue: Survival and Celebration in African American Music* (1987), still the best book on the subject, Christopher Small insists that the commercialization of the music since the 1960s—its capitulation to the financial imperatives of the recording industry—defused its challenge to "the official values and the imposed identities of industrial society [a.k.a. capitalism]." His indisputable premise is that mass-produced and distributed recordings represent a small, commodified fraction of the popular music produced in any given moment.

And yet even Small acknowledges that without records and radio— the signature devices in the early age of mechanical reproduction, and both of them "desegregated" media as far as the listener was concerned— African American music would never have gained a foothold in the larger culture, simply because, unlike the classical European competition, it was (and mostly still is) a music without a written score: the reproducible recording, the disc itself, was typically the means of conveying the music from performer to performer, and for that matter from performer to listener (lyrics and tabs on the Internet now interact with YouTube to the same effect). It's not that the artists and their audiences were always poor or illiterate; no, his point is that notation and transcription have been exceptional in this musical tradition because it's animated by an improvisational style that demands constant interaction between performers and dancers. But *my* point is that the reified technological apparatus that produced and distributed the new sounds of blues in the 1920s and 1930s, then amplified them as rock 'n' roll in the 1950s and 1960s, is not something *external* to the music. This apparatus was never a clear vessel, a mere vehicle, because the devices that *deliver* the sounds as a mass-market consumer good are inseparable from the *making* of the sounds themselves: as mechanical forms that determine as well as reveal musical contents—think of how a microphone changes the timbre of a voice, or how distortion changes the sonic range of a guitar—they're already present at the creation.

To illustrate my point, and to set the stage for my argument about the politics of "more'" in the Velvet Revolution, let me address Small directly. He dismisses disco as "a mechanical music for a dehumanized age," but he also suggests that hip-hop DJs from New York redeemed it in the 1970s by displaying "the black genius for humanizing the mechanical in surprising ways." By this accounting, the expression of human being somehow excludes the external, material, technological *forms* of that expression; the content of human nature is self-evident—a given—so it endures, waiting for rediscovery, regardless of any outward, mechanical, or environmental changes. It's a preposterous idea, and, more to the point, it undermines Small's larger argument about how African musical forms have reshaped the content of European music, not to mention the content of modern social life. But once you claim that the mechanical is foreign to the human, the conclusion is obvious:

> It will thus be clear that, whatever changes the recording of musical sounds has brought about, it has not changed the fundamental nature or social function of the musical act. The gramophone record or recording tape is an inanimate object containing coded information which can be turned into sounds by putting it into movement on the appropriate apparatus, but to turn those sounds into music, which is to say a performance, requires imaginative work on the part of the listener.

We know better than this. Small does, too. The "social function" of musical acts was changed profoundly by recording technology, mass production, and mass distribution via radio in the 1920s. Hereafter such acts didn't merely commemorate the content and mark the outer limits of a local or regional community—as live performances tend to do, particularly when ritualized as concerts. Instead these acts questioned the content and stretched the limits of every listening community. The "nature" of musical acts was also changed profoundly by the same technologies, for reasons I've already suggested; at the very least "the" human voice was made new by its microphonal equipment.

But now look at musical acts from the demand side, as Small wants us to. The "imaginative work" of listening that turns sounds into music— the imaginative work of *consumption* that eventually made the black aesthetic the mainstream of American culture—couldn't be done on African American music outside the Southern United States before the advent of mechanical reproduction and mass distribution. Until a reified recording technology produced and delivered this music, this commodity, to a wider buying public—in the 1920s—the listening that made the new sounds into intelligible music *outside the South* was impossible. In other words, until the black aesthetic became a consumer good sold in a mass market as popular music, it couldn't change the distribution of *representational* power by giving African Americans the cultural credentials they needed to speak for the future, for the people, for the nation.

In concluding, Small confronts the "basic question," What is the appeal of African American music in view of its "obvious inferiority" as measured against its classical European competition? The two most durable answers, he notes, have been the ignorance of the benighted people, who can't tell good music from bad, or the cynical machinations of profit-driven mass media, especially record companies, television networks, and radio stations. These answers often go together (the ignorance is the result of the machinations), and their political origins and effects are completely unpredictable; writers on both the Left and the Right excel at denouncing the decline of cultural standards legible in the popular preference for, say, Iggy Pop over Igor Stravinsky.

Small answers the basic question by citing a "mixture of attraction and fear in white people"—attraction to the freedoms embodied in the improvisational attitudes and the physical complexity of African American music, and fear of the very same things (the latter being, of course, what William James called *"fear of emancipation from the fear-regime"*).

We see it in the minstrel show, which defused fears of the very attractive black culture and of its subversive potential by presenting it as laughable; we see it in the commitment to jazz of many young middle-class whites in the 1920s and in the panic-stricken response to it of the guardians of public morals and public [sic] music; we see it in the similar response in the 1950s to the advent of rhythm and blues under the name of rock 'n' roll; . . . [and] we see it in the persecution of rock musicians in totalitarian countries. The list could go on, but the pattern is too clear and consistent to be accidental. The greater the commitment to the values of industrial society and its associated high culture, the greater is the fear of African-American culture and African-American music.

Really? It's an appealing argument, in part because it has precedents and corroboration from distinguished scholars of both minstrelsy and the Harlem Renaissance, and in part because it accords with our notions of the rebellion contained—in both the inclusive and the exclusive sense of that word—by rock 'n' roll. But it runs aground on the shoal of a simple fact: "industrial society," a.k.a. advanced capitalism, enthusiastically sponsors the values of consumer culture as well as "high culture." The market as organized by the recording technologies, advertising, and mass distribution of *advanced capitalism* doesn't block access to African American culture or music (if it did, there'd be no argument about the cynical machinations of profit-driven mass media); instead, it presents and delivers the black aesthetic as a consumer good accessible to all buyers. So Small's argument works better in the *absence* of capitalism. To illustrate this irony, I now turn to the politics of "more" as it developed in Eastern Europe in the 1970s, 1980s, and 1990s.

THE VELVET REVOLUTION AND THE "CONSUMER SOCIETY"

A great deal of earnest nonsense has been produced by close study of the revolutions that rocked Eastern Europe between 1975 and 1992—perhaps because they seemed such spontaneous, almost accidental events. They looked mysterious, inexplicable, mundane, and yet somehow glorious, too. The Left in the advanced capitalist nations didn't quite know what to make of it all. On that side of the political divide, people typically said, "We like trade unions, and we identify with 'dissident' intellectuals just like ourselves, but do we want 'actually existing socialism' to disappear?" Meanwhile the Right congratulated itself on winning the Cold War, maybe even ending History.

Neither side got it right because these revolutions were informed, motivated, and inspired by the politics of "more," in two related senses. First, conventional "oppositional" politics, as conducted by a party system organized around public events, electoral campaigns, and programmatic debates—or as commandeered by armed guerillas—were irrelevant to the outcome. These weren't wars of maneuver; they were wars of position. Second, the symbolic meanings of consumer goods—the significance of jeans, genres of music, even styles of hair, but also the prices of basic necessities—became central figures in the rhetoric and strategies of revolution. The constituents of this unarmed revolution didn't want to overthrow the state; they wanted more leisure, more art, more music, more time away from work—just enough exemption from necessity—to do something unimportant like read a novel or write a play or strum a guitar. They wanted to inhabit a consumer culture. Their desires produced revolutionary *political* change.

They were up against a system that couldn't quite accommodate the strange, subversive values embodied in consumer culture because that system had displaced the market and thus couldn't accredit consumer demand (by the 1980s, every Soviet satellite was borrowing in the West to import "essential" consumer goods that couldn't be procured locally because the State Plan hadn't allowed for their production). Economists in the Soviet Bloc understood the dilemma long before it acquired a cultural presence and a political standing in the late 1970s and 1980s. The "Prague Spring" of 1968, which Western observers interpreted as a daring challenge to the Kremlin, was actually a lame effort to reorganize the Czech economy (not the society) in view of lagging growth. It failed because it couldn't go far enough in the direction of what economists on the scene called "marketization"—by which they meant modifying the State Plan with market incentives and markers (prices). The Soviet tanks officially ended the experiment in August, but it was already botched by the early summer of 1968.

Throughout Eastern Europe in the early 1960s, economists were noticing a disturbing trend toward stagnation, and urging both political and economic reform (*marketization*) as the indispensable means of reinstating growth. Among these economists were Istvan Friss of Hungary, Wlodzimierz Brus of Poland, and Radoslav Selucky of Czechoslovakia, each a public intellectual who urged political change as the condition of economic progress (Brus's arguments about how socialism required markets—and vice versa—were first published in 1961, and became, via Selucky, the theoretical rationale for the Prague Spring). They argued that mere additions to the capital stock and the labor force had worked to increase per capita incomes (and thus consumer spending) in the nineteenth century, in the age of industrialization—they called this pattern "extensive growth"—but couldn't do so in the late twentieth century.

For something new had happened: the advanced capitalist countries had made the transition to a consumer-oriented pattern of "intensive growth," where a capital-saving formula amplified the effects of labor-saving machinery. In the West, these economists showed, inputs of capital *as well as* labor per unit of output kept falling, thus leaving more income available for mass consumption; but in the Soviet Bloc, these inputs of capital (investment) kept rising, according to the Plan, thus leaving less income available for consumption. On this comparative basis, they argued that standards of living as measured by consumer spending would continue to decline in the Soviet Bloc unless it somehow copied the West and made the transition to "intensive growth."

The Prague Spring was the first facsimile of the necessary transition (although there were earlier hints of it in Hungary). It was, however, a "technocratic" fix according to the reformers themselves (including Selucky). It addressed the economic problem of consumer demand in new, imaginative, market-oriented ways, but it didn't, and probably couldn't, address the key political question of how to limit *state command* of economic decisions, which in practical terms meant how to limit the power of the Communist Party. So the great discoveries of the 1960s in Eastern Europe were that a consumer-oriented pattern of "intensive growth" had become the obvious alternative to economic stagnation in the Soviet Bloc—and that the pursuit of this alternative would require massive political change. In other words, the "marketization" of resource allocation required the democratization of the political order: "genuine economic pluralism is impossible without unlimited political pluralism," as one belated reformer put it. Translation: If democracy needs markets to work effectively, markets need democracy to work properly.

The question for the disillusioned reformers after 1968 was not whether but how to make this kind of political change. They eventually decided on a "war of position," which relinquished the idea of "opposition" or "dissent," and instead cultivated a cultural politics. Poland was the exception to this rule, at least in the sense that Solidarity became an institutional thicket by 1982, including trade unions, intellectual interest groups, and finally a political arm with electoral pretensions. But even in Poland, Vaclav Havel's ideas about the crucial importance of prepolitical activity as the medium of resistance to Soviet rule became gospel truth, having circulated after 1978 in mimeographed samizdat (clandestine) format throughout Eastern Europe.

By all accounts, Havel, a playwright and essayist, was the most charismatic and influential intellectual in Czechoslovakia in the late 1970s and 1980s (and judging by the literary awards he received in the West, perhaps he was the most influential intellectual on the planet by 1980); no one was surprised as he became the DJ of the "Velvet Revolution" that lifted his country out of its Soviet orbit after 1989. The turning point in this career was not the Prague Spring, when he was a bit player; it happened a decade later, when he became the spokesman for Charter 77, a human rights group formed in protest of the state's prosecution of a rock group called Plastic People of the Universe. Then in late 1978, he wrote a long essay, "The Power of the Powerless," the samizdat manifesto that made him famous throughout Europe, and meanwhile made him dangerous enough to be jailed by the Czech government. Here he argued for a political consciousness—or rather an attitude—grounded in "areas of life that [have] nothing to do with politics in the traditional sense of the word."

Like Gompers, like Gramsci, and like Du Bois, Havel knew these were the areas of an unofficial second culture, a "hidden sphere," an "independent life of society," a set of "parallel structures"—parallel to the state—that composed a civil society, the middle term between state, family, and individual: "Culture, therefore, is a sphere in which the parallel structures can be observed in their most highly developed form." This society, this culture, was both beyond the reach of the state (the totalitarian Right) and invisible to those still fighting a "war of maneuver" (the socialist Left), because the seizure of state power was never its goal. Like Gompers, like Gramsci, and like Du Bois, Havel assumed that "political reform was not the cause of society's reawakening but rather the final outcome of that reawakening."

Havel's premise was that a "post-totalitarian society" had emerged in the aftermath of the 1960s, in both East and West; so the former stood as a "warning" to the latter, as the harbinger of an ugly future: "In the democratic societies, where the violence done to human beings is not nearly so obvious and cruel, this fundamental revolution in politics has yet to happen, and some things will have to get worse there before the urgent need for that revolution is reflected in politics." Like Small, Havel sometimes called this post-totalitarian political order an "industrial society," or a "technological society," as a way of suggesting that its suffocating bureaucratic routines cut across any differences between capitalism and socialism.

And like most recent theorists of "late capitalism," Havel also equated industrial society and consumer culture. He broadcast this indictment as follows: "The Soviet bloc is an integral part of the larger world, and it shares and shapes the world's destiny. This means in concrete terms that the hierarchy of values existing in the developed countries of the West has, in essence, appeared in our society. . . . In other words, what we have here [in Eastern Europe] is *simply another form of the consumer and industrial society*, with all its concomitant social, intellectual, and psychological consequences." Indeed, Havel claimed that industrial society—whether Socialist or capitalist, East or West—was inert, passive, "soporific, submerged in a consumer rat race," because its constituents had been "seduced by the consumer value system." The "general unwillingness of consumption-oriented people to sacrifice some material certainties for the sake of their own spiritual and moral integrity" was a self-evident truth, already beyond argument.

Havel notwithstanding, the revolution in Czechoslovakia was fueled by the same politics of "more" that ignited the workers' revolts in Poland of the 1970s—food price increases were the spark every time—and fanned the flames of *perestroika* in the heart of the Soviet Union in the 1980s. In the 1970s and 1980s, more consumer goods were, in fact, more available in the Soviet Bloc because the authorities kept trying to meet consumer demand by borrowing from the West to import scarce items like children's clothes (they could do so because Soviet oil revenues sky-rocketed after 1973). But they couldn't keep up, because, as Steven Kotkin puts it, "Although people had more, they were demanding more on the basis of wider horizons." And those horizons were, of course, the distant, wavering lines they could see on TV series imported from the West, which they watched for clues about material life (as well as entertainment), looking into the refrigerators with the actors as if they were on the scene. Those horizons were the confident bass lines they could hear on taped music imported from the Americas, which they listened to for ways of being in a world elsewhere (as well as enjoyment), won-dering what way of life could make sense of this noise. Those horizons were the sights and sounds of consumer culture.

The Velvet Revolution was no exception to this rule. In fact, Havel admits as much in explaining the origins of Charter 77 and the subse-quent political itinerary of Czechoslovakia. Here, for example, is the narrative he offers in "The Power of the Powerless," that pathbreaking essay in his underground oeuvre:

> Undeniably, the most important political event in Czechoslovakia after the advent of the Husak leadership in 1969 [after the Soviet invasion and the end of the Prague Spring] was the appearance of Charter 77. The spiritual and intellectual climate surrounding its appearance, how-ever, was not the product of any immediate political event. That climate was created by the trial of some young musicians associated with a rock group called "The Plastic People of the Universe." . . . Everyone understood that an attack on the Czech musical underground was an attack on a most elementary and important thing, something that in fact bound everyone together: it was an attack on the very notion of

living within the truth, on the real aims of life. The freedom to play rock music was understood as a human freedom and thus as essentially the same as the freedom to engage in philosophical and political reflection, the freedom to write, the freedom to express and defend the various social and political interests of society.

In short, Charter 77, the Czech equivalent of Poland's Solidarity—the "parallel structure" whose members would dominate the nation's post-Soviet government—was founded in response to the arrest and trial of four men who had formed a rock band called Plastic People of the Universe.

There was enough irony in the name of the band to alert knowledgeable listeners to the subversive possibilities of the music: not to worry, it said, we're just pretending to be hapless consumers. But its genealogy and Havel's explanation of Charter 77 suggest that the detonating event in the Velvet Revolution was the reflexive defense of what had become both a common good and a consumer good—the black aesthetic embodied in rock 'n' roll.

The Plastics got their name and their aura from their affiliation with the obvious and the esoteric. To begin with, the name recalled a song, "Plastic People," recorded in 1967 by Frank Zappa and the Mothers of Invention. It mixed bemused spoken dialogue with the already classic rock sound of "Louie, Louie," changing tempo, timbre, melody, whatever, following the CIA through Laurel Canyon and telling listeners to "watch the Nazis run your town." The song's paranoia was pointed, ironic, and hilarious—that is, perfectly suited to the wary, weary temperament of the Prague Spring and its aftermath.

The name of the band also recalled Andy Warhol's multimedia project of 1966–1967, the "Exploding Plastic Inevitable," which featured the Velvet Underground as the house band. The voices and the music on these occasions sounded like Bob Dylan had wandered into a disco, at least until John Cale turned up the amp and sped up the sound toward the end of a song; before then, it was all slide guitar verging on the plunky feel of a banjo, nasally vocals coming and going like strange weather over major chords as the strobe meanwhile lit up the dancers in their cages.

If you listened closely enough, you could hear the entire history of North American music in these ragged performances. That was probably the point, and it wasn't lost on the Plastics.

But this name, Plastic People of the Universe, came from yet another world elsewhere. This was the world delivered to the band by its manager, Ivan Jirous, an art historian, cultural critic, and close reader of Roland Barthes, the French semiotician who treated plastic—the signature material of postwar capitalism—as a wondrous, lovely, but also "disgraced material," as the cartoonish lack of substance that defined consumer culture: "So, more than a substance, plastic is the very idea of its infinite transformation; as its everyday name indicates, it is ubiquity made visible . . . it is less a thing than the trace of a movement . . . because the quick-change artistry of plastic is absolute: it can become buckets or jewels."

The quick-change artistry of the Plastics was antiauthentic; it was mostly earnest make-believe except in the context of official Soviet sincerity, in that belated parental space where everything gets done for your own good because you don't know any better, where you pretend to understand the rules and that gets you by. They knew they were already disgraced, "imitation materials" as Barthes put it, practicing the kind of artifice that "aims at something common, not rare," something reproducible, not unique, something that was already circulating beyond the local ambit of their sound system. At the outset, the band got its avant-garde standing from its imitative abilities—from its covers in English of songs by the Velvets and the Fugs (the translations were the work of the Canadian Paul Wilson, who was recruited by Jirous, who meanwhile promoted the band in much the same way Warhol had promoted the Velvets). The Plastics copied the Velvets' early droning sound from bootleg tapes smuggled into Czechoslovakia, they copied the Fugs' strident yet playful lyrics using the same illegal sources, and they copied the dress code and attitudes of rock 'n' roll as played in Greenwich Village, ca. 1968, from album covers and Wilson's wardrobe.

But they were licensed by the Czech government—they were part of the Prague Spring. As in Russia, where every factory had its own in-house band by the late 1960s, the Czech authorities didn't treat rock 'n' roll as decadent or subversive; they saw it as a weird consumer good imported from the West in response to the insistent demands of people who wanted "more." They revoked the Plastics' license in 1970 as part of a larger crackdown on participants in the Prague Spring—but *the band played on into the 1970s without interference from the state*, covering the Velvets and the Mothers and the Fugs in English until 1972 (when Wilson left the group), and then using the poetry of Egon Bondy, the banned Czech philosopher, as the lyrical content of its original music. The three remaining band members and Jirous were arrested in 1976; all four were convicted of "disturbing the public order" and sentenced to prison terms of eight to eighteen months. Their crime wasn't rock 'n' roll. The authorities weren't singling out the music, bizarre as it was; they were trying instead to silence Bondy once and for all.

In any event, however you catalog the crime, the music came from the farthest Western outpost of consumer culture. The Mothers, the Velvets, and the Fugs were avant-garde bands, to be sure, but they had recording contracts, they played concerts, and they sold lots of mass-produced records made with industrial technology (I know; my sister bought them). If the records hadn't circulated worldwide as consumer goods, the Plastics would never have been able to copy the music, the attitudes, and the styles these industrial artifacts made both audible and reproducible. So when Havel invoked the "freedom to play rock music" as a basic human freedom and cited the Plastics, he was actually invoking the freedom to *listen* to the new sounds imported from the headquarters of both capitalism and consumer culture; for without its audience, which appeared en masse and in public—and not just in Czechoslovakia—the band would never have drawn the attention of the authorities. In 1976, this basic freedom meant access to the consumer good that was the black aesthetic embodied in rock 'n' roll. No less than the constituents of the Velvet Revolution, then, and no less than Gompers and Du Bois, Havel was demanding that a consumer society of free time, leisure, and play be released from the deadening constraints of industrial society. Despite his *theoretical* opposition to consumer culture, he was preaching, and practicing, the politics of "more."

Søren Kierkegaard, one of Havel's (and Bondy's) favorite philosophers, once said, "We live forward, but we understand backward." The

aphorism, at once painfully obvious and insightful—you've heard it before in this book—alerts us to the strange possibility that Havel might
have been right when he asked whether the Eastern European experience of the 1970s looked like the future of the Western democracies. I
don't mean the feverish rhetorical questions that conclude "The Power
of the Powerless," where he cites Martin Heidegger, another favorite
philosopher, to mourn the "ineptitude of humanity face to face with the
planetary power of technology." I mean this very pointed question: "And
do we not in fact stand (although in the external measures of civilization,
we are far behind) as a kind of warning to the West, revealing its own
latent tendencies?"

Eastern Europe *was* far behind the United States in the 1970s, and
still is when judged by those "external measures." But the late twentieth-
century revolutions there do make me think we might understand our
contemporary predicament backward; they do make me think that the
two fundamental questions raised there are immediately relevant to our
own time and place. Those questions are, Can we make the transition
to "intensive," consumer-led growth by embracing the politics of "more,"
by fighting a prepolitical "war of position"—in other words, can we break
the grip of a mindset that insists, on principle, that rewarding saving and
investment rather than consumption is the key to growth? And, beyond
that, Can we use markets to limit state command of economic decisions?

No matter how we answer, our very own *perestroika* is upon us. No
matter how we answer, the politics of "more"—the consumer culture
etched in the "age of surplus"—looks like a usable past. Economic change
since 2007 amounts to a crisis, to be sure, but, like the Great Depression
of the 1930s in the West and the stagnation of the 1960s in the East,
it's also an opportunity to rethink the sources of growth. More important,
it gives us a *second* chance to solve what Keynes called the real, the permanent, problem of humankind—and that is how to use our "freedom
from pressing economic cares, how to occupy the leisure, which science
and compound interest will have won for [us], to live wisely and agreeably and well."

CHAPTER SEVEN

The Wand of Increase
Advertising Desire

WHAT'S THE MATTER WITH ADVERTISING?

One of the charges against consumer culture that sticks like Krazy Glue is its undeniable affiliation with modern advertising—the place where creative people go to sell their souls by persuading the rest of us to buy stuff we don't need. You can't have a consumer culture like ours in the absence of advertising. Of course there were plenty of advertisements before mass consumption came of age in the twentieth century; in the nineteenth century, the new print media (back then the only media) were often decorated with "notices" that explained how buying canned goods, patent medicines, and metal plows would improve readers' lives without impairing anyone's character. But that's a different story, because you can have advertisements in the absence of consumer culture, just like you can have big business—joint-stock companies, giant oil trusts, even outright monopolies—in the absence of a specifically corporate kind of capitalism.

So, if I'm here to defend the consumer culture of our time—the time of corporate capitalism—I need to make a case for advertising as we know it, where style is substance, character is fungible, and truth is as transient as the homeless men we've learned to ignore. But isn't that something like making a case for, say, adultery? Isn't that too hard a sell?

Or is it too easy to make this case? Could advertising be the thesaurus of our real feelings, the indispensable, vernacular language we use to plot our positions on the emotional atlas that is everyday life? Could we hear it as the siren voice of the restless and the romantic among us, speaking on behalf of real needs we didn't know we had, making irresistible speeches, and always quoting the commodity form? Could advertising be the last utopian idiom of our time? To all of the above, my answer is yes.

But let's see. Let's consider the charges against advertising. We've all pressed them at some point in our lives, even when we were working for an ad agency. I certainly have. For example, I've said, to my kids, "I'm sorry, we're not going to get you this, uh, toy, it looks bigger there on the screen than it actually is, you see the commercial is, ah, misleading us, they're lying about the size of the thing, it's just not that big, and it's dangerous, too." I've also said, to my students, "Yes, advertising creates demand for goods we don't need; in fact it creates a longing for freedom—for release from the grip of necessity—and then tries to channel that longing into what's for sale in the market. They make it sound like you can buy your freedom by consuming goods: 'You say you want a revolution?' Buy those Nikes! Oh, please." And so on. Like I said, we've all been there, done that, and we were thinking these pure thoughts even as we were planning to buy the things made desirable by the advertisements we knew how to resist.

So let me draw up a more formal complaint against advertising, and then, having studied it, ask what we plaintiffs have in common with the defendant. All this by way of suggesting that maybe we need advertising because it always speaks, playfully and insistently, to our fondest hopes of *interrupting* reality and finding freedom in the here and now, in our everyday lives—where, like it or not, we create identities by means of commodities, buying and selling what we want to be. And if not always, then maybe advertising speaks more effectively to these subversive ends than the voices we hear in the alternatives, which preach abstention from the subtle tyrannies of everyday life, and send us—now equipped as sober missionaries—in search of an abstemious afterlife.

Here's that formal complaint:

- Advertising is deceptive. In violation of modern scientific assumptions and methods, it treats appearance as reality; it skims surfaces and ignores depths; it celebrates variety rather than utility, chance rather than law. Advertising doesn't provide information, it exerts influence, and it does so by inciting and magnifying irrational impulses, particularly by using sex to sell almost everything (including, for example, motor oil and pesticides). It places the highest value on the ephemeral—fashion, above all— as against anything that endures. It teaches us to emphasize the exterior and the ornamental at the expense of our inner lives: as the perfection of rhetoric, it's the sworn enemy of authenticity.

- Advertising disfigures the visual landscape and the aural field of our time. From billboards on highways and commercials on TV (now also at the movies) to the voice-over blare of radio—and now in so-called remarketing, where a tracking cookie in your browser sends the same ad to every website you open—there's no escaping the sights and sounds of things for sale as brought to you by. . . . Only an eco-vacation or a New England zoning law will let you off the hook, and even then you've got plenty of equipment or groceries to buy. But let's suppose we've all learned from looking at the neon juggernaut that is Las Vegas, as Robert Venturi famously urged us to; still, the compelling visual and aural cues we get from most advertising are designed to sell us crap—shoddy goods that can't last, and stuff we don't need, anyway. It's all unnecessary artifice, and it makes us fat, stupid, or sick.

- Advertising creates desires, in fact, where there were none, thereby fueling insatiable appetites for disposable consumer goods and validating the tyranny of economic growth as an end in itself. *Fortune* magazine forthrightly summarized the project in 1947: "the creation of new and daring, but fulfillable, consumer demands, demands that would not occur if advertising did not deliberately incite them." In this sense, advertising is both the symptom and the cure of excess productive capacity, or "overproduction" as that excess was called in the late nineteenth and early twentieth centuries (a term revived by Vance Packard in 1957, in his best-selling

indictment of advertising *The Hidden Persuaders*); for it has
no cultural purpose and no intellectual purchase in the absence of surplus goods, which, if merely brought to market
without fanfare, would increase supply but not demand,
thus depressing prices and profits. The economist Neil Borden explained the "enormous growth of large-scale national
advertising" in the first half of the twentieth century—he
was writing in 1941, before the postwar boom—in exactly
these terms: "The quest for product differentiation became
intensified as the industrial system became more mature,
and as manufacturers had capacity to produce far beyond
existing demand." Well, all right, not exactly. My translation:
advertising as we know it, as the avant-garde of consumer
culture, makes no economic sense before the "age of surplus," without the absurd excess of material goods capitalism could deliver by the 1920s.

- Advertising is, then, the dialect of desire. It can't acknowledge any limits to satisfaction, or speak to real material needs.
Its response to every query is: "More." But it is a stunted,
brittle language that creates "effective demand" by training
the unruly desires it engenders on specific commodities—it
channels those desires into the price system, turning them
into things with market values, meanwhile turning *us* into
things who carry "brands." It puts everything up for sale:
nothing worth having is priceless, not even love, loyalty,
friendship, family, or children. So advertising is anything but
the vernacular of a "pleasure economy": by convincing us to
spend more on the stuff we don't need, it persuades us to
work harder at the jobs we don't want, just as Simon Patten
predicted in 1907 (see Chapter 5). In the name of desire, it
creates generic demand; in the name of the genuine individuality that comes only with freedom from compulsion, it
encourages conformity.

- Advertising encourages a peculiarly insidious version of conformity by triangulating our desires; it teaches us to value

things as others do, even when we're most intent on customizing the insignia of our individual identities. Indeed it teaches us to see ourselves as if we're *things*, from the standpoint of others rather than from the inside out, from the enduring, authentic interiors that constitute our genuine selves (this dangerous perspective is the extremity of what the eighteenth-century political philosopher Jean-Jacques Rousseau called *amour propre*). We know that buying certain things, or frequenting certain stores, puts us in a cohort of consumers who've already "branded" themselves with the help of ads, and we understand this product placement of ourselves before we make the purchase or arrive on the chosen scene; we're joining up with strangers, hoping to be recognized by them as one of them (and yes, sometimes as athwart them). In fact, this recognition by others is the key to most purchases we make as consumers who've been persuaded by advertising; for the ads have already conjured a social background or stylistic genre for us (Classical, Preppie, Hip, Avant-Garde, Goth, Punk, etc.), a place or a brand where our quirky tastes will sometimes look new but will always be intelligible. By understanding the dialect of advertising, and speaking it with our purchases, we're learning to desire what others do, to be like them.

SELLING WITH SEX: THE CASE FOR ADVERTISING

It's a pretty convincing complaint. But of course there's another way to tell this story. So let me respond, almost in order, and then see where we stand. I'm not reporting so that you can decide. When I'm done, I want you on my side, but that's where the conclusions are mostly questions.

Advertising did adjourn the modern scientific opposition between appearance and reality, surface and depth, variety and utility, chance and law. In doing so, however, it was either slightly ahead or just abreast of intellectual and artistic innovation in the twentieth century. It's preposterous,

I know, to characterize such innovation in a single phrase, or even in an entire monograph, but for my purposes here's what the significant intellectuals and artists of the last century agreed on: these dualisms, these oppositions, and the Newtonian physical science that underwrote them, are contestable truths, on trial like every other received tradition.

Nothing was immune from this innovative contagion, not the fixed relation between time and space (Einstein, Picasso), not the permanent mind-body problem (Freud, Bergson, James), not even the irrevocable differences between males and females (Gilman, Key, Mill). The discussion of these distinctions had long been animated by both an ancient metaphysical and a modern scientific notion, which held that a natural, enduring reality existed apart from its representation—its *appearance* in words or images—and that the purpose of representation, whether in words or images, was to achieve a closer approximation of this natural, enduring reality. But now, as early as 1905, these distinctions were in question, and would remain so into our own time. Advertising was always in the interrogative camp, along with the artists and intellectuals who tried to get beyond the received tradition. Yes, it was often the calculating stepson along for the ride, hoping, like Robert Downey Jr., to score off the idiot excesses of his parents, but sometimes it reached innovative conclusions on its own—particularly in the 1960s, as Thomas Frank argued in a brilliant book on the subject, *The Conquest of Cool*, and as the cable TV series *Mad Men* demonstrates more poignantly.

In adjourning the opposition between appearance and reality, surface and depth, variety and utility, chance and law, advertising stakes an antimetaphysical claim along with the twentieth-century philosophers we value most—William James, John Dewey, Ludwig Wittgenstein, Martin Heidegger (did I just say Heidegger?)—and validates the claim by voting for the importance of all things irrational. Freud taught us that reasonable decisions have unreasonable origins; advertising is the practical, consistent embodiment of this fundamental psychoanalytical insight. Put it another way. Like James, Dewey, Wittgenstein, and Heidegger, Freud taught us that desire and reason aren't mutually exclusive ways of knowing, not any more than values and facts are antithetical; they're inseparable. Evolutionary psychology has recently proven the point by showing that the

cognitive capacities of the human brain have developed as adaptive responses to social and sexual possibilities. In this sense, when advertising
appeals to the irrational, it's just acting on what we already know about
how cognition works. Information never comes undressed—and if it
came rhetorically naked, stripped to its essentials, we'd complain about
its prurient content.

Advertising does make fashion its origin and its destination, and it
does use sex—sexuality, not the promise of fornication—to sell things
you can't use in bed unless you stretch the definition of intimate lubri-
cant to include WD40. But fashion and variety have been the enemies
of utility and uniformity since these categories squared off in the eighteenth century, when Enlightenment thinkers put them in contention,
typically as an intellectual prize fight between the flighty female and
the steadfast male. Advertising refuses this either/or choice in its flamboyant embrace of fashion; it tells us that variety is more interesting (at
least!) than uniformity, and that maybe the boundaries between them
aren't worth observing because they're so arbitrary. Change, flux, the
dissolution of everything we take for granted, these are the premises of
advertising: "All that is solid melts into air," it says, quoting Marx, so we
might as well buckle up and prepare for takeoff.

The argument against fashion hasn't changed much since the eighteenth century. It's the same old "scientific" argument for a fixed natural
reality as against appearance, image, illusion, and distortion, as if repre-
sentations are not themselves real, as if reality is an inert, external set
of material facts we all agree on, as if we know what an objective, God's-
eye view of the world would look like. In the late twentieth century,
many historians of advertising indicted fashion, the constant redefinition of style enforced by advertising, on these very "scientific" grounds.
Stuart Ewen's complaint was (and is) typical: "Modern style speaks to
a world where social change is the rule of the day, where one's place in
the social order is a matter of perception, the product of diligently as-
sembled illusions." Notice that social change looks like a problem from
this standpoint. Or again: "On the one hand, style speaks for the rise of
a democratic society, in which who one wishes to become is often seen
as more consequential than who one is [sic]. On the other hand, style

speaks for a society in which coherent meaning has fled to the hills, and in which drift has provided a context of continual discontent."

All true, except for that third person ("one"), who multiplies too quickly. Fashion or style does speak for these new worlds, where your place in the social order isn't determined by your origins, and its argot is advertising. Fashion or style does speak to the lack of "coherent meaning" imposed on you by your superiors, whether they're political commissars, college professors, cultural custodians, or earnest managers—all better educated than you are—and its argot is advertising. Fashion or style is the informal language of modern individualism out of control, for better or worse, and it finds the words it needs in the slang of advertising. As Virginia Postrel puts it, "the more influence accorded individual preferences, the greater the importance of fashion." It exists, she declares, and here I fully agree with her, "because novelty is itself an aesthetic pleasure."

But advertising does sell with sex(uality). The real question is not whether but how it does so. We take it for granted that until our post-millennial moment, the female body was tendered as the currency of desire in advertising, and we typically read this offer as the exploitation of women for profit. But isn't it something more than that? Before the 1960s, women as rendered by advertising were wifely, maternal figures, just as they were portrayed in TV sitcoms (the exception to this rule, as all others, was *The Honeymooners*). Then they almost disappeared in the "creative revolution" of the early 1960s, which put ad agencies at the forefront of change in visual and verbal styles by turning print and television advertisements into artifacts of the avant-garde. When women reappeared as the foreground of print ads in the late 1960s, they were positioned as either a parody of earlier "sexual" solicitations, or as figures with their own physical presence, looking at something beyond the frame of the ad; in both cases they were drawing your attention *away* from the goods on display. And if they were looking right at you, as Catherine Deneuve did for Chanel, the "you" constituted by their gaze was neither male nor female. This new spatial configuration was consistent with the "sexual revolution" that was meanwhile convulsing the larger society by giving women control of their bodies. The nude or half-naked woman who appealed directly to men, as if the product were the female body itself, hereafter appeared mainly on calendars hung in garages and base-ments, where working-class men read *Hustler* and indulged their rude fantasies.

So yes, advertising sells with sex(uality), but again, the question is how. Could it be that our opposition to sex in ads is yet another iteration of the historical correlation between unwanted social change and the metaphorical figure of the prostitute—the woman who would peddle intimacy as a commodity? Since the eighteenth century, prostitution has appeared at—and as—the cutting edge of the market's expansion into spheres of life where it hadn't yet intruded. Sex for sale has seemed, for about two hundred years, the perfect example of what Thomas Carlyle (yes, Marx, too) called the "cash nexus," the epitome of a profit motive without limits. In the late nineteenth century, for example, prostitution signified the demise of true womanhood and its attendant, the family organized by desexualized maternal affection; but meanwhile, with the emergence of romantic notions of love, it also sig-nified the degradation of the new conjugal choices available, at least in theory, to both men and women. In the late twentieth century, it signified new sex roles—male prostitutes now became as visible as their female predecessors—and then, with the rise of an adolescent sex trade in South Asia and Eastern Europe, it came to represent the moral depravity of the economic phenomenon called globalization.

Let me put my central question another way, hastening to preface it by saying that I mean it as something more than mere provocation or polemic. Could it be that in selling with sex, advertising disturbs us pre-cisely because it reminds us that under capitalism the prostitution of our bodies, our selves, is eminently possible—that the boundary between the public and the private, between commerce and intimacy, isn't fixed, and can't be? By the same token, could it be that in understanding our bodies as objects in their own right, according to the logic of advertising, we come to understand them as things—yes, things, "desiring machines"—subject to our scrutiny and manipulation, thus as more rather than less malleable? Could it be that in seeing our bodies from this new cognitive distance, now abstracted from where we were, we come to understand them as invitations to thought as well as limits on our thinking?

I've been tacking toward the next question all along. Could it be that the unwanted social change we correlate with the apparent prostitution of the female body in advertising is, in fact, the liberation of this body? To all of the above, once again, my answer is yes. Does that mean I'm in favor of prostitution, or the exploitation of the female body for profit? No, it means that selling with sex disturbs us for the same reason it convinces us. We know that the experience of our desires is pleasurable; we know that sexuality can't be legislated, not anymore; and we know that women should have full control of their bodies, their selves. But somehow we also feel that when female sexuality—or any other kind— is unbound by matrimonial, monogamous, or familial commitments, it gets dangerous, because then its purpose is mere pleasure, not the diligent reproduction of the species. Advertising has spoken to and for our ambiguities in this regard as no other idiom has (with the possible exception of middlebrow fiction, and, more recently, cable television). In doing so, it has reintroduced us to the most disturbing of the disruptive characters—the prostitute, the adulteress—who stood athwart the bourgeois moral order of the nineteenth century, and it has finally taught us that the consumer is neither male nor female.

Advertising has no use for what is priceless unless its practitioners are doing public service ("This is your brain on drugs"). In this fundamental sense—in the sense that it takes the commodity form as given, a permanent part of the real world, not a big problem—it remains the sworn enemy of authenticity. I mean that it has no use for virtuous personalities produced by abstention and release from market forces; for these would be individuals without consumer preferences to shape. And yet in the absence of *surplus time* outside the labor market—without the time away from work we call leisure, when we do what we want— advertising would have no purchase on our imaginations. So advertising not only acknowledges certain limits on the scope of the commodity form or the reach of the market, it also requires those limits as a condition of its ability to sell us stuff: it locates freedom somewhere after work, beyond compulsory labor, in the culture of consumption, where diligence and productivity need not apply. Its attitude toward authenticity is, then, as ambiguous as ours: we're all divided up in time, living forward and understanding backward.

All right, advertising is ironic and ambiguous about authenticity, just like its audience, just like us. Does it have to clutter every bit of scenery, from the highway to the online magazine, from the airport—where you cringe under huge screens crammed with news you don't want—to your handheld device? And in crowding these horizons, does it have to sell us pure crap, the stuff that makes us fat, stupid, or sick? I hope not, but let's consider a simple historical fact: until the Internet, there was never an "information delivery system" that stood apart from profit motives and commercial calculations (go ahead, think of your favorite pastoral escape, the baseball game, and now recall that the home field was always teeming with ads; the only exceptions to the rule are political pamphlets and samizdat, but these are hardly "disinterested" formats). And even there, in cyberspace, every website is looking for advertisements, every reputable publication with an online edition is now figuring out how to charge readers for accessing content.

David Potter, the much-honored historian of the American South who wrote a neglected book called *People of Plenty: Economic Abundance and the American Character* (1954), understood the symbiotic relation between advertising and mass communication better than anyone before or since—and he was writing at the end of the dark age, just before TV supplanted radio as the characteristic medium of home-delivered news and entertainment:

> Students of the radio and of the mass-circulation magazines frequently condemn advertising for its conspicuous role, as if it were a mere interloper in a separate, pre-existing, self-contained aesthetic world of actors, musicians, authors, and script-writers; they hardly recognize that advertising *created* modern American radio and television, *transformed* the modern newspaper, *evoked* the modern slick periodical, and remains the *vital essence* of each of them at the present time.

Advertising is to information as recording technology is to music: neither is something added to what is already finished aesthetic content, because each is an essential component in the *production* as well as the distribution and reception of the goods (see Chapters 5 and 6). Avant-garde artists in the twentieth century have taken this commercial connection for granted in appropriating the visual styles of ads, on the one hand, and comics, on the other, and so have consumers of poster art since the 1960s. By this accounting, Andy Warhol stands at the end, not the beginning, of a long line of painters, sculptors, photographers, and filmmakers whose sensibilities were shaped by an engagement with the strange possibilities of the commodity form—from Marcel Duchamp and Francis Picabia to Marsden Hartley and Stuart Davis, from Man Ray to Billy Wilder. Look at the same commercial connection from another, more prosaic angle. The so-called free press we take for granted—it's never been absolutely free from venal collusion or constitutional constraints—has been able to protect itself from state control (not influence) precisely because it's always been subsidized by private enterprise rather than the state. This relationship is now changing, of course, as reading and viewing publics learn to scroll past ads and see only what they want; the very nature of the press as we know it is changing accordingly.

But still, advertisements do constantly urge us to buy crap like double bacon cheeseburgers—about seven hundred calories *without* the fries and the Coke—and, to that extent, they turn everything, including the food chain, to shit. Meanwhile they "differentiate" products to the point of absurdity, so that every aisle of every grocery bristles with at least three versions of the same damn thing, giving us choices between ointments, laxatives, or beverages we don't even need. This ugly process is what the social critic Laura Kipnis has called the "crapification" of American culture—the process that's made us fat, stupid, or sick. No one in his right mind would defend it. And yet I can claim that the enfranchisement of consumers is the beginning of a practical solution to the problem so conceived.

Consider the so-called obesity epidemic. If it is, in fact, a problem on the scale our hysteria around it would suggest (see Chapter 9), the obvious solution is to redistribute income so that poor neighborhoods can consume the amazing variety of calories already available in affluent areas, rather than buy the relatively cheap calories compacted into burgers and fries at the nearest fast-food joint. In other words, the "crapification" of American culture can be slowed or stopped by economic measures that promote a society that's more equitable, more democratic, and less fat as well—a society that's more healthy all around.

For now, the poorer neighborhoods don't have access to Trader Joe's, Whole Foods, or farmers' markets, so their inhabitants buy what's available; if they had higher incomes, the fast-food joints would move their menus upscale at a quicker pace, the boutique grocery chains would open stores in neighborhoods that can't yet sustain them, and the farmers from upstate would clamor for space on the cross streets. Meanwhile the advertising agencies would be pitching the product in local tabloids. "Buying locally" in this sense need not mean sacrificing the pleasures of food produced in worlds elsewhere: the energy and/or environmental costs of transporting fruits, vegetables, and fish in the Western Hemisphere, for example, are quite small when compared to the costs of the refrigeration we need at both ends of the food chain.

DESIRING MACHINES

Just as no one can doubt that advertising sells with sex, no one can doubt that it creates desires. The real questions are, How and for what? And since every criticism of advertising's creative power is based on a distinction between need and desire, we also have to ask, What's the big difference between them?

Freud is the great theorist of desire, the so-called drives or urges that make us human. In his view, these were sexual urges, but he defined sexuality so broadly as to drain it of any copulative meaning. For the infant, every surface, limb, and orifice is a novel source of sensation, in part because he or she hasn't yet mapped the boundary between what is internal and what is external; the child is "polymorphously perverse," as the saying goes, heedless of propriety and instinctively devoted to the pleasure economy of a porous, leaky body. As the child matures, it learns to contain itself, and, what is the same thing, it learns to redirect its desires away from its original attachments, which were first to itself (narcissism) and then to its parents (incest).

This redirection takes two general forms, according to Freud, either repression or sublimation, and it is precisely these modifications of instinctual urges that make us neurotic— they divide us up in time—and thus human. In such terms, to be human is to translate and project your restless, primal, original desires onto the world in forms that, in turn, change you and the world, making both new. Of these fundamental desires, however, the most basic seems to be an urge toward "individuation" or separation, getting out from under the control of others—looking, always, to become a genuine self, an autonomous being who is nonetheless capable of commitment to others. To be human, in other words, is to want to be free, without knowing how. Or is that desire a need, a drive, a permanent dimension of human nature?

By this accounting, the baseline of our desires is not given, it's instead amplified and changed by their modification—by sublimation, their formal expression or representation in the external, material world, as in a work of art or an act of kindness, or by repression, their ruthless containment within an internal, psychic world, as in a conscience made guilty by unseemly urges. Either way, the modification of desires is more significant than their origin because it's more consequential, and—this is the hard part—there's no telling which modification works better in civilizing any given individual. In the long run, though, sublimation is clearly better for us as a species, because it turns us outward, toward the world and its mysteries, and in doing so it creates the postinstinctual armature of everyday life we call culture.

Advertising plays on these distinctions, but it tends, always, toward sublimation. It refuses repression. It sells freedom. Now you may think that the idea of freedom sold there is impoverished—it's too individualistic, say, or too attached to material measures of autonomy and well-being. But the fact is that advertising doesn't sell you particular commodities; it purveys a way of being in the world that is free of compulsion—free of necessary labor, the work you do because you have to—on the assumption that when at your leisure, you're free to choose an identity that might accord with the goods on offer. In that crucial sense, it remains a utopian idiom, where more work and improved productivity aren't allowed.

Forty years ago, in one of the first manifestos of women's liberation, Juliet Mitchell glimpsed this unintended consequence of advertising as a kind of ideological dialectic:

A person's physical energies can be visibly harnessed and exploited. Buying mental energies is riskier. . . . Expanding the consciousness of many (for the sake of expanding consumerism) *does* mean expanding their consciousness. And the products of this expanded consciousness are more elusive than those of the factory conveyor belt. The ideologies cultivated in order to achieve ultimate control of the market (the free choice of the individual of whatever brand of car suits his individuality) are ones which can rebel *in their own terms*.

Soon after, Daniel Bell suggested that all the cultural contradictions of capitalism—just to begin with, the opposition between bourgeois restraint and bohemian release—are captured in the post-Protestant, anti-Puritan attitudes of advertising: "It is the mark of material goods, the exemplar of new styles of life, the herald of new values."

But how so? How does advertising sell freedom, expand consciousness, herald new values? Let's start with Roland Barthes—he's the French theorist who indirectly inspired the Plastic People of the Universe, the Czech rock band we met in the last chapter. Here he is analyzing an advertisement for a powdered soap called Omo. When he gets there, to the name of the thing, go ahead, fill in the blank with a car or a garment or an appliance, and you'll realize that ads never work as inert labels for the things themselves: "Advertisements for _____ indicate the effect of the product (and in superlative fashion, incidentally), but they chiefly reveal its mode of action; in doing so, they involve the consumer in a kind of direct experience of the substance, make him an accomplice of liberation rather than the mere beneficiary of a result; matter here is endowed with value-bearing states." Now think of all the ads you've ever seen, and you'll realize that Barthes is right—they work best when they *displace* your attention from the goods on offer, toward states of being where you could buy them and put them to social uses, but don't have to.

For example, think of any beer commercial. Does it sell the beer or the identity constituted by the fellowship of beer drinkers who surround and validate the person at the center of the visual frame or the billboard narrative? You might say both—or all three, beer, identity, fellowship

—but it is this very multiplication of meanings that Barthes noticed, and that meanwhile the brewer wants you to experience. "Few stronger emotions exist than the need to belong and make meaning," as a contemporary ad agency executive puts it. "And brands are poised to exploit that need." Or, as the woman in charge of a recent Kids Foot Locker campaign laid it out for a skeptical interviewer: "We wanted to be able to show them [the kids] the empowerment they could have with the shoes." Or again, as a fierce critic of youth marketing patiently explained in a scholarly paper: "Instead of black cultural products denuded of their social context [these products are presumably musical recordings], it is now primarily the *context itself*—the neighborhood, the pain of being poor, the alienation experienced by black kids. These are the commodifiable assets." Hello? We buy stuff because we want to be poor and alienated in the 'hood? We're in the market for what is priceless, what we can't possibly obtain by purchasing it? Well, yes, that's the nature of desire, with or without advertising on the scene to engage our attention.

So Rob Walker, our best critic of consumer culture, is right to conclude that "people do not buy objects, they buy ideas about products." Nevertheless I want to revise his conclusion by suggesting that people buy ideas, period—the ideas peddled in advertisements don't adhere to specific products; they migrate, they scatter, they never settle down. The "secret dialogue" between what we buy and who we are, as Walker puts it, has been audible since the early twentieth century, when the majority of Americans started earning so-called discretionary income—something beyond what food, clothing, and shelter cost them. But there's never been a fixed relation between the idea in play and the product on offer, because time and money have intervened.

If we could buy the product as soon as the ad appeared, no one would debate the economic effect of advertising—and no one would doubt that advertisers control our desires as well as create demand from them. But we can't make that purchase in real time, right then, so the idea of the thing can now run loose; it can spill into all the other areas of our waking lives, onto other objects and situations. In a barter economy, this temporal (thus cognitive) interval between the moments of exchange is erased: I trade this thing for that thing, right here, right now.

When money comes between us, I can wait, so can you, and the equivalence between "this and that" gets stretched to the point where fundamentally different things acquire values that are equal. Time is money.

And precisely because money intervenes, these values divide into use values (personal satisfactions) and exchange values (prices). When we buy clothing, for example, we're not simply getting what we need to cover ourselves. The shoes we wear protect our feet, no matter what price we paid for them, but they also adorn our bodies and invite admiration from others; we bought them for many reasons apart from mere need. Notice, then, that the use value of those shoes is plural, immaterial, and irrational—we need to cover our bare feet, but we want to look good or "make a statement." We need what we want, and vice versa. And what we want is, by its very nature, without limit. We're never satisfied because we're human beings, not because we're prompted by advertising. As Freud among others explained, desire is the basic content of human nature. It's inexhaustible because it's the law of dreams: either you keep wanting, you keep moving, or you die.

Advertising sells freedom, expands consciousness, and heralds new values in another strange way, by sponsoring a critique of consumer culture from within the precincts of commodity fetishism. Once upon a time, as Thomas Frank tells the story of the 1960s—and as *Mad Men* has more recently dramatized—Madison Avenue became the epicenter of cultural rebellion against corporate conformity. It did so by creating ads that interrogated advertising itself, forcing consumers to question the sources of their own preferences, and, in doing so, expanding their consciousness of themselves one way or another. Frank's astonishing account of the "creative revolution" that convulsed the business in the early 1960s shows that the cutting-edge agencies treated the margins of the culture as the key to the future—they bet everything on the so-called hippies and the outsiders, knowing that these badly dressed figures were a small fraction of the buying public, and a cranky one at that. By his account, the admen didn't co-opt or appropriate the counterculture; instead, they were part of it, and maybe they were its masterminds.

More recently, advertisers and their clients have become active, creative participants in the "culture jamming" that some younger consumers have adopted as a stratagem in what they understand as a guerilla war against corporate economic power—or rather a friendly skirmish with the creative folks at the ad agencies. Here the techniques perfected in selling you the pleasures of life in a hoodie (see "social context" above) are deployed to elicit and redistribute the angers and desires of people who won't be middlebrow consumers until they have kids. And the techniques work. The dialogue between the jammers and the advertisers— and their corporate clients—is now more interesting than anything you can read about the evils of corporate power, because the second-generation jammers know they're always already branded. Their question is what to do about it, not how to escape it.

These jammers know what the avant-garde artists of the twentieth century knew—that the most tasteless and grotesque artifacts, let's say greeting cards or urinals, can be made beautiful by resituating them in new structures of feeling, new circuits of meaning. And vice versa, the most tasteful and alluring objects can be made absurd, even frightening, by the same procedure, by taking them out of context. See the magazine *Adbusters*, where iconic images from vodka advertisements, for example, are used in an anti-alcohol campaign that takes its cue from the anti-tobacco campaign of the 1980s: here the shape of an Absolut bottle looks just like a hangman's noose.

The jammers know the things themselves aren't that important except as the material devices we use to distinguish between our needs and our desires, and then to express both. For example, as a thing in itself, a Hallmark card is banal at best. But as a thought, as a moment in a gift exchange, it can be touching and precious, perhaps even becoming a priceless reminder of a loving relationship. The jammers also know that authenticity is unaffordable if the price you have to pay is abstention from market forces. The founding father of *Adbusters*, Kalle Lasn, is a true believer in what he calls an "authentic culture," and yet the first step he prescribes in his program to "win the battle for ourselves and for Planet Earth" sounds like a marketing campaign (and he of course cites the antismoking ad campaign of the 1980s as the template of his own activism): "We build our own meme factory, put out a better product and beat the corporations at their own game."

Everything the jammers do is animated by the assumption that of course we want others to notice what we wear, what we drive, what we do with the things we buy, and of course we want to appreciate ourselves from the standpoint of others: of course our selves are social. But this assumption violates the founding principle of modern Western civilization, which requires us to think of our individuality as something that develops only in opposition to tradition, community, society, whatever seems to enclose us in situations we didn't choose. So the jammers have perfected what William James and W. E. B. Du Bois called a "double consciousness," a way of seeing themselves from the outside in—and this way of seeing themselves doesn't permit conformity. Instead, it requires innovation and individuality based on mastery of the "received tradition": you have to be conversant in the language of markets, advertising, and commodities in general if you want to get ironic and playful with it. You have to understand how to play the game of consumer capitalism if you want to rewrite the rules. Put it this way: you don't have to master the American Songbook, but—as the Ramones would remind you—if you want people to listen when you punk out, you have to be able to play at least three chords.

In these terms, "culture jamming" is a colloquial, grassroots version of what high theorists like Judith Butler and Louis Althusser have called "resignification" or "disarticulation"—fancy words that are synonymous with the resituating of artifacts by avant-garde artists I've just mentioned. The jammers themselves are big fans of the French Situationists, who used the word *detournement* (literally, "turning around," or, more colloquially, "hijacking") to mean exactly the same thing, a subversive rerouting of images and ideas. Now Butler, a close reader of French intellectual history, is a fierce critic of "heteronormativity," another fancy word that means heterosexuality has become the gold standard of monogamous relationships (thus the peculiar notion that marriage happens only between a man and a woman): anything else is a deviation from this norm. But she criticizes feminists for assuming that heteronormativity is a closed system, and for assuming, as a result, that any participation in it merely prolongs its stranglehold on our bodies. Here is how Butler makes the argument against Monica Wittig:

Wittig appears to believe that only the radical departure from hetero-sexual contexts—namely becoming lesbian or gay—can bring about the downfall of [the] heterosexual regime. But this political consequence follows only if one understands all "participation" in heterosexuality to be a repetition and consolidation of heterosexual oppression. The pos-sibilities of resignifying heterosexuality itself are refused precisely be-cause [it] is understood as a total system that requires a thoroughgoing displacement. The political options that follow from such a totalizing view of heterosexist power are (a) radical conformity or (b) radical revolution.

Just so, I'd say, with respect to the culture jammers and their ambigu-ous agendas. They use the language of marketing, prices, advertising—the dialect of desire—to resituate and resignify and disarticulate commodities in general. From their standpoint, consumer capitalism has too many fissures and contradictions, not to mention fun places, to be grasped as a closed system that won't change without a frontal assault, a war of maneuver, or a mass exodus. Jammers believe they can partici-pate in it without validating all its oppressive idiocies; like hipsters, they work at the margins, but they know they're insiders, creating "punk cap-italism" by hacking at the mainframe. So they can refuse the either/or choice between (a) radical conformity and (b) radical revolution that has disabled almost all thinking about consumer culture since the 1950s. They can start with this question: We don't buy food for its nutritional value, and we don't buy clothes for their protective value—these are the only things we really need—so what are we doing here, when we're shopping, and what is to be done?

CHAPTER EIGHT

News from Nowhere

Advertising Utopia

THE HERALD OF NEW VALUES

I've already mentioned Thomas Frank's account of the "creative revolution" that shook up the advertising business in the early 1960s. Let's return to it now as a way of revisiting the question of participation in consumer culture, from the standpoint of both consumers and advertisers. The shocking thing about Frank's argument is not that the admen were taking the pulse of a rapidly changing culture—that's their job—but that they identified themselves and their corporate clients with the outer edges and the radical results of the cultural changes defined by civil rights, youth rebellion, and women's liberation. How is that possible? Doesn't "big business" oppose progress—by this I mean the regulation and socialization of market forces in the name of equity among classes, genders, races, and nations—because progress endangers profits? The answer isn't anywhere near self-evident.

For a century, leading historians have argued that big corporations uniformly opposed the legislation of the Progressive Era precisely because it socialized market forces—either that or CEOs wrote the laws themselves to exploit their market power—and then they fought the New Deal of the 1930s and the Great Society of the 1960s on the same grounds. This historical argument looks to be confirmed by our recent experience with health care and financial reform: the opposition was led by corporate lobbyists. If that weren't confirmation enough, there's always the evidence of corporate malfeasance, corruption, criminality, and mere cruelty that goes by the name of "globalization."

But there's another way to tell this story, too. In the early twentieth century, when large industrial corporations first became the dominant structural element in the U.S. economy, their founders and executives were eager to find both public and private means to subdue the anarchy of the free market; that's why they joined the movement for banking reform that invented the Federal Reserve, and that's why they signed on to the analogous movements that gave us the Federal Trade Commission and, before that, the Food and Drug Administration. They had no stake in a price system that put them at the mercy of small producers in deciding what to charge for their products; they wanted stability and predictability because they had enormous amounts of fixed capital in play, and because unmanaged economic crisis threatened both social and political order. So these corporate leaders didn't just accept government regulation of market forces when it was imposed on them; they created it, and not just to take advantage of it. Meanwhile they perfected private means of socializing markets (trade associations, business councils, chambers of commerce, civic federations, and the like). The same story of corporate involvement rather than simple opposition can be told about the New Deal and the Great Society.

So we're shocked by Frank's rendition of the "creative revolution" in advertising because we're used to treating large corporations and business executives (small entrepreneurs are still OK) as the faceless, bureaucratic enemy of progress as such. We don't want to hear that the admen and their corporate clients were on our side in the 1960s and after because if we believe this, we can't treat consumer capitalism as a closed system to be displaced by "radical revolution." Nor can we treat corporations as the uniform, obvious enemy of our progressive agendas. Instead, we have to treat progress as a cross-class project that involves every social stratum, including—or maybe especially—the segment of the population that excels at selling us stuff we don't need.

Not to worry, Frank and his fellow critics of consumer culture have a way around this uncomfortable conclusion. Yes, they say, the admen bet everything on the counterculture, where "Just Do It" was the imperative of everyday life long before Nike turned it into a slogan. But, you see, they did it to profit from the desires of innocent consumers, people who would never go near Haight-Ashbury or Greenwich Village, people who would never experience the reality of immediate experience as lived at the margin by the romantic and the restless among us. The admen mainstreamed the counterculture to enhance and perpetuate corporate power, and they did it by convincing us to buy more stuff. They were peddling false consciousness.

This is the same logic that convicts working musicians of "selling out" to the A & R men and their bosses at the record companies, thus enhancing and perpetuating the dead hand of corporate power—more white noise—rather than staying poor and striking a blow for authentic art. This is the same logic that accuses successful writers of pandering to the popular tastes of the market, writing the kind of chick lit or detective fiction or scatological horror that is formulaic enough to be lucrative, rather than striking a "literary" blow for the benighted people who should be reading what's good for them. This is the same logic that insists we discover truth and make progress only when we're safe inside an ideal zone of use value, outside the market, where exchange values haven't yet invaded and disfigured the creative process, where our souls are still beautiful.

At best, when dressed down as bohemian rebellion, it's a pseudo-realistic logic of weary resignation, because it leaves the world as we know it intact. It lets us ignore or escape reality rather than interrupt it and rearrange it, by resituating or resignifying the everyday objects that crowd our lives—the objects that inevitably come with price tags, unless you live off the grid or on the set of *Avatar*. At worst, when dressed up as academic piety, it's a childish logic, because it blinds us to the unintended consequences of what we take to be the wrong motives, and again removes us from the real world, where people work for a living and buy the best they can. We want the agents of progress to share our noble purposes, no matter when they lived, so that, for example, we doubt the radicalism of the American Revolution because it was led by slaveholders. By the same token, we don't want advertising, corporate profits, or consumerism to be listed as ingredients in the counterculture of the 1960s. The fact remains that all three were crucial components of this progressive moment, not least because it was then that they conspired to make the black aesthetic a transnational consumer good.

Moreover, the "creative revolution" of the 1960s was not an exception proving the rule that profits and progress don't mix. Into the 1970s, 1980s, and 1990s, ad agencies continued to be *sources* as well as benefi-ciaries of cultural and economic change—mainly by placing risky bets on the marketability of black musicians, athletes, and comedians. As they had once gambled on marginal figures who seemed to stand outside the frame of the market, they now rolled the dice and put their clients' money on images of people who had been systematically excluded, by law and every other means, from the promise of American life. Their risky bets paid off in profits for them and their clients, of course, but they paid off in other more important ways, by depicting the black aes-thetic as the mainstream of American culture, both at home and abroad (see Chapter 6).

The 1980s were the turning point. As the late Leonard Wynter con-vincingly tells this story, the pivot was a commercial that aired on Super Bowl XIII of 1980, featuring the hulking black defensive tackle "Mean" Joe Greene and a ten-year-old white kid who offers him his Coke. It was a one-minute spot that dramatized two acts of kindness—an exchange of gifts—between people who might as well have been from different planets, even as late as 1980. Its effect on the advertising business and their clients was electrifying. By 1984, Coke and Pepsi were in a bidding war for the services of Michael Jackson, Lionel Richie, Whitney Houston, and Tina Turner. Meanwhile Vanessa Williams was crowned Miss Amer-ica, Eddie Murphy starred in a movie (*Beverly Hills Cop*) that tied *Ghost-busters* for the top-grossing film of the year, and *The Cosby Show* debuted on ABC as the number-one TV series. Wynter calls this new trend the "commercial browning" of America, and rightly insists, as Thomas Frank had done in his study of the 1960s, that the admen were *creating* it, not merely capitalizing on what the "culture industry" already knew. The culmination of the trend was the 1999 Budweiser commercial that fea-tured four young black men; in an unprecedented move, an all-black cast carried the general-market campaign for the country's best-selling brand of beer. Or was the culmination of the trend reached even earlier, when the NBA sold its brand to worldwide TV audiences at the very moment five black starters became commonplace? Either way, "Whassup?" What's happening here?

THE DANGERS OF ABUNDANCE

As late as the 1930s, in the midst of the Great Depression, Simon Patten's signature ideas and phrases were still idiomatic reflexes among social scientists and journalists. Stuart Chase, a contributing editor at the *New Republic*, published a book called *The Economy of Abundance* in 1934, for example, and repeatedly cited Rexford G. Tugwell, a former student of Patten's and a current member of FDR's "brain trust." At the same moment, in a book called *America's Capacity to Consume*, the economists at the Brookings Institution noted that policy makers (like Tugwell) assumed the validity of Patten's theories: "The same view is often expressed in the statement that the age of scarcity has been replaced by the era of abundance, an era in which the great problem is how to make effective use of the leisure time which the age of technology has thrust upon us. Of more significance than the mere expression of this view is the fact that it is being embodied, more or less consciously, in governmental policies." Meanwhile public intellectuals like Lewis Mumford and Archibald MacLeish wrote about the displacement of workers and the redefinition of work this "age of technology" had caused. Both noticed the problem of consumer demand in the absence of full unemployment, but emphasized the promise of a society freed from the bonds of necessary labor—both welcomed the end of work as all previous generations had experienced it.

By the 1950s, Patten's optimistic idiom had all but disappeared. The postwar decade was the dawn of consumer culture as we know it, and yet David Potter's book of 1954, *People of Plenty* (mentioned above), is one of the very few attempts to assess the social psychology of economic abundance, and its conclusions are uniformly bleak. He mentions a "scarcity economy," to be sure, as if Patten were only one generation removed, but he seems by this to mean the moment of the Great Depression—and he never cites Patten himself, or for that matter any social theorist who wrote before the 1940s. The presiding spirit of the book is instead the Frankfurt School as attended by David Riesman, the author of *The Lonely Crowd* (1950)—you can tell by the title that this is a book about the "other-directed" sources of conformity—and by Paul Goodman, the author of *Communitas* (1947), the most biting critique of consumer culture until Philip Rieff and Herbert Marcuse went him one better in the 1960s.

So Potter does a lot of hand-wringing about the scary "social effects" of advertising, deciding, in the end, that it reduces the range of individual choice and exalts "the materialistic virtues of consumption" as against the genuine benefits of real work. He lifts this idea directly from Goodman, who is quoted at length in the chapter on advertising. Here is how Potter introduces it: "In the society of consumption . . . production is only a means to the end of consumption, and therefore satisfaction in the [sic] work disappears. The workman accordingly focuses all his demands upon suitable working conditions, and high wages, so that he may hasten away with sufficient time, wealth, and energy to seek the goals of the consumer." Sam Gompers and the politics of "more" already mystify—or rather disgust—the political imagination of higher education (again, see Chapter 5).

To drive the point home, Potter quotes Goodman, who declared that any exit from the dignity of honest labor delivers us unto Rousseau's nightmare of *amour propre*—where the regard of others is the only measure of self-worth—and who also insisted, in a solemn parody of John Bunyan, that this evasion can be completed only in a "great city" like New York: "And the chief drive toward such goods is not individual but social. It is imitation and emulation which result in the lively [consumer] demand. . . . The heart of the city of expanding effective demand is the department store, [where] all things are available according to desire—and are on display in order to suggest the desire. The streets are corridors of the department store; for the work of the people must not be quarantined from its cultural meaning."

This is the voice that replaced Patten's in the postwar years—so that by the 1970s, Susan Sontag, Goodman's dear friend, could spit out "consumer society" as a convenient epithet, an incidental profanity, in explaining how the cinematic aesthetic of fascism was too dangerously appealing for routine exposure to the tasteless masses. Meanwhile consumer culture had become the object of critique from *within* the advertising industry itself. What happened? How did the promise of abundance become an embarrassing problem and then a dangerous proposition? To answer that question is to understand why advertising, the herald of the new values attending abundance, got such a bad name, from itself among others.

I have two tentative answers—call them hypotheses—drawn from my research as an intellectual historian of the twentieth century. First, events in Eastern Europe caused significant defections, both social and intellectual, from the ranks of western Communist parties. The Soviet Party Congress of 1953 renounced Stalin's legacy, leaving a lot of fellow travelers in other countries wondering why they'd been defending him all those years, and persuading many of them to quit the party and the cause. Their disillusionment led directly to the reconsideration of Soviet Marxism, and that allowed for a "cultural turn," a new skepticism about the economic determinants of social change, among left-leaning intellectuals and activists alike. This disillusionment was magnified by the savagery of the Soviet response to the Hungarian uprising of 1956.

The intellectual results were a vast improvement on what had passed for serious analysis of society and literature—for example, Antonio Gramsci, the renegade Italian Communist imprisoned by Mussolini, soon became a new beacon of Marxist theory, as did Raymond Williams, the presiding spirit of the British New Left. Meanwhile writer Harold Cruse, a would-be playwright disgusted by his experience as a Communist Party hack, freed himself from the party line and produced wholly original work on the central importance of black nationalism in American life. William Appleman Williams, Richard Hofstadter, Hannah Arendt, Daniel Bell, and C. Wright Mills led comparable breaks from the prison house of Marxism guarded by Soviet authority, remaking their disciplines by making their escapes (but never relinquishing their claims on Marx's key ideas). But with few, mostly British, exceptions, the opportunity cost of this vast improvement, this "cultural turn," was a pointed neglect of political economy. Hereafter only professional economists and vulgar Marxists were willing to pronounce on these matters, and most of what they said was either unintelligible or inane. The economics of abundance were now the province of historians like David Potter, who looked to Frankfurt School students (Riesman and Goodman) for intellectual guidance. And from their standpoint, abundance was a lie sold to the spastic, ignorant masses by advertising. Simon Patten and his interpreters could now be forgotten, or treated like shills for false consciousness.

Second, the cultural turn in the social sciences incorporated theories and models stressing the irrational as against the ideological, in effect replacing Marx with Freud or Max Weber, and installed European social theory—again, the Frankfurt School was the place to be—as the critical antidote to the complacency of American pragmatism. Susan Sontag's intellectual career is an extreme version of this trajectory, but it is exemplary, too. For the questions requiring some form of theoretical address in the immediate postwar world were, How did fascism happen? What was its appeal? The "cultural turn" seemed to produce better answers than the inherited alternatives, especially since the Soviet Union, the habitat of vulgar Marxism, looked to be a close relative of fascism in the family tree of "totalitarianism."

The Frankfurt School notion of an "authoritarian personality" that needed the dictates of charismatic leaders—now here was an idea with traction among intellectuals who doubted that the masses had the coherent egos (the psychological resources) required to resist the techniques of propaganda perfected by the Nazis for political purposes and by the "culture industry" for economic purposes. When David Riesman, an obscure Harvard sociologist, translated this notion of the "authoritarian personality" as the "other-directed individual" whose inner direction had failed him, he became an overnight sensation. His book *The Lonely Crowd* became a best seller, and he was soon designated an intellectual celebrity by an appearance on the cover of *Time* magazine in June of 1950. And then David Potter made the obvious connection, correlating Riesman's new character type with the ideal consumer who emerged as the result of "the element of abundance." Suddenly all of middlebrow America agreed that the masses could be stirred to action after all, and agreed also that if they began moving their slow thighs and started slouching toward Washington, the center would not hold. But the high-brow intellectuals who attended the Frankfurt School had led the way to this consensus.

I now quote Potter at length because the correlations he made between abundance, consumerism, and the passive "other-directed individual" became staples of cultural criticism in the 1960s, culminating in the idea of "One-Dimensional Man" made both rigorous and popular by Herbert Marcuse, another Frankfurt School alumnus. Notice how the citation of Riesman authorizes the pronouncements that follow.

> Prior to the attainment of abundance, Riesman remarks, people are concerned primarily with increasing production. In their own tempera-ment this requires hard enduringness and enterprise; in their external concerns it requires concentration upon dominating the physical en-vironment; in their personal economy it requires thrift, prudence, ab-stinence. But once abundance is secured, the scarcity psychology that was once so valuable no longer operates to the advantage of society, and the ideal individual develops the qualities of the good consumer rather than those of the good producer. He needs now to cultivate in-terests that are appropriate to an enlarged leisure, and, since he is likely to be an employee rather than an entrepreneur or to be engaged in one of the service trades rather than in production, the cordiality of his re-lations with other people becomes more important than his mastery of the environment. In his personal economy, society expects him to consume his quota of goods—of automobiles, of whiskey, of television sets—by maintaining a certain standard of living, and it regards him as a "good guy" for absorbing his share, while it snickers at the prudent, self-denying, abstemious thrift that an earlier generation would have respected. In short, he has become an other-directed man.

Translation: the end of the self-made man—the entrepreneurial, "inner-directed" man who read his own moral compass—coincides with the advent of abundance, which in turn requires the pliant, white-collar employee who goes along to get along. This new man is an "other-directed individual" who waits for instructions from bosses and advertisements rather than striking out on his own. Like Willy Loman, he wants to be well liked, and that desire makes him an abject consumer of whatever the authorities purvey, whether it's political truths or aesthetic judgments. As such, as a mere desiring machine, he's the perfect constituent of the political demagogue or the sophisticated copywriter who speaks *for* the inert masses, not *to* self-determining, "inner-directed" citizens capable of making their own choices. So this new man explains the gross appeal of fascism. By the same token, he explains the insidious effects of advertising: both prospered from the Big Lie.

If these correlations seem far-fetched, we need only look at how they inform a recent best seller by Matthew B. Crawford, *Shop Class as Soulcraft* (2009)—a book that treats skilled manual labor as the obvious alternative to the enervating consumption of goods that comes with "the full flowering of mass communication and mass conformity" in the late twentieth century. Here is how Crawford draws together the threads of his argument: "Because craftsmanship refers to objective standards that do not issue from the self and its desires, it poses a challenge to the ethic of consumerism . . . [and] renders the social narrative of the advertisement less potent. The craftsman has an impoverished fantasy life compared to the ideal consumer . . . [but] he is also more independent." Like many previous political theorists from Aristotle to Jefferson, Crawford deduces political consequences from this difference between the artisan—the producer—and the consumer: "If the modern personality is being reorganized on a predicate of passive consumption, this is bound to affect our political culture." He explains in words that David Potter, David Riesman, or any other student of the Frankfurt School could have used, but notice, too, the classical republican equation of economic and political independence (the same equation the Populists wrote in the 1890s): "Since the standards of craftsmanship issue from the logic of things rather than the art of persuasion, practiced submission to them perhaps gives the craftsman some psychic ground to stand on against fantastic hopes aroused by demagogues, *whether commercial or political* [my emphasis]."

These correlations first became commonplace in the 1950s, as intellectuals cobbled together interpretations of fascism and communism under the heading of "totalitarianism." By the 1960s, writers of every origin and orientation had abandoned the very idea of abundance, calling it an ideological aberration that obscured the fundamental facts of American life—facts like the poverty on view in the cities ("the ghetto") as well as Appalachia, the "economy of death" dictated by the Department of Defense, and the rural idiocy of suburbs enabled by massive federal spending on superhighways. This reckoning proved that the basis of the new consumer culture was actually a false bottom. An "age of surplus," a "pleasure economy"? These were the puerile dreams of American innocence, not the waking life of a world power at war, spending almost every tax dollar on weapons of mass destruction. Deprivation, alienation, and reification defined everyday life in these United States, not to mention the less-developed parts of the planet. No matter: the hidden persuaders on Madison Avenue kept selling fables of abundance.

EROS AND CIVILIZATION

Again, this quasi-academic, middlebrow revolt against consumer society was generated by high theory and validated by certain strains of popular culture. Let's take a brief look at the high theory, to see how it informed what we still take for granted. In the late 1950s and early 1960s, Norman O. Brown and Herbert Marcuse reinvented psychoanalysis as a theory of culture, on the one hand, and a philosophy of history, on the other. In *Life Against Death* (1958), a book that achieved cult status on campus by the late 1960s—I preserve my copy of the original paperback edition with duct tape and rubber bands—Brown took Freud's metapsychology so seriously that he treated the master's theory of a death instinct as a useful hypothesis subject to empirical tests from the historical record. Freud notwithstanding, the concluding section of the book is the most lyrical and damning indictment of money, property, and capitalism since Marx.

But in the last substantive chapter ("Filthy Lucre"), where money and excrement get equated—everything has turned to shit—Brown renounced both repression and sublimation as symptoms of the death instinct, on his way toward a plea for an adult rendition of the child's polymorphous perversity. In this sense, he advocated an end to alienated labor, just like the Marxists always had, but he went well beyond them by claiming that the real problem was not the external domination of workers by capitalists; instead, it was the neurosis at the heart of human nature, the "compulsion to work," the urge to change the world. So long as that sickness went untreated, nothing could change. He explained that the "drive to sublimate is the same as the drive to produce an economic surplus" because—as Marx himself had noted—the satisfaction of a need merely provoked new needs. "Such a [drive] makes man eternally Faustian and restless," Brown concluded, "and therefore precludes happiness; it also precludes the possibility of [what Freud called] an 'economy of abundance.'" For it renders us unable "to distinguish real human needs from (neurotic) consumer demands."

Brown was of course in dialogue with Marcuse, who had argued in *Eros and Civilization* (1955) that sublimation could be a polymorphous, socializing urge to connect; he insisted that in surreal works of art and in social movements calling for an end to compulsive, useful, productive labor, it had recently taken "nonrepressive" cultural forms. Marcuse took his cue from Geza Roheim, the anthropologist who framed his studies of Australian aborigines as psychoanalytical case studies. "The difference between a neurosis and a sublimation is evidently the social aspect of the phenomenon," Roheim claimed in *The Origin and Function of Culture* (1944): "A neurosis isolates; a sublimation unites. In a sublimation, something new is created—a house, or a community, or a tool—and it is created in a group or for the use of a group." Marcuse followed this lead, and was able, as a result, to glimpse a "nonrepressive civilization" already residing in, perhaps even emerging from, the "traditional culture, intellectual as well as material." Like many social scientists of the 1950s, he saw that the explosive forces of automation might soon reverse "the relation between free time and working time on which the established civilization rests." He saw that these forces could realize "the possibility of working time becoming marginal, and free time becoming full time."

Like Brown, then, Marcuse was looking for a way beyond the compulsion to work, and insisting that an end to alienated labor was the precondition of a nonrepressive civilization. But in 1955, at any rate, Marcuse had a prognosis and a course of treatment for the diseased civilization he had diagnosed so carefully. Brown had only a diagnosis, and, as he put it in concluding his book, "a way out" of the insane asylum that was advanced industrial society: the patients consigned to this bedlam could not be cured, so it was best to give up on them and move on to live possibilities in another place. That radical attitude fed directly into the gathering consensus on the wholly neurotic, self-destructive nature of a consumer society and its reified cultural apparatus—a consensus that required abstention, withdrawal, and release from a reality steeped in money, property, advertising, and excrement.

And then the hugely influential cultural critic Susan Sontag seconded Lionel Trilling's assessment of *Life Against Death* as "far-ranging, thoroughgoing, extreme, and shocking," plus "the best interpretation of Freud" available. Her praise of Brown was both effusive and just plain wrong (there was nothing "immanent" in his critique of consumer capitalism: Martin Luther and Jonathan Swift are the last historical figures he consults). But her loud endorsement of 1961, reprinted in *Against Interpretation* (1965), drowned out Marcuse's hopeful prognosis, and made Brown's bleak diagnosis the highbrow standard of argument about the promise of American life. David Potter's more hesitant, more academic indictment of "consumer society" and advertising now had serious, strident backing from the leading public intellectuals of the day.

Meanwhile, Marcuse changed his mind. By the time he came to write *One-Dimensional Man* (1964), he had followed Brown—also Sontag, and every other reputable intellectual—down the road of retreat from an advanced industrial society that was clearly beyond redemption because it brandished an abundance of material goods as compensation for alienation without end. It was a poignant reversal that had the quality of a confession and an indictment, all at once, as if this Promethean author addressed an absent judge, an unseen god, a Stalinist tribunal, or a Gestapo interrogator; in any case it was a performance that ratified the hopeless verdict on contemporary consumer culture delivered by

Goodman, Brown, and Sontag, among others. It still informs most critical thinking about so-called consumer society.

For Marcuse, advanced industrial society was "one-dimensional" in the sense that it had turned the once-tabooed truths of "disruptive characters"—"the artist, the prostitute, the adulteress, the great criminal and outcast, the warrior, the rebel-poet, the devil, the fool"—into goods and services available to anyone with disposable income. What had been fantastic, oppositional, alien, subversive, and utopian before the advent of consumer society was now commonplace because it was all for sale. So the world elsewhere of genuine literature, classical music, and high culture—the transcendental outpost of art that had pointed beyond the oppressive realities of everyday life—this vertical "second dimension" of society had now been flattened into the material reality of the market.

Here is how Marcuse himself put it: "If mass communications blend together harmoniously, and often unnoticeably, art, politics, religion, and philosophy with *commercials*, they bring these realms of culture to their common denominator—the commodity form." Those commercials had created "repressive needs" that induced "euphoria in unhappiness." But this was not Hegel's heroically unhappy consciousness, the Stoic of antiquity who understood his alienation and accepted his terrible destiny—a character Marcuse had studied carefully in his first book, *Reason and Revolution* (1941); no, this was a new state of mind. This was a new psychological place where the hunger for approval was so great that it had materialized Rousseau's *amour propre* and made the authoritarian personality your suburban neighbor: "Most of the prevailing needs to relax, to have fun, to behave and consume in accordance with the advertisements, to love and hate what others love and hate, belong to the category of false needs."

The older, high culture of the West was not just endangered, then, it was extinct. Where "its authentic works [had] expressed a conscious, methodical alienation from the entire sphere of business and industry, and from its calculable and profitable order," the new consumer society had taken up permanent, smiling residence in that very sphere, this very order. Nothing was safe from the clutches of the commodity form, and so the oppositional force of culture as such, that vertical second dimension, was out of reach, maybe even invisible, except to the most disruptive, the most dangerous of characters, outlaws all. When alienation can be bought and sold as if it were a pair of shoes rather than an artistic property—as if it were something peddled or prized by anyone with enough money—"exchange value, not truth value, counts." The danger of abundance was just this, the conversion of the artist's methodical alienation into a consumer good available to all, even the least reflective yahoo. So, either the price the artist had to pay for his abstention from the "sphere of business and industry" would keep climbing, amounting in the end to some kind of exile from the common, commodified experience of humankind, or the very idea of art would expire, having become the province of graphic designers at the glossy magazines.

Marcuse's aristocratic bias in favor of a pretechnological, almost feudal culture was explicit and mournful at the same time; he knew he celebrated a world that was already irretrievable. And yet the book became a sensation, a touchstone of cultural criticism, a talismanic text in the 1960s. It was popular in spite of itself, something like the advertisements pitched with winks and nods and gentle elbows by the avant-garde agencies at the same moment. It was a two-faced argument in the sense that it was a search for "thoughts and principles not marketable"—this is Ralph Waldo Emerson speaking—and, at the same time, an earnest bid for a hearing in the marketplace of ideas. But it carried no trace of hypocrisy.

And so there's no paradox at work here. To abstain from the market is to fall silent, to refuse to trade truths with your fellow citizens; to write for the market is to make your ideas intelligible to the masses, to treat your thoughts as so much merchandise. Like Marcuse, you assume that falling silent is worse than the alternative, and so you keep writing, knowing that some great writers, from Melville to Salinger, have gone dark overnight because the trade-off became an either/or choice. You try to avoid that choice. As an author who wants readers, you proceed as if the commodity form is *constituted* by its opposition between exchange value and use value, and you acknowledge, then negotiate, this opposition every time you buy or sell a commodity, whatever the site of the transaction may be—whether you're writing a "serious" book and hoping it reaches a wide audience anyway, or claiming exemption from interest in what Oprah says, meanwhile hoping for validation from the sales figures. The measure of your contemporary influence is written in those figures, but still you somehow know that the worth of your ideas will be recorded in a different ledger, sooner or later, and you're right. The prices of certain things can't make sense—they can't let us find equivalence where difference resides—if everything has a price.

One-Dimensional Man completed the postwar movement that made the idea of abundance a joke and the spectacle of consumer culture a disgrace—the movement that deposited Simon Patten and his early, sympathetic interpreters in the dustbin of history. By the 1970s and 1980s, it was impossible to find a respectable intellectual who was willing to defend either the idea or the spectacle (or Patten). Academics were especially eager to denounce both, of course, in keeping with the radicalization of higher education. But the Left's worries about the reach of the commodity form were confirmed by the Right, and the universities weren't the primary source of doubts about the insidious effects of advertising. As Marcuse himself acknowledged, his argument against the dangers of abundance was derived from muckraking, wildly popular books by Vance Packard, as well as his own rarefied background as a student of Max Horkheimer, Theodor Adorno, and the larger curriculum of the Frankfurt School.

Packard's breakthrough book *The Hidden Persuaders* (1957) topped best-seller lists for a year after its publication. Its broad appeal was a result of its debunking form and style—the way it addressed "rational citizens" as readers who couldn't possibly fall for advertising pitches based on mere prurience. The first-person pronouns helped. The ad agencies had recently learned "the lore of psychiatry and the social sciences in order to increase their skill at 'engineering' our consent," Packard explained, but once forewarned of these invitations to irrationality, we, the people, were also armed against them. So the book worked in part as a touching homage to the admen "who still do a straightforward job and accept us as rational citizens"—the good guys, the ones whose words still adhered to real, valuable things. The new "depth approach" of the motivation researchers at the agencies was, by contrast, an affront and a threat to democracy; for it persuaded with style, meter, rhythm, voice, and so on, always on the assumption that consumers don't know what they want and would lie to you about it if they did.

The bizarre quality of the book—or rather, the pleasure of reading it—lies here, in the gap between its solemn commitment to the ideal consumer with the impregnable unconscious and its gleeful ridicule of real consumers, whose preferences were obviously driven by unspeakable, irrational urges. Packard pretty clearly couldn't help himself in emphasizing those urges. In his opening chapters, he shows with painstaking detail that in the early 1950s, the advertising agencies and their clients kept doing surveys with the expectation that the customer was making reasonable decisions about the utility of the products on offer—but kept discovering instead that the customer was motivated more by colors, packaging, and style, in cars or detergents, than by any comparison of benefits against costs. The agencies thereupon did some different homework and decided, as a result, to visit the inarticulate sources of consumer motivations (read: desires), the social-psychological places where reason was a tourist without a dictionary. They had no choice if they wanted to sell more consumer goods.

So Marcuse could cite the best-selling Packard because they agreed that the masses were plainly benighted, obviously manipulated, and more than ever in need of redemption by exhortation—in need of rescue from the false consciousness imposed on them by the "culture industry." Across the board, then, from the lowbrow Packard on toward the middlebrow Potter, unto the highbrow Sontag, everybody understood that consumer society was a terrible affliction, that abundance was a very Big Lie, and that advertising was the sales headquarters for both.

NEWS FROM NOWHERE

No one doubts that advertising has been the headquarters of consumer culture, just as no one doubts that banking—the financial sector—has become the headquarters of corporate capitalism. Still, the question that remains is how to characterize the goods it sells. In this chapter, I have twice suggested that advertising is a utopian idiom, and should be valued as such. Let me now flesh out that suggestion by enlisting

Herbert Marcuse, of all people. My goal here, of course, is to challenge the intellectual consensus on consumer society and abundance that he helped create.

In the pivotal Episode 6 of *Mad Men*, year one, Rachel Menken, a potential client of Don Draper, the creative director at the advertising firm Sterling Cooper, describes Israel as "more of an idea than a place"; she's trying to say that it's more of a pretext than a destination, more of a protest than a plan. The ever-intuitive Don understands her, so without a beat he says, "Utopia." She nods, but splits the word into the two meanings her Barnard professors had taught her: "a good place, and the place that cannot be." In his own erudite way, Marcuse agreed with Rachel and Don. In *Eros and Civilization*, Utopia appeared as the before and after of alienated labor, as an elusive idea that had forever haunted the artistic imagination—the place that cannot be—and as an impending stage of human development, a good place for the conduct of the good life. But Marcuse was of two minds: until he came to write *One-Dimensional Man*, he refused to decide between these definitions because the use value of the idea had acquired an exchange value, a real price and a real place in the world. To put it another way, the universal appeal of the utopian attitude toward necessary labor—who doesn't want to stop working and enjoy the rest of life?—had a particular meaning for him in 1955, a very specific, material articulation he called "automation."

In *Eros and Civilization*, Marcuse argued that the "ultimate form of freedom" would require release from compulsion in its most familiar human shape: necessary labor. "It is the sphere outside labor which defines freedom and fulfillment," he insisted, "and it is the definition [the idea] of the human existence in terms of this sphere which constitutes the negation of the performance principle." That would mean the negation of what Freud called the reality principle, which contained the pleasure principle by freezing instincts in the name of civilization, by putting us to work rather than play. But Marcuse wasn't advocating the ignorance or the evacuation of reality. He was suggesting that in its new guise as the "performance principle," the reality principle now looked like "surplus repression": it looked like a punitive urge that produced individual anxiety and social stupidity instead of just getting us back to work on Monday.

Once upon a time, mere survival in a savage world required the deferral of gratification; once upon a time, the development of civilization required repression: less play, more work, that was the price of our exit from the state of nature, according to Freud. But had this price now become too much to bear? Yes, Marcuse answered, very quietly, by suggesting that the premise of Freud's basic theorems was material scarcity, and that perhaps the premise needed revision in view of new historical circumstances. "Behind the reality principle lies the fundamental fact of Ananke or scarcity (*Lebensnot*)," he began, "which means that the struggle for existence takes place in a world too poor for the satisfaction of human needs without constant restraint, renunciation, delay. In other words, whatever satisfaction is possible necessitates *work*, more or less painful arrangements and undertakings for the procurement of the means of satisfying needs."

Now Utopia is always a story of how a society meets its end, told from a standpoint removed from the ending. So it's often situated in a *place* that denies this fundamental fact of scarcity, most poignantly in medieval peasant vacations from hard labor like "The Land of Cockaigne," where nourishment fell from trees and flowed through streams. In modern Utopias such as those by Thomas More, Edward Bellamy, and George Orwell, the fundamental fact of scarcity is still denied—but now because labor has been rationalized, not abolished. Either way, this narrative *place* was a precinct of the imagination: it was a world elsewhere, like the second, oppositional dimension of funny, angry art made by those "disruptive characters" Marcuse celebrated in *One-Dimensional Man*. It was a legible world, to be sure, but it wasn't inhabitable except as an attractive (or, in Orwell's case, repulsive) idea, so it resembled what certain organized religions call heaven (or hell): it "happened" before or after historical time, as an extraordinary alternative to everyday life. It was more of an idea than a place.

In *Eros and Civilization*, though, this world once elsewhere seems close by, right next door, ready to move in. It feels measurable, like a real place, so it doesn't sound utopian: unlike heaven (or hell), it's not "otherworldly." Here is how Marcuse sketches the new neighborhood: "If the construction of a non-repressive instinctual development is oriented, not on the subhistorical past, but on the historical present and mature civilization, the very notion of utopia loses it meaning." Translation: if we've reached a stage of civilization where scarcity is no longer the norm, and alienated labor is no longer even necessary, then Utopia isn't a world elsewhere, it's the here and now, it's everyday life. Then what?

Then a new, nonrepressive reality principle would be in the making—a principle in accordance with an era of abundance, when the "general automatization of labor [would] reduce labor time to a minimum." This new principle would preclude "productivity" as an essential value or purpose of a good life. "Man is evaluated according to his ability to make, augment, and improve socially useful things," Marcuse noted, but went on to say that "this notion of productivity has its historical limits." And with automation, those limits had been reached: "The utopian claims of imagination have become saturated with historical reality." He hadn't yet read the social scientists who studied the impending end of work—they would figure prominently in his next book, *One-Dimensional Man*—but he sensed that a passage beyond socially necessary labor was already under way. He sensed that the Philistines' resentful defamation of mere indolence and idle inquiry would soon cease, because improved productivity was pointless in a society that could make many more goods with much less effort.

Marcuse didn't want abundance (as conventionally understood) to serve as the condition of this impending release from the grip of repression: "The reconciliation between pleasure and reality principle does not depend on the existence of abundance for all." Even so, he grasped the strange psychological—maybe even political—possibilities residing in an organization of labor that turned producers into spectators, making workers into mere watchmen and regulators:

> Rationalization and mechanization of labor tend to reduce the quantum of instinctual energy channeled into toil (alienated labor), thus freeing energy for the attainment of objectives set by the free play of individual faculties. Technology operates against the repressive utilization of energy in so far as it minimizes the time necessary for the production of the necessities of life, thus saving time for the development of needs *beyond* the realm of necessity and of necessary waste.

So technology had delivered on its promise, after all. Marx had similarly located the realm of true freedom beyond necessity, but in the distant future, at an address far removed in time from the scene of socially necessary labor. Marcuse located it in our vicinity, in an unfinished but actual historical moment called "advanced industrial society," where machines and robots—"automation"—could do the hard work. That's why he claimed that the very notion of Utopia had lost its meaning: it was now a *place* as well as an idea. But then it regained its meaning, for him and countless others, because, in the 1960s and after, the fact that "the utopian imagination had become saturated with historical reality" became a problem rather than a promise. This historical reality, this *place*, now looked one-dimensional; for everything, even the "methodical alienation" that important artists needed to accomplish their subversive work, had been reduced to a commodity: consumer society had arrived.

I can't claim that since Marcuse lost his faith in the liberating potential of technology, we've reached the *place* where alienated labor is over and capitalism gets canceled—so that Utopia finally loses its meaning. But I can claim that an economy of abundance is a historical reality. And then I'll claim that it is only, or mainly, in advertising that the *idea* of this good place is preserved, as a badly folded but still legible map of a "sphere outside labor."

Marcuse insisted that such a sphere—a place somewhere beyond the realm of necessity—was the domain of "freedom and fulfillment," and also suggested that automation had already laid the economic groundwork for it. In making this suggestion, was he on firm empirical ground, or was he in some kind of philosophical stupor? I think he was on to something more measurable than metaphysical. I think the obvious trend of economic development since 1919 is the reduction of socially necessary labor time—because since then the use of technology has minimized the time required to produce the goods essential to the survival of civilization as we know it, and has enlarged the "sphere outside labor which defines freedom and fulfillment." At any rate that's the argument of Part 1 in this book.

Once upon a time, my argument goes, economic growth required "additional labor," either more living labor, more people at work in the present—what we call the *labor force*—or past labor, work already completed and now congealed in the form of tools, plant, and equipment—what we call the *capital stock*. And then, around 1919, additional labor of *either* kind became unnecessary to increase the production of goods. In the 1920s, for example, the output of nonagricultural goods grew 60 percent but the labor force in manufacturing, construction, and transportation declined, and so did the capital stock per industrial worker. For the first time in human history, growth happened in the absence of net additions to the goods-producing labor force or to the capital stock. Suddenly a new horizon was visible; for the world that had always been "too poor for the satisfaction of human needs without constant restraint, renunciation, and delay" was whirled away. Now more work—additional labor of either kind—had become unnecessary, even impossible; in that sense, the satisfaction of human needs no longer required constant restraint, renunciation, and delay. An economy of abundance, maybe even a "pleasure economy," had come of age. So the deferral of gratification had begun to look pointless.

I'll put it another way. After 1919, net private investment becomes pretty much irrelevant to growth. This means that both corporate profits and personal savings become more or less redundant, because corporations don't need their after-tax profits to invest in new plant and equipment—they can expand output just by replacing and maintaining their existing capital stock out of depreciation funds earmarked for that purpose—and because banks don't need to gather the personal savings of households so that they can loan to corporations wanting to finance increased investment by borrowing. This atrophy of net investment also means that, between them, increasing profits and savings will strangle balanced growth. On the one hand, both these forms of "saving"—another word for restraint, renunciation, and delay—will limit consumer spending, the single most important component of aggregate demand, because they withdraw money from the share of national income otherwise available for consumption. On the other hand, both of these forms of saving will accumulate as idle surpluses that fuel speculative markets, then inflate bubbles, and finally cause full-blown economic crises—as they did in the 1920s, and in the age of the "global savings glut," ca. 1983–2009.

So Marcuse was on solid empirical ground when he suggested that the historical reality of his times contained the nonrepressive, post-industrial promise of a "sphere outside labor" where "freedom and fulfillment" would reside. He defined that reality too easily, and too narrowly, by constantly reaching for the word "automation"—and then he gave up on it. But still, and again, he was on to something in spite of himself, in spite of the fact that he couldn't see that the commodity form had delivered the goods he so eloquently defended—in spite of the fact that he couldn't see how consumer culture was the "sphere outside labor" he so desperately wanted.

DON DRAPER'S UTOPIA

For a moment in the 1950s and early 1960s, the "good place" Marcuse mapped was both a surpassing idea and a location in time—it was both a categorical imperative and an impending reality, an ethical principle and a historical circumstance, an "ought" and an "is." Then it divided up along with the loyalties of everyone else in the late 1960s. But advertising has remained as the publicist of the place that *could* be, that sphere outside labor. I mean that since the expiration of actually existing socialism, it's only or mainly in advertising that the idea of this "good place" is still preserved—so that Utopia remains as a vital part of our imaginations, constantly invading our everyday lives, urging us to violate the demands of increased productivity and to interrupt reality with minor misdemeanors or great refusals, whatever removes us from the realm of necessity and projects us into a world of leisure, indolence, receptivity, and consumption.

Look anywhere, in any mass-market magazine, at any TV show, at any ad, and what do you see? There's no necessary labor on view unless the spot is aimed at potential buyers of pickup trucks, manly men wearing jeans who presumably work with their hands. But even here, in this minor sales province, the men watch as the truck takes a terrific beating, or they drive the thing with enthusiasm: whether watching or driving, they're not working. Nobody's seen working in advertisements because the point is to "sell happiness," as Don Draper puts it, and that, as always, means freedom from compulsion, freedom from necessity, "freedom from fear" (here he's quoting FDR). The product is certainly in sight, but it's the idea of release—not abstention—from these scary and yet tiresome realities (compulsion, necessity, fear) that counts.

"People do not buy products"—this is again Rob Walker speaking—"they buy ideas about products." And again I would amend his conclusion by saying that they buy ideas, period. Or rather, I would revise my own conclusion and say that the things and the thoughts are interchangeable parts of our experience as consumers. Advertising is the "place" where the movement between these parts, these moments, is transacted, thus reminding you of that world elsewhere, that "second dimension" of existence where you can be yourself because you're not working for somebody else, where you can be as devout or as disruptive a character as you like.

But this transaction isn't exceptional anymore, it's not something reserved for the Sabbath, the holiday, or the carnival, no, now it gets done on a daily, maybe even hourly, basis, because advertising has brought the once-rarefied experience of the world elsewhere into your everyday life by means of the commodity form. This world is brought to you by a paying sponsor whose greedy vulgarity is obvious, so you understand, and you probably admire, its antagonism to every kind of *spiritual elevation*—you're transported, but you're not uplifted, and that is the point, to stay in the here and now rather than leave the world as it is behind. Until now, it's true, what advertising invokes is more of an idea than a place, more like a map or a video game than something you can experience in three dimensions. But for now, that's utopian enough.

Or is it? When Don Draper responds to his potential client's cryptic remark about Israel with "Utopia," you have to wonder why. Before the lunch with Rachel Menken, he was sifting through startling photos of Jews—pictures from both the death camps and Israeli fashion magazines, mysteriously interspersed in the portfolio provided by another potential client, the new Israeli tourist bureau. In the staff meeting that follows, he notes that this place is a hard sell because it has a "quasi-communist government" and equips its women with guns. Now at lunch with his Jewish informant (soon to be his lover), he says "Utopia" when she defines Zionism for him. Why? Because he's been reading *Exodus*, courtesy, again, of the Israeli tourist bureau?

Rachel Menken isn't the only outer borough of personal experience Don visits in his search for the right thing to say—the words that would make him whole and sell the product with the same expressions. He has a girlfriend in the Village, a bohemian artist who reminds him of the animal spirits missing from his commute between ad work and family life in the suburbs. He visits her that same night, still pondering those doubled meanings of Utopia, still wondering how to sell Israel. There he meets Roy, another bohemian artist, but much younger, who of course accuses him of "perpetuating the lie," building the "tower of religion of mass consumption," the new Babel.

Don Draper is himself a wanderer, in flight from his own origins, having stolen another man's identity, and he stays in disguise, in character, to conceal his secret, even turning his back on his little brother. He lives a lie, so he knows how to perpetuate one. His response to Roy is as cynical as the kid's provocation: "People want to be told what to do so badly that they'll listen to anybody." The proof of Don's proposition arrives soon after at the Gaslight, a Village club where the unlikely trio endures two awful, droning performances by nobodies. And then Ian, the musician they've come to watch, gets on stage and sings "By the Rivers of Babylon," a vaguely reggae tune. As historical events go, this is at least improbable because the lyrics were ancient (Psalm 137), but they weren't set to music and recorded until 1978. The chronology is beside the point, however, because the refrain is this: "And we remembered Zion."

That's what Don remembers as the song carries the camera through shots of a pensive Rachel, of his wife and daughter sharing lipstick, of his boss zipping his lover's dress in a Midtown hotel room, then back to Ian's scruffy face and sorry mandolin. He remembers his own exile from his past, his former life, and his uneasy assimilation into this new world, this abundant, urban America. "Zion" has always been a shorthand definition of an imagined community that feels imminent but isn't extant: it's an urgent idea whose time has not *yet* come, as in the "promised land," but somehow it also means a journey you have to make, an inevitable return to where you've never been, and so you know its residence is the future, not your past. It's not a place, not now, maybe not ever, and yet it calls you home all the same. This is the Utopia Don Draper remembers in the Gaslight. He remembers the principle of hope, the idea and the *possibility* of the place he wants to sell—to himself among others. He remembers the future.

I measure his remembrance in this manner because in the very next episode he returns to the downtown scene of his extramarital transgression and announces that neither consumer society nor advertising can be implicated in the crimes of fascism, as per the specifications of Susan Sontag and Herbert Marcuse, among other important intellectuals then as now. In the artist's loft, having smoked some pot and come undone, Don tries to pull himself together but has to confront Roy and his friends, who press a familiar complaint straight out of *The Hidden Persuaders*: "You invent want." The adman has three responses, and none of them puts him in the camp of Vance Packard's good guys. "The universe is indifferent," Don says. "There is no 'system.'" And, most important, "There is no Big Lie."

He's emphatic, and effective as far as we can tell. He reminds us that what he wants, and what he sells, is the same thing, "freedom from fear." It's a New Deal slogan, of course, a cliché that he casually translated in Episode 1 as "the smell of a new car." But it's just that possibility of embodiment in this world, in everyday life, of the pleasure principle, that he represents. Don Draper can't care about the next life because he's barely got a grip on the one he's living. "This is it; this is all there is," he says to Rachel when they're finally in each other's arms, and he says it knowing he's a liar and a thief, soon to be an outcast again. We know better than he does even as we succumb, with Rachel, to his fragile charms. But the man is selling something worth having, this "freedom from fear," and he believes there's a mass market for it. So he personifies the restless utopian urge that otherwise appears in *Mad Men* as drunken revelry—as compensation and reversion, as something to be forgotten tomorrow morning, not remembered and embedded in everyday life, where it might begin to reshape the future.

Marcuse called on two big names, Alfred North Whitehead and Theodor Adorno, to make sense of that utopian urge: "This Great Refusal

[Whitehead] is the protest against unnecessary repression, the struggle for the ultimate form of freedom—'to live without anxiety' [Adorno]. But this idea could be formulated without punishment only in the language of art. In the more realistic context of political theory and even philosophy, it was almost universally defamed as utopia." And now this idea is formulated without punishment, with reckless pleasure, only in the grotesque and yet idiomatic language of advertising, where commodities come alive and speak clearly, as if Walt Whitman himself—not Dick Whitman, Don Draper's real name—had summoned them, and was begging us to live as he did, without anxiety in a world so reified money doesn't just talk, it smiles. Here's old Walt at the conclusion of "Song for Occupations": "When the minted gold in the vault smiles like the night-watchman's daughter, / When warrantee deeds loafe in chairs opposite and are my friendly companions, / I intend to reach them my hand, and make as much of them as I do of men and women like you."

It's hard to watch Dick Whitman/Don Draper reach out to us and protest against unnecessary repression when he's all dressed up in a suit and tie, meanwhile pitching the ultimate form of freedom on the job— "to live without anxiety," free of fear—and in his not-so-personal life. But this unlikely agreement between him and Theodor Adorno on the essential meaning of freedom sells me on the idea of Utopia as Herbert Marcuse peddled it in *Eros and Civilization*, and as advertising still purveys it.

CHAPTER NINE

It Beats Working

Why Consumer Culture Is
Good for Your Soul and Our Planet

THE PATHOS OF PRODUCTIVITY

Ask anybody. Americans have a neurotic relationship to work. You might even call it a perverse relationship, because for us the meanings of work are so many and various and profound that they make us look like a bundle of contradictions. We believe that work is where we learn the real worth of honest labor—it's an indispensable introduction to a life well lived, we say, and a constant reminder of the proper alignment between effort and reward. It's where we build character. But we also believe that work sucks—in The Office, nothing counts except the delusions of the morons in charge, so we know that honest labor in The Cubicle is impossible. It's where we divert ourselves with Twitter, porn, and Facebook.

We believe that the duration and intensity of our effort should determine our incomes. So we resent the bankers, the lawyers, the middlemen, and the "welfare queens" because they deduct their incomes from the sum of value created by hardworking people like us: we know they're vampires, maybe even "vampire squids" like the traders at Goldman Sachs, sucking the lifeblood of the American Dream. But we also believe in what the philosophers call the "criterion of need," which tells us that the unfortunate deserve our charity and that getting something for nothing is not necessarily a sin. So we admire the rich for their cunning, we have faith in the luck of the draw, and we still have sympathy for the poor.

This perverse combination of beliefs is mostly a legacy of the Reformation, the great upheaval of the sixteenth, seventeenth, and eighteenth centuries that split Western European Christians into warring factions of true believers. The Protestants who rebelled against the Holy Roman Catholic Church won their wars in central and northern Europe (in the areas now known as Germany, the Netherlands, and England), and, in doing so, they brought new attitudes toward labor, luxury, and consumption into the world—the attitudes we now summarize as the "Protestant work ethic." The mariners, renegades, and castaways who successfully colonized the Eastern Seaboard of North America in the seventeenth and eighteenth centuries were, by and large, products of this new ethic, so it had lasting effects here in the United States, even after immigrants with very different attitudes started arriving in the nineteenth century; in fact, it wasn't effectively challenged as a central principle of American culture until the 1920s, when young, urban, bohemian intellectuals filed everything that was stunted, ugly, and repressive under the label of Puritanism.

The Protestant work ethic brought three new attitudes into the world. First, it sanctified labor as a material means to the end of salvation: you could save your soul by working hard, by "staying in your calling," as Martin Luther put it, where the Devil would teach you to suffer and God would teach you to persevere. Second, it changed the perceived relation between necessity and freedom. Until the Reformation and the emergence of modern market societies in Western Europe, you perceived this relation as an either/or proposition; if you were immersed in goods production, in socially necessary labor, you knew you were unfree, because if you worked, you did so at another's behest. You were by definition a slave or a serf. Consumption or control of goods beyond what was necessary to sustain everyday life was, then, the insignia of the free man, the nobleman, who didn't produce those goods. So, too, was the life of the mind—only men (and only *men*) free of the claims of necessity could be philosophers or priests.

The abolition of these oppositions was at least implicit in the new Protestant work ethic; it was made explicit by the Anglo-American revolutionaries of the seventeenth and eighteenth centuries, Protestants all, who defined themselves as free and fit to rule the world precisely because they produced the material conditions of their lives. From their standpoint, the realms of freedom and necessity intersected in the bustling area of life they learned to call "civil society"—the new space opened up between the state and the family, the marketplace where anonymous laws of supply and demand, not the commands of noblemen and their retainers, moved goods and organized labor. From their standpoint, those who consumed goods without producing anything of value were parasites on the body politic, probably throwbacks to a feudal past; these indolent creatures lived off the surplus created by those who mixed their labor with their property, those who produced goods of real value.

Finally, the new Protestant ethic made work the site of self-discovery and self-determination. In doing so, it repudiated the two basic truths inherited from the ancient and medieval worlds—the truths that had certified *politics* and *reason* as the proper dimensions of the real individual, the genuine self. On the one hand, this new ethic demoted politics. Where the inherited tradition insisted you could achieve selfhood only as an enfranchised citizen who shaped political debates with your voice and your virtue, Protestants said you could ignore politics and still become your true self—the one you tried to be in the eyes of God—while at work, in your calling.

On the other hand, the same Protestant work ethic demoted reason. Where the inherited tradition specified reason as the unique human capacity that separated us from plants and animals, always pointing us upward toward the otherworldly place where God abides, Protestants inserted blind faith and the strenuous, "horizontal" exertions that followed. Reason was merely useful, they insisted, just another form of calculation, and a secondary one at that. So the life of the mind now looked like a problem: at worst it was an unaffordable indulgence, and at best it was a costly distraction from the reality that mattered. Acting on that reality by means of work, by staying in your calling and changing things, was more important than standing back from the material world and thinking abstractly along with the philosophers and the priests who were exempt, in any case, from the demands of necessary labor.

Americans still live by these attitudes—not because we're Protestants all, but because we're modern individuals who believe that the past isn't merely a limit on what each of us can achieve: we believe that, with a little luck and some hard work, we can become the people we set out to be. In electoral season, we often use that belief to belittle the life of the mind, and to indulge ourselves in what Richard Hofstadter called the anti-intellectualism of American life. And at this late stage of the American Dream, we're more haunted than inspired by the attitudes of the Protestant work ethic, because the key figure here, a legible relation between effort and reward, makes no sense in these times—when big bankers get bailed out by big government for making big mistakes even as unemployment compensation runs out for the people they put on the street. But still, the inspiration remains, we keep talking about "just compensation," and the haunting isn't over, not by a long shot.

In fact, I would claim that we can't live comfortably with the pleasures of consumer culture (not to mention the life of the mind) precisely because the Protestant work ethic still haunts us—because we believe along with Marx, who got the idea from Hegel, who got it from Luther, that human nature just is the metabolic exchange with nature that we call work: "He grasps labour as the essence of Man" is how Marx put it in explaining why he admired Hegel, who called Luther the founding father of modern philosophy. I admit that this intellectual genealogy of our discomfort with consumerism must sound slightly absurd in a political culture animated by fears of socialists and intellectuals, especially but not only in the last election cycle.

And yet since the nineteenth century, most Americans (Abraham Lincoln included) have viewed capitalists as would-be aristocrats who consume and control wealth without producing anything of value—just as most Americans now view big bankers and their benefactors in government. In 1883, for example, in sworn testimony before a Senate committee, officers and members of the Knights of Labor explained why capitalists, lawyers, drunkards, and whoremongers—each an affront to civilization—couldn't join the organization (it was more than a trade union, and by 1886 it would have more than 700,000 members). When a senator objected to these admission standards by saying that an investor "ought to have some share in the benefits derived from the improved machinery for which he pays," the witness, John S. McClelland of Hoboken, New Jersey, and an elected officer of the Knights, replied, "If he has accumulated money to build the machine it must have been taken from labor, because the capitalist performs no productive labor himself." In complaining about one of the more egregious robber barons of the day, another witness, also a member of the Knights, made the same point even more memorably: "Jay Gould never earned a great deal, but he owns a terrible lot."

We still think this way, in terms of "productive labor," and we condemn the robber barons of our own time—the Wall Street bankers and their outrageous bonuses—accordingly. We still believe that we produce ourselves by acting on the world, by producing goods, and so we know, without thinking, that consuming goods is somehow *passive*, reeking of indolence, luxury, idleness, and, yes, a certain "femininity." We're still slightly suspicious of the eggheads and intellectuals in our midst, particularly the teachers and professors (they get the summers off, don't they?). And we still think our souls are at risk if we're not doing something useful. So, as Americans who know what hard work can bring, we're intellectually and psychologically armed against consumer culture. We like shopping—most of us do, anyway—but we know we spend too much money on too many unnecessary items: we want our genuine, objective needs to contain our unruly, subjective desires, and we rely on work to provide this containment, or rather we rely on the income we get from work to serve as the proper limit on those desires. In these various ways, we still suffer from the "pathos of productivity"—an almost Puritan belief in the redeeming value of producing as against consuming, saving as against spending, working as against whatever comes after.

MATTHEW CRAWFORD PUTS US BACK TO WORK

This pathos is on bright display almost everywhere you look these days, as Americans of all political persuasions mourn those good jobs that once sustained the fabled middle class, those well-paying jobs in man-ufacturing now exported to offshore platforms and less-developed countries in Latin America or Asia—those boring, backbreaking jobs in factories and foundries that our fathers kept, against their own wishes, as down payments on our futures. But the same pathos is nowhere more conspicuously displayed than in the back pages of the *New York Times Book Review*, where best sellers are divided into strange and arbitrary categories, so that nobody mistakes a new book by J. K. Rowling for one by Philip Roth. Here, every week, you will find a quarter-page list with the title of "Advice, How-To, and Miscellaneous," which is an encouraging place because you can find at least two books that tell you how to turn your hobby into a paying job, convert your neuroses to productive pur-poses, and at last become a useful citizen of our invisible republic. And here, from time to time, in this same statistical space, you will also find a learned, almost academic book by Matthew B. Crawford called *Shop Class as Soulcraft: An Inquiry into the Value of Work* (2009). It sold 25,000 hardback copies within a month of publication in June 2009, and by now it's racked up at least a half million; these are huge, even startling numbers for a nonfiction book in the age of the Internet.

The backstory of the book is worth our attention, because it suggests how deep the pathos of productivity runs in American culture. Crawford was working for a K Street think tank devoted to debunking scientific claims about global warming when he wrote an impassioned piece about the value of manual labor that appeared on an obscure website. The conservative journalist David Brooks touted the piece in his regular op-ed column for the *New York Times*, which led immediately to a book contract, an excerpt published in the *New York Times Magazine* (May 21, 2009), and on toward the book's remarkable success in the market-place of ideas. Crawford had clearly struck a chord, touched a nerve, lit a fire, broken the bank, rocked the cradle, hit a homer—everything but started a fight—because everybody seemed to agree that his celebration of work was just what we need to recover from the lack of productive authenticity in our time. Certainly the enthusiastic blurbs on the hard-cover dust jacket came from all over the place, from Richard Sennett and Jackson Lears on the Left to Harvey Mansfield and Rod Dreher on the

Right. The Left: "Matthew Crawford has written a brave and indispensable book. . . . No one who cares about the future of human work can afford to ignore this book" (Lears). The Right: "It is a superb combination of testimony and reflection, and you can't put it down" (Mansfield).

The publisher's intellectual framing and commercial placement of the book were similarly ecumenical, with an appreciative interview appearing in Truthout.com, a strenuously left-wing website, and also in *Reason*, the journal inspired by Ayn Rand, and in several venues in between these political extremes. The author photo perfected this image of a man who covers all bases—a man who calls himself both a philosopher and a mechanic (like Robert Pirsig, the blueprint), a man of the people, to be sure, but a man who is also athwart them, trying to change their minds. He leans against a wide dark wooden doorframe—this is not a residence—dressed for work in blue jeans and a dark shirt with sleeves rolled, no desk or computer in sight, just him and two gleaming motorcycles in view. There's not much light here, everything except the chrome on the machines is brown and muted, so we could be looking into an antique shop or a Stickley ad except that there's not enough furniture in sight.

In his right hand the author holds a long shiny wrench, in his left he grips the handlebar of an ancient but restored motorcycle—you can tell it's old by the shape of the handlebars and the repainted color of the gas tank—and together the pose, the costume, the tool, and the machine appear as *impediments*. This man is blocking us, casually but clearly, from entry into his domain, his repair shop: he's visually athwart us as viewers and as readers, standing between us and what he presumably wants us to know by looking inside the book, or by seeing what happens in the shop. The handlebar he clutches points down and across his body, but we know it's the accelerator, and when gripped in this backward way, it looks no less like a weapon in waiting than the wrench in the right hand. I see this picture and I have to ask, Is there something the author or the publisher doesn't want us to know about the work the philosopher does inside the book, or about the work the mechanic does inside the shop? What are they hiding, or rather, what are we not supposed to see?

Let me ask the same question in another, less conspiratorial tone. What is the *secret of work* in this book? How does Crawford propose to reintroduce the material realities of manual labor into our lives, and thus make us more authentic personalities? And why do we agree with him? Why is this book so wildly popular, particularly in the suburbs, where, according to Nielsen BookScan, two-thirds of its sales are concentrated? To begin with, Crawford defines craftsmanship as the antidote to the passivity of consumer culture. He repeatedly distinguishes between "active engagement and distracted consumption," between purposeful creation and idle choice, between the sturdy selves socialized by their work and the fragile individuals privatized by their purchases: "To fill the void that comes with isolation, and give it a positive cast, we posit the ideal of the sovereign self, unencumbered by attachments to others and radically free. This is the consumer self that puts its stamp on the world by buying things." As we saw in Chapter 8, Crawford deduces alarming political conclusions from these distinctions, going so far as to suggest, along lines drawn by Susan Sontag, that passive consumers are the "psychic ground" on which demagogues can arouse the kinds of "fantastic hopes" that once fueled fascism.

In the end, however, Crawford's defense of manual labor comes down to a specification of reality itself, what the philosophers call *ontology*. He wants us to strike through the "layer of abstraction" that comes with a computerized consumer culture and face reality as the craftsman knows it—as unforgiving material that is wholly external to our purposes and completely indifferent to our desires or ambitions. In other words, he wants us to understand the "things themselves" as a world unto itself, not as theoretical artifacts or linguistic conventions subject to the academic arts of persuasion we call rhetoric. "Practiced submission" to the unchanging logic of these material things in themselves teaches us "mechanical realities," and these are useful facts because, unlike the consumer goods we desire today and discard tomorrow, they "do not arise from the human will."

So it seems that manual labor, working with and working on things with your hands, is the only means of knowing reality as Crawford specifies it here, as a fixed externality. By his accounting, mere consumption of goods can't give us this fundamental knowledge of the world that exists apart from us, because in consuming things we never enter and experience that external, material world—and so we need not heed its hard limits. Thus our ability to assess either the world or ourselves is impaired. "The consumer is disburdened not only of the fabrication [the making of things], but of a basic evaluative activity," Crawford explains, because he or she lacks the *objective* standards drawn from acknowledging something, anything, outside the wishful imperatives of what he calls the "sovereign self."

Crawford makes three large claims, then, and these are clearly in keeping with the sensibilities of both academia and the buying public; again, this is a best-selling book endorsed by famous journalists and leading scholars, learned men you could honestly call public intellectuals. First, artisanal, hands-on work, involving the production or preservation of goods with measurable value, can save you from the enervation of The Office and The Cubicle, where abstraction, conformity, and cynical performance rule out personal authenticity. Second, the same kind of work can teach you the real limits of your individuality, your freedom, and your knowledge; it can educate your desires. And finally, work so conceived can offset the moral and political effects of your pseudo-sovereign "consumer self," the easy prey of the adman and the demagogue. In short, working hard with your hands will protect you from the slough of despond that is consumer culture, where boredom, absurdity, and passivity preside. Welcome to *Fight Club*. Or should I say, welcome back to the Protestant work ethic?

Quite apart from the sales figures, the appeal of this book is simply undeniable, unavoidable—even to someone like me, and I'm trying to persuade you that leisure is a better laboratory for "soulcraft" than work. Following my earlier lead, you could explain the book's appeal by reference to the residual force of the American Dream and its key informant, that Protestant work ethic. But there is something else happening here: like the Senate testimony of John S. McClelland in 1883, Crawford's book is a proentrepreneurial and yet anticapitalist manifesto. In other words, it's an argument against the corporate kind of capitalism that has prevailed in the United States for at least the last hundred years. In these pages, the market as founded on private property is both the ally and the enemy of self-mastery, exactly as both appeared in the programs of the Knights of Labor. Crawford's hundreds of thousands of readers are responding to this ambivalence because it makes sense of their recent experience with the market as an economic reality and a moral calendar, and—more importantly—because it is in keeping with Americans' long-standing suspicions of corporations and capitalists as such. No wonder the endorsements of this book come from Left and Right and everywhere in between: we're still rooting for the self-made man, still railing against the big bankers and the bloated bureaucrats.

Crawford makes a poignant case for and against the market, as both the setting of productive labor and the scene of extreme alienation. I quote him at length from his concluding paragraphs, where he rises to the philosophical occasion with political rhetoric—and vice versa—just as his acknowledged predecessors, from Aristotle to Heidegger, always did:

> When the conception of work is removed from the scene of its execution, we are divided against one another, and each against himself. For thinking is inherently bound up with doing, and it is in rational activity with others that we find our particular satisfaction[s]. A humane economy would be one in which the possibility of achieving such satisfaction is not foreclosed ahead of time for most people. It would require a sense of scale. We in the West have arranged our institutions to prevent the concentration of political power, with such devices as the separation of legislative, executive, and judicial functions. But we have failed utterly to prevent the concentration of economic power, or take account of how such concentration damages the conditions under which full human flourishing becomes possible (it is never guaranteed). The consolation we seek in shopping serves only to narcotize us against a recognition of these facts. . . . It is time to dispel the longstanding confusion of private property with corporate property. Conservatives are right to extol the former as a pillar of liberty, but when they put such arguments in the service of the latter, they become apologists for the ever-greater concentration of capital.

Notice that our *intellectual* failure to face the *political* fact of corporate power is a direct result of our addiction to consumption—if we weren't doped up on shopping, nodding out at The Mall, we'd understand our predicament. Then we'd be able to do something about it: our intellectual capacities, now freed of contamination by desire for the drug of consumer goods, would be available for the required political tasks, among them a redefinition of property that reduces the market power of corporations. As it is, under the stupefying regime of consumer culture, our attention is diverted from the realities that matter.

It's a compelling position because it beckons us toward a future that somehow resembles the past, when large corporations and lazy bureaucrats didn't come between us in our daily transactions with others. That's where we all long to live, in a simpler past—ask any competent psychotherapist or professional historian. In this sense, what finally makes Crawford's position convincing is an unstated assumption rather than an argument, and it's an assumption his readers bring to the book without prompting from anything except their routine encounters with American culture: with great learning and good writing, he's validating the common sense of Americans, what we already know without thinking much about it. You know the refrain. It goes like this: consuming goods is a passive, silent, selfish reflex that keeps us from experience of the real world—it keeps us from society, from politics, from everything except the console, the keypad, the monitor, the remote, and the cell—so producing goods must be morally, intellectually, and politically superior to consuming them.

ANOTHER COUNTRY

Let's see, finally, what happens when we drop that assumption. Or rather, let's see what happens when we turn it into some questions. Does consumption remove us from material reality, or from "rational activity with others"? Is production better for us in either sense? Is consumption all that passive, silent, and selfish? Is *work* the true habitat of the genuine self, as almost every philosopher since Luther has claimed, so that it must be the site of any attempt at social change or individual redemption? My uniform answer to all of the above is, "*No*, goddamn it," and I say this loudly, "in thunder" as Herman Melville heard Nathaniel

Hawthorne's voice in the wilderness. But I intend my answering as explanation rather than refutation—as the key that unlocks the secret of work as Crawford wants us to experience it. I mean to explain the purloined reality he has hidden in plain sight.

I'll begin with the material and social realities of consumption, aiming to illustrate two basic facts. Then I can claim that the work Crawford himself describes as "soulcraft" has long since moved to the borough of leisure and rented a place in the neighborhood of consumer culture, where we make furniture, knit sweaters, collect plates, perform music, produce plays, repair motorcycles, prepare meals, fix cars, play ball, build decks, and customize vans for the same reason—for fun rather than a monetary recompense (a wage, a salary, a profit).

At the risk of repetition, let me emphasize this last point. I'm going to claim that the reality Crawford brings into focus is quite simple, and painfully obvious. Indeed it's been right there in front of us all along, like Edgar Allan Poe's purloined letter: the work we want to do, the work that nourishes our souls, is almost always a form of consumption or sacrifice we indulge when *at our leisure*: it's not the work we do for wages, for the boss, for the person with the paycheck; it's what we do in our free time. The "soulcraft" that keeps you alive is the producing that's freely given for irrational, unprofitable purposes, as when you cook something—anything—for a hungry child or a hungover friend or all those bizarre relatives you invited for Thanksgiving, or when you write something that makes sense of a world gone mad, or when you construct something that has no possible use except the marvel of the making and the pleasure of the admiring.

So, the first basic fact is that whether mediated (reified) by the commodity form or not, most acts of consumption are motivated and saturated by sensuous pleasures that rightly get excluded from acts of production, where unruly desires will undermine the discipline, regularity, and exactitude typically required by the task at hand (unless of course we define "acts of production" as displays of artistic talent like the composition of a poem). In other words, most acts of consumption place us in a world dense with sensation, difference, and surprise—a material but fluid world that responds to our touch, a world that won't be standardized and can't be subordinated to anybody's equation, as it must be when it appears to us as an inert assembly of inanimate things. As consumers of goods, we come to know this world as anything but a fixed externality; and yet as consumers we need not *master* the same world in order to know it, as producers of goods must do: we can take it or leave it.

The second basic fact is that whether mediated (reified) by the commodity form or not, acts of consumption tend to socialize rather than isolate the participants, because these acts are normally *less instrumental* than acts of production: they don't "privatize" your experience; they turn you inside out. On the one hand, when you've finished that restaurant meal or worn that expensive dress or bought that Christmas gift, what you're left with has no exchange value, no price you might quote as if it were still for sale; at any rate you can't be aiming to profit from what you've eaten, used, or bought. You're no better off except in ways that the market can't calculate, because when the transaction is completed, there's no check you can cash as payment for "services rendered" or as compensation for your consumption. What you've done could be called sacrifice because you've used something up; you've spent what had been saved by somebody, probably you, but if it's someone else your pleasure is no less.

When you've finished that meal or worn that dress or bought that gift, on the other hand, you've made yourself part of an economy— you've exchanged goods and expended resources—but not so you can accumulate assets; for unless you were dining alone, your purpose has been to renew or create circuits of feeling among friends, lovers, associates, acquaintances, family. In terms of economic theory, you've done something pretty useless—or rather something that can't be measured except as expenditure. And notice that even if you ate by yourself, you ordered food that was consistent with a self-image derived from reliable sources outside yourself, and your satisfaction; the "surplus" produced by what you ate can't be permanently saved or privately hoarded as though calories are a currency you can deposit in a deviant food bank. You measure the profits or dividends from these transactions as solidarity, togetherness, or community rather than monetary gain that is yours alone. So they place you in the vicinity of archaic but still vital *gift economies*, where excess and expenditure, even sacrifices, are normal.

When you're at work, by contrast, you're doing pretty much what you have to, even (or especially) if you're self-employed. And the real purpose of the work you're doing is a monetary recompense, a wage, a salary, or a profit. Acts of consumption are almost always means to social ends: as unforced sacrifices of accumulated assets, they create or sustain bonds of friendship and love, and not merely when gifts are the things getting exchanged. The obvious exception to this rule is *hoarding*, when unused and unusable shit piles up in the garage—or when unused but usable savings pile up in the bank accounts of both corporations and individuals. Acts of production, at least as organized by the market and experienced as "socially necessary labor," are almost never means to social ends. The monetary recompense you receive in return for the work you've done is a means to a means—it gives you legitimate access to a share of the goods others have produced, but it doesn't bind you to anybody, certainly not to the employer or the customer who has just paid you. These transactions are complete upon payment in full, so you can walk away from them without a care. You may well develop a friendship with your employer or your customer or your fellow worker. But this relation will be created after work, off the clock, at your leisure, or it will be sustained by the absence of monetary recompense, by the common purpose and the sexual tension created by the work you have to get done together: the only professional friend you have is your therapist, and you know he won't consort with clients after hours. You will fall in love with your coworker, but not *just* because you admire his or her professional competence.

All right, then. Let's go shopping, eat a meal, and see how it feels, materially speaking. At that point, we might be able to gauge both the social and the spiritual dividends of consumption.

Nobody shops alone. You may go by yourself, and buy things only for yourself—no gifts, no frills—but still, you're never alone. When you choose a garment from the rack, you're wondering how it will look on you, so you're already seeing yourself from the outside in, as if you were another person; this observer is perhaps someone you love, but it is certainly someone whose admiration or attention you want (and this latter someone could be a stranger). Your identity is in play, and at play, because you've brought these imaginary observers with you. In 2010, for example, I did what the anthropologists call fieldwork: I accompanied my girlfriend on many grueling expeditions to the Dollar Store on Amsterdam and 162nd, way Uptown, and to Barney's New York—a decidedly upscale clothing store in Midtown, on Madison Avenue. One day in Barney's, when I asked her what she was thinking as she took an expensive item from the rack, she said, "Everything I look at, everything I pick up, I'm asking myself, 'Who am I?' 'Is this too young or too old?' But it comes down to, 'What will this look like on me, when somebody else is looking at me?'" As she said it, I realized that this "somebody else" wasn't me, and that I ask myself the same questions when I shop for clothes—we all ask them, because we're all participant-observers in the same social ritual. We all know that who we are depends, more or less, on what others make of us, how they see us, and that these others are mostly the absent causes we call strangers.

When you try on the garment you've chosen from the rack, its material or fabric is something you touch, handle, hold, and measure with your hands; then you experience it more directly, against your skin, or as something that follows the contours of your body. "You know what body goes in the clothes, how it'll feel," as my girlfriend explained. "'Fit' is the wrong word; it's not strong enough. You want to know how the thing *feels*." But that feel, that immediate sensation, is partly a function of the occasion(s) you're buying for. Your audience and its expectations can't be there in the dressing room with you, and yet they're never absent from your silent, skin-deep calculations. Work or leisure, funeral or wedding, indoors or out, family or friends? . . . The question is, *Where* am I going to wear that? So how the garment feels right now, as you put it on and look in the mirror, is determined by the opinions you attribute to the individuals, some of them strangers, who will see you wearing it elsewhere, on a future occasion, at another place and time.

When you're shopping for clothes, therefore, you're never removed from the garments, the material things themselves; you're always handling them, and meanwhile you're changing the way they fold and drape as they wrap your body. But you do divide yourself up in time, you do step back from that body, your self, as you try to see it as others would. As you abstract from your "sovereign self" in this sense, the transactions between you and the mirror become "impersonal" and thus "social" at the very same moment, and in the very same way. You become the person you want to be—you appear as that special figure of your own desire—insofar as you leave yourself behind, and see yourself from another point of view. So material reality and social implication are essential moments in your shopping because your very own self is at stake.

You may want to ask whether this "external" perspective on yourself is good for you. What about the enduring, authentic, internal core of your self that you call your character? But notice what the question itself presupposes—an original, natural self that somehow subsists outside of time and change, absent the flux of unexpected events, always abstaining from the jagged edges of existence. There's never been such a thing, and that's a good thing. If you can't change your mind in view of novel circumstances, and if you can't see yourself from another person's point of view—sometimes this person is who you used to be or who you want to be—you're a god or a monster, probably both. Rousseau notwithstanding, we all need the regard of others to understand who we are and might become. We want a double consciousness because it constantly reminds us that we're not alone in the world even when we're all by ourselves and can do exactly what we want.

But eating is different, right? This is a private matter compared to shopping, because it's just you and the food you're digesting. Let's start there, with the food right in front of you, and then move outward. Somebody cooked it unless you're a single person eating soup from a can at the counter of your galley kitchen (and even then it was somehow prepared). What went into the cooking? Shopping first, in the stores—probably plural—where the cook found the ingredients, held them in his or her hands, smelled them with serious intent, maybe peeled back some of their layers. Then the preparation, mainly the chopping and the arrangement of the raw materials, including the oils and the unguents and the liquids, in a sequence that would make sense of the kitchen's space, the timing of the meal, and the unpredictable desires of both cook and consumer.

And then of course the actual cooking of the edible substances takes place. There is nothing passive about this process except my voice in describing it, and it is so deeply embedded in the particularity of the ingredients—their sight, their smell, their weight, their feel, their *taste*— that to call it a material reality would be laughably redundant. These ingredients are separate things, to begin with, but they're transformed by their penetration, reduction, and mixture, becoming moments in a meal that must be greater than the sum of its parts. In other words, they're transformed by the work of the cook: the things themselves aren't a fixed externality; they're moments in a fluid world that is nonetheless profoundly material.

Now remove yourself from the restaurant kitchen you've imagined as the site of these culinary stages and you know what "real work" is and where it abides. It's the unforced labor you do for fun, for friends, and for family, not for a wage, a salary, or a profit—it's what you do at your leisure, when you're a consumer rather than a producer, when you expect nothing except enjoyment from what you're doing, when your soul is enlarged by displaying or giving away what you've made, what you've cooked. This making, this cooking, is "socially necessary labor," but only in the sense that the work you do at your leisure creates a local society by extending the circuits of emotion, affect, and purpose you want and need as a normal human being.

That is the secret of work Matthew Crawford discovered in writing his celebration of manual labor: the purloined reality on display here is the "soulcraft"—the moral life—that is more legible, and more attainable, in consuming and serving goods than in the strenuous life of producing goods through manly exertion. Crawford cites the "intrinsic satisfactions" of full engagement in real work—these are what the philosophers call "internal goods," the moral qualities we acquire and recognize when we do something for its own sake, like play ball with abandon but forget the final score. Then he writes, "It may be telling that it is leisure activities that come first to mind when we think about intrinsic satisfactions— athletics, for example, or hobbies that we enjoy. Such activities are ends in themselves, and we pursue them without anyone having to pay us to do so. Conversely, with work, getting paid is really the main point."

Just so, I would say. While we're at our leisure, engaged in acts of consumption, from buying expensive clothes at Barney's and exchanging gifts with loved ones to eating good food prepared by friends or strangers, we glimpse the utopian edges of everyday existence—because now we can look past the "pathos of productivity," because what we're "accomplishing" has no measure in the scheme of values we call the labor market, because we're not getting paid for what we're doing. We've evacuated the realm of necessity, the place of *work*; now we're treading on possibility in the province of hope. In consuming goods, we're sacrificing rather than saving resources, so we're resisting the urge to accumulate, and learning to forget the lessons of frugality: we're teaching each other that extravagance and exuberance and generosity are what we love about ourselves.

It beats working, anyway. Our goal is not to improve ourselves by changing the way we work, but to *work less*; we want to reduce the scope of necessary labor in our everyday lives. And as I demonstrate in Part 1 of this book, we have at last reached the point in human civilization where we can afford to do so.

THE CARE OF THE PLANET

Or can we? What is to be done about the environment? I've been claiming all along that the moral life of consumer culture—at least as I've sketched it here—might serve as a better critique of capitalism than the celebration of craftsmanship and small business that still animates Marxism, existentialism, phenomenology, Populism, and the American Dream—all of them essential ingredients in Matthew Crawford's best-selling recipe for the good life. But consumerism seems to exclude the mindful care of the earth; at any rate the *sacrifice* of resources I'm recommending as an economic agenda and a moral compass doesn't seem consistent with environmental integrity. It looks like the kind of indulgence we can't actually afford in the age of global warming.

And this of course is the crux of the matter. My defense of consumer culture as an intricate and productive moral life—quite apart from its economic significance—has always ended here, at the barrier of Nature as it's been conceived by the critics of the commodity form. Let me try now to push beyond this barrier, to see whether we can suture what seem to be the mere opposites of human being and natural life.

We're not invaders, us humans. We're not intruding on a natural world that would be better off without us (absent our "footprint," as we now say). We're as much a part of Nature as the soil itself, because since the Neolithic revolution our planting and harvesting—which allowed our settling down in the places we called cities, then civilizations—have been changing the physical and even the chemical composition of the earth. So the "material reality" of the world is not a fixed externality that operates according to laws of motion we didn't devise: most of the "things themselves" that make up this earth, including the trees and the deserts, wouldn't be there without us, because, God help us, we were present at their creation.

Our responsibility for the integrity of the environment is only increased by admitting this historical fact—and the admission need not involve huge intellectual controversy. It's just another way of saying we owe each other everything. But to acknowledge our responsibility for an environment that is *not* a fixed externality, and that would be an environment that includes human beings as a natural element, this, I believe, is to defend rather than reject consumer culture.

I'll work backward in my defense, from the theoretical to the practical, from the general to the specific, from good ideas to good food. We've heard countless times that "hyperconsumerism" is the enemy of the planet, and we've seen the evidence—in the plastic snow that covers mountains in the third world, and in the indestructible garbage that creates huge islands in the Pacific. But consumers are the best hope we have if our goal is to reexamine the premises, the practices, and the promises of economic growth and development. For when consumers engage in what we recognize as economic activities—buying and using goods—their purpose is not the endless accumulation of exchange value, greater wealth in the abstract, more money in the bank.

Consumers instead want what Marx (following the ancients) called use values. These aren't merely physical, local, and parochial values that naturally correspond to the human needs we produced, once upon a time, with the slight extensions of our bodies known as tools. No, use values are the medium of human desire, and thus have no inherent limit. And yet they *are* an alternative to the endless accumulation of exchange value precisely because they don't last; they can't be saved or stored up against a future. Unlike money in the bank, they're worthless if left unused and unspent. They accrue no interest: they decay, they expire, they "depreciate." So you can't put off their appreciation in the here and now unless you can hoard the things you buy, just keep piling them up in your basement or your garage or your memory—but then you might as well be accumulating assets to deploy in the next life, just like the acquisitive individuals inspired by the profit motive. These use values come and go; you have to be ready for them. So conceived, they're qualitative limits on accumulation—economic growth—as such. At any rate we might learn to treat them in this manner and, while we're at it, realize that consumer culture is their last redoubt.

THE FOOD REVOLUTION

In theory, this notion of use value and its address sounds at least plausible. In practice, in history, it looks irrefutable. The archive is vast, but its most convincing results come from the records of American eating—from the "food revolution" of the late twentieth century started by James Beard, Julia Child, Craig Claiborne, and Alice Waters; later narrated by Eric Schlosser, David Kamp, Marion Nestle, Warren Belasco, and Michael Pollan; and meanwhile enacted by us "foodies," us consumers. This unfinished revolution has already changed the way food gets produced, prepared, and consumed, and will continue to change the way we (and the rest of the world) eat. Perhaps the best way to summarize it is to follow Pollan's lead and call it the deindustrialization of food.

In the half century following World War II (and as a direct consequence of the mass production that won the war), the production and distribution of food in the United States were centralized, systematized, and homogenized under the corporate auspices of "agribusiness." The

share of food expenses in household budgets fell accordingly, and remarkably, even as eating out became a normal moment in family routines
(to the point where, by 2001, 36 percent of the calories consumed by
Americans came from restaurants rather than home-cooked meals). This
was the golden age of TV dinners as well as live television, when Mc-
Donald's reshaped the landscape in the most fundamental and literal
ways, by creating factory farms in the countryside and planting those disturbing yellow arches in every big city and small town. Frozen food, pack-
aged food—dinner out of a box—and fast food were now commonplace.

Meanwhile Big Science conquered the world by dividing whole foods
into "nutrients" as well as splitting atoms into strange new particles. By
the 1970s, nutritionists, in effect scientists who treat foodstuffs as the
sum of their chemical parts, were agreed that one essential ingredient
in any human diet—fat—was a problem, and urged its reduction. They
got their way, with the help of margarine, corn, and beef producers who
lobbied Congress, so that by the 1990s, Americans were eating right,
working out, and gaining weight: the triumph of scientific nutritionism
coincided with the emergence of an "obesity epidemic" fed by the so-
called Western Diet, the odd, deadly combination of sugar, saturated fat,
and animal protein. As Pollan and Nestle show, the turning point came
in the late 1970s. That was when, thanks to all kinds of legislative incentives, corn and soybeans became the staple crops of American agriculture, more feed—mere feed—for cows, pigs, and chickens, and also
when high fructose corn syrup became the basic ingredient in the American diet (it's everywhere; look at any label in the grocery store).

But at the very same moment, Beard, Child, Claiborne, and Waters
were reinventing American cuisine, providing consumers with new ideas,
foreign possibilities, and different promises, and, by the same token,
equipping them with alternatives to industrialized food. I place the emphasis here on *consumers*, because these ideologues of the food revolution
weren't interested in the housewives and the home economics that Irma
Rombauer celebrated in *The Joy of Cooking*. Beard, the gay man from
Seattle by way of the West Village, wrote his first best-selling cookbook
about the manly art of grilling outdoors. Child, the difficult child of privilege once removed—someday we'll think of her as the Herman Melville

of the late twentieth century—wrote her masterpiece on French cuisine and reenacted its fables on TV as if we had all the time in the world, as if we were off work for good. The point of *Mastering the Art* and *Cooking with Julia* was not getting dinner on the table; it was savoring the exotic ingredients, mixing things up, enjoying the process, maybe even setting the food on fire, as if the kitchen were the proper setting for sacrificial rites: everything was animated by the participles of those titles, by the present tense, by *spending* time.

Claiborne was another gay man, another exile in waiting, always expecting expulsion from polite society and always in flight from its norms. His columns in the paper of record nevertheless redefined food, remade restaurants, and refined the palates of most Americans (his column was syndicated, and his two *New York Times* cookbooks were best sellers). And Waters, well, how often does a French restaurant (Chez Panisse, it was called) lead to educational movements, mass-market magazines, and mistaken identities? Together these visionaries—it's not too much to call them revolutionaries—made the preparation and consumption of food into new ideas and new folkways, without ever trying to make us healthier.

And yet, for all the butter they began with, they did make us healthier by persuading us to be both more rational and more romantic as consumers, willing to scout out the best ingredients, to linger over their preparation, and to savor the spectacular results. As Belasco demonstrates, their food revolution started as a protest against industrialized eating—a consumer boycott of what postwar capitalism did to the food chain. In that sense, it was an original and crucial dimension of what we have come to know as the environmental movement (which is why Alice Waters's new cookbook is called *The Green Kitchen*).

Again, it's changed the way we cook and eat food, and so it's changed the way plants and animals get raised, harvested, and delivered to the grocery stores: the difference in our modes of consumption has made a big difference in the mode of production. Not enough of a difference, of course, but the destructive environmental effects of a completely industrialized food chain were first revealed by people who appealed to the use values of consumers—their customers and readers—in resisting those effects. Their intellectual heirs, the narrators of the food revolution, have followed this lead by continuing our education as both rational and romantic consumers—by alerting us to the idiocies of the Western Diet on the demand side, by exploring the insane cruelties of animal slaughter on the supply side, but mainly by reminding us of the sheer pleasures of eating. They're always teaching us to demand more (never less) than what is available in the market as it stands.

But even the best of them succumb to what I've called the "pathos of productivity." They can't see that the unfinished food revolution they have chronicled (and fostered) is, at bottom, a consumers' movement, a consumers' good. The brilliant Michael Pollan, who's done more than any other writer to explain the awful effects of industrialized food, is a perfect example of this partial blindness. In last year's food issue of the *New York Times Magazine*, he lovingly described a weekend of cooking everything from a whole goat to a loaf of bread in an outdoor brick oven, along with five California chefs, bakers, and purveyors, perfectionists all. These experts cooked so much great food that a lot of guests, mostly neighbors, had to pitch in to polish it off. This is how Pollan concluded the piece: "I realize I've gotten at least as much pleasure from working together to create these meals as I have from eating them. Sometimes producing things is more gratifying—and more conducive to building community—than consuming them, I decide. Our guests seem merry and convivial, but there's something special about the camaraderie of the kitchen crew."

Pollan said something slightly but significantly different in an earlier essay for the *New York Review of Books* (June 10, 2010): "Though seldom articulated as such, the attempt to redefine, or escape, the *traditional role of consumer* has become an important aspiration of the food movement. In various ways it seeks to put the relationship between consumers and producers on a new, more neighborly footing, enriching the kinds of information exchanged in the transaction, and encouraging us to regard our food dollars as 'votes' for a different kind of agriculture and, by implication, economy." Here Pollan clearly assumes what Matthew Crawford, Juliet Schor, and Ben Barber do, that the "traditional" consumer is the passive, privatized, prepolitical type who buys whatever the advertisements and the supermarkets offer. Even so, I think Pollan's rendering of the cultural reality is useful because it suggests that the consumers educated by the food revolution are *social* selves with political weight and ambitions. They're people who, like the culture jammers, have changed capitalism by noticing, stretching, and contorting the meanings of commodities: "The modern marketplace would have us decide what to buy strictly on the basis of price and self-interest; the food movement implicitly proposes that we enlarge our understanding of both those terms, suggesting that not just 'good value' but ethical and political values should inform our buying decisions, and that we'll get more satisfaction from our eating when we do."

Those ethical and political values are of course the use values that Marx and the ancients placed in opposition to the exchange values (prices) permitted by the marketplace (in fact, Marx once remarked that the "moral and political element" was a key variable in the price of labor power, regardless of market imperatives). But only consumers, the buyers who can't profit from market exchange—whatever they buy, wear, or eat will soon lose its value—only consumers must always factor these use values into their calculations. That simple fact is worth emphasizing: only consumers have a vested interest in acquiring use values at the expense of exchange values. But they develop that interest in full view of the commodified status of whatever they buy, wear, or eat. As they do, they turn the market to their specific social purposes, bending it, in the long run, toward their will. As they do, they transform the commodity they've bought from a possible fetish with only generic, symbolic meaning—just an exchange value—to a real thing, maybe even the thing itself, because from now on its symbolic properties will be local memories, loving gestures, spoken words, and usable pasts—just a use value— rather than a price or a profit.

Most of you have bought a greeting card or a plastic toy that hundreds of thousands of other consumers have bought with the same thing in mind, and in hand. But you know that once you sign the card or wrap the toy, it doesn't feel generic anymore, because when you give it away, the recipient can't be a stranger: you've created or sustained a highly specific social bond, possibly an intimate relationship, and you've done that by handing over a mass-produced item. You also know that both you and the recipient are going to make unique use of this item: you'd be offended if someone else borrowed your inscription, and you'd be surprised if anybody else could play with this pointless plastic device in the same way.

"A SOMEWHAT DISGUSTING MORBIDITY": WHEN FAT IS THE POLITICAL ISSUE

All along I've been arguing that the empowerment of consumers is both possible and necessary. The economic argument of Part 1 is that saving for a rainy day or piling up profits in corporate coffers is a recipe for disaster: any transfer of income shares that increases corporate or high-end incomes at the expense of consumer spending will lead directly to speculative markets, bubbles, and crisis—as in the 1920s and the age of the "global savings glut" after 1983—because growth is no longer driven by new/net private investment (or capital formation, if you like). So if we want sustainable growth, we need to increase consumption at the expense of both higher personal savings and higher corporate profits. But that political project will require a redistribution of income on the one hand, and the socialization of investment on the other. Meanwhile, it will require an intellectual fortification of consumer culture.

That fortification is the purpose of Part 2. I've claimed here that consumer culture is not the crematory of progressive politics, not the abject creature of advertising's Big Lie, and not the principal cause of spiritual impoverishment or environmental degradation. I've argued instead that consumer culture enables a new politics that still animates revolution in our own time, that it harbors a utopian urge that reminds us of how much we hate the socially necessary labor we call work, and that it contains moral complexities that allow for the mindful care of our souls and our planet.

In effect I've been arguing along the lines laid out in the early 1930s by John Maynard Keynes, who also wrote in the immediate aftermath of an economic crisis that changed everything. Don't get me wrong; I'm no

Keynes—I'm not even an economist—and his theoretical mantle has been ably assumed by Paul Krugman, Dean Baker, and James Galbrath, among others. I mean that his interest in the moral questions raised by the decay of capitalism must now become our concerns. Either that or the "pathos of productivity" will regulate the intellectual response to our crisis, and so will disfigure the future we hope to give our children, and theirs.

In 1930, in "Economic Possibilities for Our Grandchildren," an essay published in the *Nation and Atheneum*—a studious magazine, like our *Atlantic Monthly*—Keynes pondered something his fellow economists had been trying to measure for a decade: "unemployment due to our discovery of means of economizing the use of labour outrunning the pace at which we can find new uses for labour." He called it "technological unemployment" and italicized the phrase. But like Herbert Marcuse, who called it "automation," Keynes suggested that the new reality was a cause for celebration, not mourning: the new kind of unemployment was "only a temporary phase of maladjustment." The "revolutionary technical changes" that had put so many people out of work meant that "mankind is solving its economic problem," he exclaimed, and he italicized this phrase as well, insisting that these changes held an almost miraculous promise of conquering scarcity and ending the struggle for subsistence that had preoccupied the human species since its departure from the instinctual habitat of plants and animals.

Keynes was trying, as he put it, to "lead us out of the tunnel of economic necessity into daylight." He had glimpsed the dawn of "the age of *leisure and of abundance*" made visible in the 1920s and still legible, as he saw it, in the catastrophe of the Great Depression. Here is how he concluded: "But chiefly, do not let us overestimate the importance of the economic problem, or sacrifice to its supposed necessities other matters of greater and more permanent significance." On his way to this counterintuitive conclusion, he reminded us that we had the chance to "return to some of the most sure and certain principles of religion and traditional virtue"—but he did *not* mean a return to the Protestant work ethic. He meant instead that the eager embrace of austerity, the solemn deferral of gratification, and the saintly renunciation of desire were residual symptoms of the "economic problem" that abundance could adjourn.

Like W. E. B. Du Bois, who complained at the very same moment that his opponents were "still thinking in terms of work, thrift, investment, and profit," Keynes saw further and knew better than the economists who prescribed harder work, more saving, and less consumption as the obvious cures for what ailed us. He put his faith in our better angels, those "delightful people who are capable of taking direct enjoyment in things, the lilies of the field who toil not, neither do they spin." They walked "in the paths of virtue" because they took "least thought for the morrow."

Keynes was even more lyrical in predicting that we would soon be able to treat the profit motive as something like a personality disorder—something to be included in the diagnostic manuals of psychotherapy. "When the accumulation of wealth is no longer of high social importance, there will be a great change in the code of morals," he began. Then he gleefully explained the implications:

> We shall be able to rid ourselves of many of the pseudo-moral principles which have hag-ridden us for two hundred years, by which we have exalted some of the most distasteful of human qualities into the position of the highest virtues. We shall be able to afford to dare to assess the money-motive at its true value. The love of money as a possession—as distinguished from the love of money as a means to the enjoyments and realities of life—will be recognised for what it is, a somewhat disgusting morbidity, one of those semi-criminal, semi-pathological propensities which one hands over with a shudder to the specialists in mental disease.

Eighteen months later, Keynes wrote a piece for the *New Republic* that was less lyrical and yet more pointed. It was called "The Dilemma of Modern Socialism." He claimed that the ethical imperatives of the "ideal society" known as socialism could now be realized in the historical circumstances of the Great Depression—not by the generalization of thrift and the sainthood of frugality, but rather in the "economically sound reforms" required for recovery. The opposites of "ought" and "is," values and facts, desire and reason, had finally come together:

It happens that the most pressing reforms which are economically sound do not, as perhaps they did in earlier days, point away from the ideal [of socialism]. On the contrary, they point toward it. I am convinced that those things which are urgently called for on practical grounds, such as the central control of investment and the distribution of income in such a way as to provide purchasing power for the enormous potential output of modern productive technique, will also tend to produce a better kind of society on ideal grounds.

So again the emphasis was on the passage beyond necessity—the new prospect of freedom—that was revealed, not postponed, by the extraordinary circumstances of economic crisis. Like Du Bois, Keynes understood that two events had conspired to make the consumer the key figure in any realistic discussion of the future. The first event was the trend toward the *expulsion* of human labor from goods production as a result of technical innovation: before the 1920s, the sector of the workforce that built all that laborsaving machinery grew faster than any other sector, and then, around 1919, it started shrinking (this is why "technological unemployment" became a stock phrase in the 1920s). New investment in goods production—whether capital goods or consumer goods—now looked impossible as well as unprofitable (in *The Treatise on Money* [1930] Keynes had already noted the huge discrepancy between rising profits, absent investment, and soaring productivity, using data from the 1920s in the United States). The second event that had conspired to make the consumer the key figure for both of them was what Keynes delicately named "the ruin of the old system," and what Du Bois bluntly called the "collapse of capitalism."

For both of them, both writing in the early 1930s, the end of work—original sin once removed—and the beginning of a new stage in human civilization were suddenly obvious, and each, end or beginning, appeared as cause and effect of the other. So, in this spastic transition we call the Great Depression, they both saw promise where most others saw disaster: they saw comedy—not humor, but maybe a happy ending—where most others saw tragedy. We've sampled Du Bois in Chapter 5; there's no need to recapitulate his seminal ideas about the impending age of the consumer. But we should now listen to Keynes as he awkwardly arrives at the conclusion that when socially necessary labor recedes—when the "economic problem" has been solved—then consumption becomes the solution:

> For until these latter years, the chief effect of new machinery was to render *labor*, i.e., man's muscles, more efficient. Economists could plausibly argue that machinery was cooperative, not competitive, with labor. But the effect of the latest type of machinery is increasingly, not to make men's muscles more efficient, but to render them obsolete. And the effect is twofold: first, to furnish us with the ability to produce consumption goods, as distinct from services, almost without limit; and second, to use so little labor in the process that an ever increasing proportion must be occupied either in the field of supplying human services or in meeting the demand for durable [consumer] goods.

I'm in perfect agreement with Keynes on this sequence as history—Part 1 is my empirical test of his claims—but I cite his authority, not his enthusiasm. For we know that the solution to the economic problem may not always be the solution to the moral problem. In fact, we've learned over many years that the economic and the moral dimensions of our lives are supposed to be separate spheres (unless of course we're at work for ourselves, where necessity and freedom intersect, but even then we're tempted to cut corners). For example, the rational economic decision to dump toxic waste to save disposal costs, or to invest in high-risk assets to maximize profits, may well impose unwanted effects—"externalities"—on populations that don't want to be affected, but it will probably be more profitable than the alternatives. Or conversely, and more to the point, higher consumption may be good for the economy as a whole, but it may well impose unwanted environmental effects on the larger society, the moral community, and its natural environment. Even your scrupulously well-informed decisions as an individual consumer could sustain the exchange value of a commodity produced by immoral acts in a remote location (a sweatshop in Thailand, say).

So let me put the proposition and the questions that follow as plainly as I can. In my view, consumer culture is good for the environment and our souls as well as the economy. I wouldn't have argued the case if I didn't think the three stories fit together in framing a new social edifice that's worth inhabiting. You wouldn't have come this far in the argument if you didn't think of it as real estate you wanted to inspect.

But if consumer culture is such a good idea, why are we so fat?

Isn't the "obesity epidemic" the soft underbelly of the argument? Put it another way. If abstention, delay, and renunciation are bad for us—if consumer culture is good for us on moral as well as economic grounds—why are we now witness to a deadly excess of overeating? Why are so many people impervious to what Pollan calls the food movement? Are they suffering from a new version of "false consciousness," thus unable to see that the objective reality of their caloric intake will soon destroy them? Don't they understand that they're exploited by a food industry willing to market poison if it's profitable? Why are they unwilling—or is it unable—to restrain themselves in the name of their own health? Why can't they defer the gratification of bad calories?

Ask Keynes. If we've solved the economic problem, as he thought we had all these eighty years ago, what follows? If we—us consumers—are enfranchised by a redistribution of income, as per my economic argument, wouldn't we all just get fatter?

Possibly. But the evidence works both ways. And when it comes to fat, well, it's the exuberance we love to hate because, unlike collateralized debt obligations and other financial derivatives that have no location in space, obesity has a convenient address and we already know how to solve the problem: Consume less. Save more. Get fit. I mean that our obsession with obesity is another iteration of our problem with consumer culture. It's excess, pure and simple. We fear it because it crosses every boundary we've been taught to respect and obey, including the "interpersonal space" that's supposed to keep us separate as individuated bodies unless we're having sex with someone else (as opposed to sex with ourselves, which we call masturbation). It oozes, it overflows, sometimes it obliterates those boundaries and makes us wonder what we're missing. It beckons us toward something that might be mere pleasure—in any case, it leads us back toward a medieval experience of the grotesque, when bodies outweighed minds in the natural order of things. And it leads us forward in time, too, because it reminds us of death: these fat people are killing themselves.

As far as I can tell, there are two available readings of this obesity obsession. The first reading is what you get from the mainstream medical establishment, which includes the pharmaceutical companies that invent the diet pills and regimes, the doctors who prescribe them, and the agribusiness corporations that produce the food that requires these antidotes. All three components of this mainstream stand to profit from change in American diets. According to these sources, the central facts are that we've gained too much weight over the past thirty years (just as fat was excluded from our diets and we started working out), and that the obese among us spend way more (42 percent more) for medical treatment than people of "normal weight." These categories are derived from the body mass index (BMI), a ratio of height versus weight that echoes the actuarial imperatives of life insurance companies. In other words, we're not getting fat and happy, no, we overweight types pose a health risk that costs too much to cure: conditions such as high blood pressure, heart disease, and diabetes have become almost epidemic due to our impending obesity.

We do seem to have been putting on the pounds. In the United States, as in six other countries, *two-thirds* of all adults, including me, are overweight or obese—their BMI is 25 or over. But for once the baby boomers aren't to blame, since after the age of sixty (or menopause), you start to lose weight as your bone and muscle mass naturally decline. And for now the cure is obvious: less fat, less sugar, fewer calories, more exercise. This mainstream reading is convincing when you consult your own experience in the flyover states, where everybody eats steaks the size of a laptop while clad in khaki shorts and a colorful golf shirt tucked into that deep crevasse where belts disappear. But then you look at the numbers, and the case looks a little more complicated. Between 1973 and 2000, the official rate of obesity doubled in the United States, from about 15 percent to about 30 percent of all Americans, and yet their average daily caloric intake increased by only about 20 percent. Meanwhile deaths due to heart disease declined.

These discrepancies inform the second available reading of our obsession with fat, which debunks it by treating it as a problem of social psychology—a displacement of other issues and conflicts, including class, race, and gender. Paul Campos, Susie Orbach, and Richard Klein are the most effective advocates of this reading, but they're building on a mountain of clinical evidence compiled since the 1970s. Campos and others have argued that the so-called obesity epidemic is a statistical deception that both serves the interests of the medical establishment and diverts us from more pressing political tasks: "Obsessing about the 10 pounds of 'extra' weight that the average American adult has gained over the last fifteen years has become a convenient way of avoiding a direct engagement with any number of issues regarding America's size, excessiveness, and out-of-control consumption," as Campos puts it. (Notice that "out-of-control consumption" works for both readings: one would treat it with drugs or diets to dampen appetite, the other with political exhortation.) In a talismanic book first published in 1978, as the food revolution became part of a new feminism, Orbach argued that women have learned to use layers of fat to arm themselves against a masculinized world intent on penetrating their defenses; she successfully fit her readers for a different suit of armor. Klein argued analogously that fat signifies abundance, embodiment, femininity, even a kind of maternity, and so must be loved, not just accepted, as the obvious condition of middle age, unless of course obesity immobilizes your mother.

Much as I admire them, these readings are both correct and insufficient. For they treat fat as a big problem to be solved rather than—or in addition to—a simple fact to be explained: obesity appears as mere symptom rather than attempted cure, as a manifestation of an unhealthy, unwanted condition (out-of-control consumption) rather than a stage of recovery. Put it this way. As an attempted cure, our obsession with fat, our attention to obesity, is an ugly but effective way of asking what follows from an end to the deferral of gratification implied by the triumph of consumer culture. Do we all end up looking like Marlon Brando or Elizabeth Taylor? Some of us would hope to, I suppose, so let me ask the question differently. If a higher mortality rate among the overweight is not the issue—by all accounts, only the grossly obese are at risk of pre-mature death—then what are we afraid of?

Campos notwithstanding, we're directly engaged in a serious dis-cussion of moral (and perhaps political) choices as soon as we acknowl-edge that the size and shape of our bodies are determined by something more than our genetic inheritance, by something we do to ourselves—as soon as we say, however playfully, "You are what you eat." In this sense, the cure residing in our obsession with fat is not an answer; it's a question, and an old one at that: what is the reach of necessity, what is the role of the past, and what is the scope of our will in making decisions about who we will become?

It's the question that consumer culture poses to all of us, every day, almost every hour—but it's not esoteric or philosophical or academic, something for David Foster Wallace to answer for us, not anymore, be-cause we're able, as consumers, to buy and sell the attributes of the per-sonalities we want. That's why *fat* represents personal excess, a "disease of the will," and *thin* represents proper restraint. So conceived, obesity looks like a moral problem that each of us must address without refer-ence to external constraint or compulsion, and food as such begins to look like tobacco or alcohol, a chemical substance that can become ad-dictive and ruin your life. That's why everybody is staring at the labels, no matter how much they weigh: food now appears to us as a chemical substance, an ensemble of nutrients, the sum of its parts. But here's the rub. If you want to be thin, get rich or die trying, because if you stay poor you'll probably get fat: the single most reliable determinant and predictor of obesity is poverty.

We know that fat people congregate at the lower end of the income scale, in the poorest neighborhoods and regions, in part because we know that black people are, on average, underpaid and overweight when com-pared to white people (according to the survey data, they also feel more comfortable in their heaviness than white folks); in part we know this because we know the same things about the Hispanic men and women who deliver the food, push the strollers, and clean the toilets. We also know that more money confers more choices on consumers about where they live, where they educate their children, how they choose medical care, and how they eat. More money gives them more "votes" to cast in favor of these "enjoyments and realities of life," as Keynes put it. Obesity declines accordingly in the higher income brackets. So a redistribution of income that reversed the trends of the last thirty years—to begin with, it would address the scandal of increasing poverty among children— could conceivably do more to stop the "obesity epidemic" than any form of political exhortation or medical prescription.

If we want a change of moral season, then, we should stop treating obesity as the most disgusting morbidity of our time, a "disease of the will" verging on false consciousness, as tuberculosis was aestheticized in the nineteenth century. Obesity is a problem, to be sure, and the ways we try to solve it with changes in our diet will reveal a great deal about our selves and our choices, past and present—our solutions will become a crucial dimension of what I called the politics of "more" in Chapters 5 and 6. Still, I think Keynes was right. The most disgusting morbidity of our time is the idea that the accumulation of wealth in the abstract—more money, more exchange value—is such a worthy goal that it should regulate our time and energies, even shape our bodies and our society. But this appetite for accumulation is animated, as always, by the "pathos of productivity," by the idea that whatever surplus value we have acquired through *work* must be saved and invested, not consumed, not spent, not displayed as bodily amplitude (unless of course our bodies are the assets we bring to bear, but in the athletic or the actorly case the surplus always sprouts upward, denying the downward, medieval, retrograde momentum of the grotesque, which is merely the inarticulate acknowledgment of what time does to your body, any body).

So again, if we want a change of moral season, we should begin by changing our minds about consumer culture. When we understand that consuming goods is better for us than producing them—it beats working—and when we understand that the profit motive is a prehensile anachronism, an anal compulsion, a disgusting morbidity, we'll be able to understand that a redistribution of income away from profits and toward wages will prevent another Great Recession. What is more important, we'll be able to map and navigate a new ethical environment, where economies of scale can't be quantified because their purpose is the expansion of use values.

All along I've been saying that "saving for a rainy day" is dangerous to our economic and our mental health. The renunciation of desire and the delay of gratification—in a word, thrift—can't help us through this prolonged crisis, and increased investment induced by tax incentives won't ride to the rescue. No amount of frugality will do the trick. A greater dose of consumer culture and a higher volume of consumer spending induced by a redistribution of income will, however, address the causes of the crisis, and lay the groundwork for balanced growth in the future. To realize these social purposes is of course to treat the market economy as an instrument of our will rather than the seat of inviolable laws. As Alan Greenspan, of all people, reminded the readers of his 2007 autobiography, "Remember, markets are not ends in themselves. They are constructs to assist populations in achieving the optimum allocation of resources."

But to realize these social purposes, we need first to recognize and validate the morality of spending. We need to know why consumer culture is good for the economy, the environment, and our souls. We need to know how to be against thrift.

Bataille Made Me Do It

W riting something tends to change your mind because you don't really know what you think until you put it into words (or images, or both). Writing this book certainly changed mine, even though I can honestly say that my whole adult life was preparation for it. By way of a conclusion, I'll tell you about the change that's most relevant to the arguments of this book: the reading and the writing that went into it convinced me to eat a hamburger after thirty years of abstention from red meat.

I renounced the consumption of dead animals, shellfish included, in 1981, just as I entered the academic job market. In 1984, I modified this rule to read "no mammals" because, as a new parent, I wanted my children to eat widely and too well, but, as the owner of a dying dog—Alex was the only constant in a life that still lacked control—I couldn't quite bear the thought of eating a four-legged creature. Besides, he had become the permanent resident of my bad dreams, always already roasted and splayed on an outsized cutting board.

These local prohibitions had nothing to do with my health—I was a smoker, and I still drink more alcohol than any dietary guideline prescribes. No, these prohibitions were part of my "coming of age." They were the renunciations that marked me as an adult: they were the insignia of the maturity I could muster, the proof of the delayed gratification required by the parent I wanted to be. They were private, personal, never public, except when friends (usually in restaurants) made a point of saying I was a vegetarian, as if my abstention from mammals was something marvelous that *they* could be proud of.

This second-order abstention from mammals became so habitual that it persisted through the breakup of that marriage, the absence of my children, and the unwanted equipoise of my career. But it had become *mere* habit, so that as my life evolved after parenthood, the renunciations related to this stage of adulthood began to lose their grip on my day-to-day existence. You could say that I began to regress, to lose a vested interest in the repression of my desires, as if I were shedding some protective layer of skin—except that this molting happened inside me, where no one noticed, not even me.

Until I did notice. What were my renunciations about, I began to ask myself. I wanted to know why I had needed them, and apparently still did. I began to think that I was dying to my old self, as the Protestants used to say, as I came up with lousy answers to my own incoherent questions. As it turned out, I was right: it was a vigil; I was watching as my old self disappeared, finally becoming a closed chapter in the narrative of a life I was reconstructing. As I watched, I had to ask my newly divisible self why animals had been such useful, even talismanic devices in my ability to renounce certain fundamental pleasures of the body. Had these renunciations really equipped me with the character and resolve I needed to be a good husband and father? Clearly not: I was neither. But still.

Why did I stop eating dead animals, I asked myself, then mammals? And why did I now want to eat a hamburger, in full view of Peter Singer's stringent arguments against such a bloody act, and having just read Jonathan Foer's impassioned defense of the vegetarian life? In a word: pleasure. That's all, mere pleasure. Call it luxury if you like. Either way, it was painful because it involved new and unwelcome kinds of self-knowledge.

The smell of bacon had haunted me for thirty years. That's probably why I fried it for my kids on weekends, or grilled large slabs of marinated meat when I ran out of ideas for healthy family eating (back then I did most of the cooking). The lovely smell of incinerated flesh reminded me— and better yet, my family—of what I was missing, and again, the reminder was delicious precisely because it recalled what I was denying myself: the pleasure of eating something totally unnatural, something

altogether prepared (we don't eat wild animals, as a rule: we eat the artificial products of a food chain we've created). You can prepare vegetables, of course, but animals always take longer, and it seems they came
first in the Neolithic revolution, before the plants, when "domestication"
meant a new turn in the history of the human species.

The mere physical pleasure of eating—the indulgence, the sensation,
the seduction—finally did it for me. The turning point came in the late
summer of 2009, at a new, hip Indian restaurant in Chelsea that had
moved Bombay street food indoors and upstairs. My girlfriend had ordered tandoori lamb chops, and, with the innocent astonishment of a
delighted gourmand, she offered me a bite, knowing all about my prohibitions and abstentions. I took the bait, took the bite—I gave in—and
it was as if every part of my adult past overtook me in an instant, or
rather the past that I had banished came rushing back. I thought my
mouth would explode, and then the rest of me.

But I hadn't started writing this book yet, so the effects of the lamb
were like a familiar bass line, something you assimilate without thinking—
something that sticks somewhere in the body of your mind. Then on
a Labor Day weekend a year later, in the midst of writing the book, I
was part of a culinary experiment, a picnic on the Hudson River, which
involved the most meticulous rendering of meats, fish, cheeses, breads,
and sauces I'd witnessed since a brief stay in Japan twenty years before.
All of us got our own little basket of a dozen "sandwiches"—each of
them a tiny, precarious sculpture—prepared, as if I could make this
up, by a psychiatrist who told the origin story of every morsel. I had
to eat it all as a courtesy to the chef, but as I did so, I realized that the
pleasure of the eating wasn't just the fulfillment of an obligation to
the man who had prepared the feast (I had eaten steaks before on two
similar occasions, when it would have been impolite to announce my
abstentions). I could taste that sacrificial lamb from a year before, and
I could feel the same traces of memory and denial, but the sensations
unfolded slowly this time, little by little, as I wondered whether my
prohibitions had produced too many pleasures of renunciation over
too many years—as I wondered whether I could actually savor these
new realities.

And then I started rereading Georges Bataille, as part of my effort to measure the moral properties of consumer culture. I leavened this theoretical mix with a large dose of the practical and the empirical Michael Pollan, but they became coconspirators in the same cause, which I now read as my fortunate fall into the omnivore's dilemma.

Food and sex and death: these are the fundamental human realities, according to Bataille, and who would want to argue with him? But then he cast himself as the original outlier of French intellectual life in the 1930s and after, trying always to be in an argument with a colleague or a comrade. He played his part well: Jean-Paul Sartre, among other luminaries of the moment, detested him and his ideas. To be sure, Bataille was a fixture on the formative Paris scene between 1933 and 1939, when Alexandre Kojeve and Alexandre Koyre reinvented the study of Hegel (thus Marx) at the College de France, when the College de Sociologie convened as an informal group to study the residual meanings of the sacred, and when refugees from Nazi Germany—particularly members of the Frankfurt School such as Walter Benjamin, Theodor Adorno, and Max Horkheimer—arrived to crowd the cafés and raise the stakes of intellectual exchange. Still, Bataille was a big fan of perversity, pornography, and the Marshall Plan, all dubious propositions in postwar France: in his lifetime, he was a marginal figure. We read him now largely because the founding fathers of French poststructuralism—Jacques Derrida, among others—retrieved him from obscurity in the 1960s and 1970s.

Bataille's most substantial and controversial stance was a defense of excess, sacrifice, expenditure, and profitless consumption as the conditions of both "intimacy," which he defined as the opposite of alienated labor, and, of all things, economic growth. It seems a paradoxical stance at best—how can intimacy (the local, the micro, the sexual) and economic growth (the global, the macro, the abstract) have the same causes? But it derived from a rigorous study of medieval religion, on the one hand, and the prospects of postwar economic development on the other. These studies converged in *The Accursed Share*, a book published in 1967, five years after his death.

Unlike a barn, something built for a productive purpose, a church embodied intimacy in Bataille's terms because it signified the pointless

mobilization of resources: "For the construction of a church is not a profitable use of the available labor, but rather its consumption, the *destruction of its utility*." Intimacy was the opposite of a product or a commodity;
it required expenditure, loss, even sacrifice, but not the costs of alienated
labor. So the sacred remained as an alternative to the profane for the
same reason it remained as a rebuke to the parsimonious among us.

Bataille's understanding of postwar capitalism was clearly based on
a familiarity with Marx's famous reproduction schemes and with the
Soviet debates of the 1920s, which meant pretty much the same thing.
Those debates had turned on whether to give priority to saving and investment (capital goods) or to consumer spending (consumption goods)
in forcing the industrialization of Russia. The modern-industrial era
opened with a reallocation of resources toward saving and investment
in capital goods, Bataille observed, and thus a relative restriction of
wages and consumer goods. That allocation remained the basis of the
capitalist economy. But like the renegade economists who sowed the seeds
of the Prague Spring in the early 1960s, he saw that Soviet economic
development rested on this same basis: *extensive* growth driven by investment in capital goods—rather than *intensive* growth driven by consumer demand—was still the rule throughout industrial society. (See
Chapter 6.)

Bataille used this distinction between extensive and intensive growth
to suggest that both East and West were still devoted to the archaic
rigors of productivity rather than the novel pleasures of consumption:
"At a certain point the advantage of extension is neutralized by the contrary advantage, that of luxury; the former remains operative, but in a
disappointing—uncertain, often powerless—way. . . . Henceforth what
matters primarily is no longer to develop the productive forces but to
spend their products sumptuously." What mattered primarily, however,
was evident yet unknown, because the pressing new need for consumer
spending as against saving and investment had no representation in political discourse apart from working-class movements (which were of
course missing altogether from the Soviet scene).

The salutary effect of these movements was to allocate more resources to the production of consumer goods, in line with the increase

of wages that trade unions could negotiate. Even so, that reallocation lacked "some shining value as its aim"—it resembled the boring politics of "more" as clumsily represented by Samuel Gompers in the early twentieth century and as eloquently expressed by Vaclav Havel in the late twentieth century. Bataille admitted that it was almost embarrassing to have nothing more to advocate than the "raising of the standard of living." But, like both Gompers and Havel, he understood that the ideological weakness of this remedy—its refusal of any transcendental urges—was also its political virtue.

Meanwhile he followed the example of Simon Patten, the original champion of a "pleasure economy," and tried to change our minds about the larger meanings of consumption. So he designed his exposition of a *general* economy devoted to extravagant expenditure—as against the *restricted* economy still organized around saving, delay, and denial—for a wider audience than his comrade intellectuals. Like Herbert Marcuse, who was writing *Eros and Civilization* at the same postwar moment, Bataille insisted that to be convincing and useful, his exposition had to be historical as well as theoretical: *The Accursed Share* is the story of capitalism told as a miraculous *detour* from the continuum of human nature determined, on the one hand, by a chronic shortage of basic necessities, and, on the other, by an exuberant drive to consume resources without regard to future needs. By this accounting, exotic gift economies of the kind closely studied by Emile Durkheim and Marcel Mauss were the historical rule, whereas capitalism and its communist double were the boring exceptions.

The "shining value" of Bataille's general economy was the pleasure principle of excess, consumption, sacrifice, and waste; but this once-utopian (or ideal) state of release, expenditure, and possible atrocity— he wrote a whole chapter on the Aztecs—had now to be recuperated as the immediately practical, realistic, and necessary groundwork of modern-industrial civilization. Like Keynes, Bataille believed that the real threat to the future lay in the idle, surplus capital that had piled up on the American side of the Atlantic ledger since the 1920s; and like Keynes, he also believed that this same surplus was the sign of a material abundance that would soon redeem modernity by its seemingly profitless investment in the reconstruction of European economies (the Marshall Plan).

Food and sex and death were the fundamental human realities, according to Bataille, and they were all about excess and expenditure, not saving, conserving, or producing goods. The miraculous, miserly bourgeois interregnum had restrained, ignored, or devalued these basic forms of consumption and sacrifice in the name of "utility"—in the name of private property, economic growth, and political progress, not to mention Character and Conscience. But now capitalism couldn't sponsor these purposes unless its massive surpluses got spent unproductively and excessively, on consumer goods rather than capital equipment.

Bataille presented this argument as the inversion of conventional economic theory and a rationale for a new, postcapitalist moral universe: he felt he was on to something big, and he was right. Here is how he explained his inordinate ambition:

> I will simply state, without waiting further, that the extension of economic growth itself requires the overturning of economic principles—the overturning of the ethics that grounds them. Changing from the perspectives of *restrictive* economy to those of *general* economy actually accomplishes a Copernican transformation: a reversal of thinking—and of ethics. . . . Henceforth, leaving aside pure and simple dissipation, analogous to the construction of the Pyramids, the possibility of pursuing growth is itself subordinated to giving. The industrial development of the entire world demands of Americans that they lucidly grasp the necessity, for an economy such as theirs, of having a margin of profitless operations.

To which I say, still true, every bit of it, especially the part about us Americans. For all his eccentricity, Bataille grasped the material reality and the moral possibilities of his time—and ours—better than any economist except Keynes: he understood that thrift and saving were not the answers, whether the question concerned economic growth or ethical integrity. They were the problems, not the solutions. He wanted us to live less anxiously and more generously with abundance, excess, and expenditure. He wanted us to get over the pathos of productivity. Like Keynes, he tried to "lead us out of the tunnel of economic necessity into daylight."

I came to Bataille very late in the composition of this book. His impact on me was personal rather than theoretical—I already had an argument against thrift—but it was profound: he placed me in the scene I'd been writing about, making me a participant as well as an observer. Having digested *The Accursed Share*, I could ask myself where a reconsideration and suspension of my own renunciations would lead. The return of the repressed? "Pure and simple dissipation"? Slouching toward Babylon as Lord of the Flies? The pleasures residing in the delay of gratification are hard to give up. But would the pleasures flowing from immediate indulgence point me down that proverbial slippery slope, the one that starts with irresponsibility and ends at addiction, homelessness, or obesity? And indulgence of what, exactly?

These are the questions that any defense of consumer culture must raise, of course. But now they were addressed *to* me as well as posed *by* me: I had become my own ideal reader.

Food and sex and death, says Bataille, these forms of consumption are the fundamental human realities, and again, who would want to argue with him? But not just any food: "Sexuality is linked to the scandals of death and the *eating of meat*," he declares. How so? In a word, luxury: "The eating of one species by another is the simplest form of luxury"— more simple than sex, even, in its irrational, unnecessary consumption of energy—because the caloric yield from an acre planted in, say, wheat or potatoes is always larger than the caloric yield from an acre devoted to pasture for livestock. So eating plants is more efficient, and it's far better for us than eating animals if the purpose of eating is to provide our bodies with enough calories and nutrients—sufficient fuel—to keep us healthy, trim, and long-lived. If eating is a form of preventive medicine, as in "first do no harm," all cows are sacred.

But, as Bataille insisted, the social purposes of eating had far exceeded these bare necessities long before the sedentary cultivation of plants made civilization possible, just as the exuberant purposes of sex had far exceeded the bare necessity of reproduction long before families existed to raise the inevitable offspring: the basic human urges were to refuse "miserly growth" and to squander surplus resources. So sexuality and meat eating were "great luxurious detours that ensure the intense consumption of energy." As the negation of necessity, they were (and are) the enabling conditions of *intimacy*.

And death? To be sure, it carries the connotation of consummation, the ending of life—it signifies loss and sacrifice. It's the moment when your singularity as a member of the species is both marked (through ritualized remembrance) and adjourned: you can no longer differentiate yourself from others, hereafter only they can do that for you with words and monumental gestures. And yet it's also the moment that is yours alone. As Derrida suggests in *The Gift of Death* (1995)—and here he's following Bataille's lead—it's "very much that which nobody else can undergo or confront in my place." At the hour of your death, you become irreplaceable. In this sense, only a mortal—someone waiting to die—can know freedom, because only a mortal can understand what it means to "give up," to sacrifice a life: "By means of the passage to death the soul accedes to its own freedom."

Bataille was slightly less oracular in explaining the connection between the fundamental human realities. Death was the most costly of conceivable luxuries, he admitted, and thus the most burdensome. But the spastic consummation of the sexual act was still comparable to the ultimate sacrifice: "In this respect, the luxury of death is regarded by us in the same way as that of sexuality, first as a negation of ourselves, then—in a sudden reversal—as the profound truth of that movement of which life is the manifestation." Death is a crucial moment in the propagation of the species, then, because, like sex, it leaves what Bataille called "necessary room for the coming of the newborn." Even so, the arbitrary *excesses* of sex are finally about the *differentiation* of each of us from one another: "This squandering [of energy] goes far beyond what would be sufficient for the growth of the species." So this squandering is a down payment not on *the* soul's freedom, as Derrida would have it, but rather on *your* soul's freedom. Sex proves to you, and only you, that in the very same instant, you're all by yourself and yet you're still alive.

But let's not get carried away. In the grand scheme of things human, sex and death are profoundly important, no matter what we may think of Bataille or Derrida—or of the religious traditions they deploy in making their arguments. Food is indispensable, of course, but by comparison it looks pretty mundane. So eating meat looks rather less than heroic or even significant in *any* scheme of things. Why then do I now think of it in the way Bataille wants me to? Why did I want to eat a hamburger?

I understood my abstention from meat as a delay of gratification, a means of disciplining my desires on behalf of a future embodied as a family—embodied, in other words, as a generational bridge built by emotional saving and investment in the present. So, like most other adults whose futures are similarly invested in their offspring, I also understood the abstention, the delay, and the discipline as renewable pleasures, as gifts to my kids. These were "anonymous" gifts: my renunciations were satisfying precisely because they were a family secret, because my children knew what I sacrificed but not why. And these renunciations were even *more* satisfying when they became public, usually in a restaurant, because then I could talk about an animal rather than human beings— rather than face up to the simple fact that I wanted to contain my desires in the name of bourgeois propriety, fatherhood and family, but couldn't bring myself to do so except by summoning a dream's vision of a dog's death.

No wonder my kids often said they envied the dog's life. No wonder vegetarians are so pleased with themselves: they know their cruelties are confined to their own kind.

My abstentions, such as they were, nonetheless helped me stay in character, as husband and father, for many years. But they outlived their utility, which is a way of saying that my needs and my desires had finally parted company, making me choose between them. Or rather, to put it another way, my unconscious preparation for a role as something *other* than husband and father eventually allowed me to distinguish between the pleasures of renunciation (need) and the pleasures of luxury (desire). But then the obvious question for a pragmatist like me became how to make that distinction concrete, measurable, and useful.

Again, this is a question that any defense of consumer culture must raise. And it's now become a pressing *practical* question for Americans as they grapple with the causes and consequences of the Great Recession, as they decide that more saving/investment or more consumption is the cure of what ails the economy, and—what amounts to the same thing— as they decide that emotional frugality or expenditure is the proper structure of their souls.

My homespun answer to the question was the hamburger experiment. If I were going to take the plunge, it would have to be worth the price, in money and moral dilation. So I ransacked *New York* magazine, the Dining section of the *New York Times*, and even *Zagat's* ratings, looking for the best burger in town. Steak I had eaten twice since 1981, meat in that guise was less appealing for my purposes than the sturdy American standby that arrives as a sandwich accompanied by unpretentious sides (fries) and unassuming condiments (ketchup). The top-ranked burger joints were all over the place, but quite a few congregated appropriately in the Meatpacking District on the Lower West Side of Manhattan, so I started the experiment there, at The Homestead, a restaurant established on Ninth Avenue in 1859, where the Kobe beef hamburger goes for twenty-one dollars as a lunch special and thirty-nine dollars on the dinner menu.

It's an old-fashioned steak house, narrow, straight, and dark paneled but brightly lit, a man-made archipelago of white tablecloths, huge plates, and weighty utensils. The crowd is dense and cheerful, the sound is deafening. The menu choices are few, as they should be in a place that advertises itself as a mecca for meat-eating citizens and foodie tourists. I ordered the Kobe burger medium rare with Tater Tots (a product placement?) and my girlfriend ordered the standard Homestead burger with plain old fries; we were comparison shopping. I was extremely nervous, as if I were about to enter an operating room without a sedative, so instead of having a beer, I ordered a martini straight up. It didn't help. As both subject and object of the impending experiment—the surgeon who opens his own body—I knew I'd be changed by what happened in this room.

When the burgers came, the larger one, the Kobe, looked dangerously formless. Framed by a bun the size of a boule, it was more of a puddle to be slurped with a serving spoon than a patty to be eaten in orderly bites (the high fat content of Kobe beef, which determines both its complicated flavor and its death-defying appeal, makes it hard to cook properly). Its smaller counterpart seemed more compact—more cooked—and thus more poised to perform its culinary function. My girlfriend suggested that perhaps the Kobe was underdone and could be sent back for a searing, but I was in no mood for the delay of what was supposed to be gratification. I abruptly overruled her and, having cut the thing in half, I gathered what I could of its leaky mass and took my first bite of a hamburger in thirty years.

It was delicious. Underdone, but delicious. All those fleeting bacon fumes from weekends past took up sudden residence in my mouth. But the meat was sliding around in there, as if the chef had somehow liquefied an honored part of a pampered, grass-fed cow. I was gargling beef. So I acceded to the unfreedom of my soul, took my girlfriend's advice, and sent the Kobe burger back to the kitchen. On its return, it was much more solid and no less delicious. Even so, the junior partner in the table's choices was clearly superior in every respect: the smaller, cheaper burger got the better of us. The sheer excess of the bigger, ridiculously expensive burger was worth the price, but just this once.

I was already descending that slippery slope, thinking ahead to another, maybe better hamburger. Meanwhile my thoughts were organized by the return of the repressed, by the pleasures this experiment had produced. These weren't any better than the pleasures derived from my years of renunciation—they were *different*—but the experience of them did change me for good, and possibly for the better. For that night I realized that the delays and denials of my desires had long served a worthwhile, productive purpose; that this purpose had now expired; and that to continue to enjoy the displaced pleasures of renunciation was therefore perverse, and perhaps destructive.

The question that follows for me is the same question most Americans now face in deciding how to deal with the consequences of economic crisis and the moral complexity of consumer culture. If the worthwhile, productive purpose of surplus repression has, in fact, expired, and if the pleasures afforded by renunciation have, accordingly, become pointless, what is to be done?

I can't pretend that my hamburger experiment is the obvious psychotherapeutic complement to the macroeconomic changes I describe and recommend in this book: it's not the perfect side dish. But then the economic crisis of our time doesn't stand alone as a main dish that needs no accompaniment—it's an emotional impasse as well as a material blight. In any case, the cure for both afflictions is less work, less thrift, less production, or, if you like, more leisure, more expenditure, more profitless consumption. Of course we can *afford* to lighten up and spend more, whether you define the accumulated assets as economic or emotional. But I'm saying something else. I'm saying that we *need* to lighten up and spend more, for our own good. If we don't, we sacrifice ourselves on the altar of productivity and meanwhile sentence our children to a future of pointless repression, denial, and delay.

Georges Bataille convinced me to eat that hamburger. But it was John Maynard Keynes who prepared me to appreciate Bataille. So these two are the unlikely heroes of the book. They wrote their most provocative and still productive essays at the same moment, in the darkest hours of the twentieth century, when the rigorous claims of economic necessity seemed self-evident—and when the cultural restraints of the past seemed to be an all-purpose solution to moral panic and political depravity. They refused to be bound by these claims and restraints, but not because they ignored the relevant history. In fact, Keynes and Bataille saw further, and still speak directly to us, precisely because they used historical evidence to challenge the theoretical orthodoxy of their time.

"Economic Possibilities for Our Grandchildren" was what Keynes called his famous essay of 1930. It was a misleading title. As we've seen (in Chapter 9), the essay was a hopeful description of the change in moral season brought by a "new age of leisure and abundance." So it probably seemed incongruous, and maybe just ignorant, to readers who knew how deeply the Great Depression had already disfigured the everyday lives of working people. But this "old mole," this Keynes, has as much to teach us as the ghost who taught Hamlet to trust his instincts and do the right thing. The tunnel he dug out of economic necessity is still open, still leading us toward daylight. The opportunity he saw in the great crisis of his time is still available to us in ours.

Keynes never took the moral high road. Bataille never even looked for it. Both were too busy burrowing under, and finally through, our habitual modes of thought. Both insisted on *empirical* grounds that a redistribution of income away from saving or investment, toward wages and consumption, was the practical solution to the economic problem of their time. So their solution wasn't a saintly protest against a grim reality that could never change: it wasn't an "ought" with no purchase on what "is." Instead, they proceeded as if the ethical principle of the "ideal society"—from each according to his or her ability, to each according to his or her needs—was already legible, already measurable, in the historical circumstances they studied. To do the right thing, as they saw it, was to do the practical, necessary, available thing.

Just so, I would say once again, and now I too am speaking practically: if we want to prevent another economic disaster, and to promote balanced, sustainable growth, we must create a more perfect union— a more equal, more democratic America—by redistributing income and socializing investment. But first we need to know that the inevitable effect of redistribution—the magnification of consumer culture—is a worthy cause.

Appendix:
Capital in the American Economy:
Kuznets Revisited

Steve Roth and James Livingston

This Appendix is designed to illustrate one of the central claims of the book—that net private investment has been declining in importance for almost a century, even as economic growth has occurred. Steve Roth has prepared graphic depictions of that trend, and meanwhile explained how to read the stocks and flows measured in the National Income Accounts from which the graphs are derived.

The introductory purpose here is to suggest that there are alternatives to the mainstream of economic theory and its built-in assumptions about the importance of private investment (or capital formation) in determining rates of growth. These alternatives accord with, and speak to, the graphic depictions of investment trends that follow. They show that the "myth of investment" in Chapter 3 makes perfect sense—but only if you understand the roles (and sources) of government and residential investment.

Investment is investment, you might say, but the revenue source of the government component is federal, state, and local taxes, not corporate profits; in this sense cutting taxes on profits starves investment. And of course the residential component of investment as such contributes to the housing stock, but it doesn't increase the productive capital stock unless we turn homes into factory barracks overnight.

Famous and influential economists like Larry Summers and Martin Feldstein have strenuously argued that more private investment as such is crucial to growth, and that lower taxes on corporate profits are conducive to investment, but they've never bothered to make these distinctions. So they perpetuate the myth of investment. They're not venal servants of power; they're captives of an ideology or a paradigm—call it what you will—that assumes that more private investment is an inviolable imperative if our common goal is economic growth. Even so, their arguments obscure, deny, or obliterate the economic realities, which are that net private investment has atrophied over the last hundred years (as shown here, not because government spending has "crowded out" private spending), while economic growth has nonetheless happened.

There's been resistance to this investment-driven ideology or paradigm from within the precincts of mainstream economic theory for a half century at least. Here we'll just mention the sources of that resistance, as a way of suggesting that the rudiments of theoretical alternatives are already in place.

The detonating event was the so-called Cambridge capital controversy started by Joan Robinson in 1954, amplified by Piero Sraffa in 1960, and addressed by eminent theorists such as Paul Samuelson, L. Pasinetti, A. Bhaduri, Maurice Dobb, and Ian Steedman. This transatlantic debate, pitting economists at MIT against those at Cambridge University, turned on the utility of "production functions"—those equations that seem self-evidently useful in explaining the different factors, including labor, that variously contribute to growth as such. The question that never got settled was how to measure the marginal productivity of capital. One side held that the equations posited what they were supposed to prove. The other held that they worked as heuristic devices, in effect admitting that the empire of neoclassical theory was a nudist camp. Either way, the importance of capital, and thus of private investment, was already a question in the 1950s.

Meanwhile Moses Abramovitz, Simon Kuznets, Robert Solow, Solomon Fabricant, Kenneth Kurihara, Anatol Murad, Harold Vatter, Burton F. Massell, Harry T. Oshima, and others were suggesting either that capital formation contributed very little to growth, or that net private investment was declining as a percentage of GNP, even while growth continued apace. For these economists, technological change had made labor and capital so productive that both were being displaced: the labor-saving machinery that had once caused "technological unemployment" was now supplemented by capital-saving techniques that made all factors of production mere watchmen and regulators. The implications were recognized early on by the arch-Keynesian Alvin Hansen, but best summarized by Edmund S. Phelps, a Nobel Prize winner, in 1962: "Technical progress is organizational in the sense that its effect on productivity does not require any change in the quantity of the inputs." Again, the contribution of capital formation and private investment to economic growth had become a question.

At the same time, Eastern European economists such as Istvan Friss, Wlodzimierz Brus, Radovan Richta, and Radoslav Selucky noticed that in the West, "extensive" growth fueled by expenditure on capital goods was giving way to "intensive" growth fueled by demand for consumer goods. The Prague Spring was already waiting beneath the frozen ground of the Plan and its priorities. And here, too, the question raised was, What role does investment in nonconsumable goods—capital formation—actually play in economic growth?

The final piece of the new puzzle was the emergence of "human capital" as a concept and a category of investment, at precisely the same moment, between the mid-1950s and the mid-1960s. Its advocates were promarket theorists like Gary Becker, but their findings were consistent with Solow's startling conclusions, and they suggested, accordingly, that public investment in education and technological change driven by extramarket forces were more significant than investments driven by traditional profit motives in making the labor force a new factor of production. So once again the question became, What exactly is it that capital does, or rather, what are capitalists for?

That's one of the questions this book raises. In an effort to provide an empirically grounded answer to that question, the rest of this appendix provides an overview of capital in the American economy since 1930.

To begin with, a little historical background:

The estimation of national income was initiated during the early 1930s, when the lack of comprehensive economic data frustrated the efforts of Presidents Hoover and Roosevelt to design policies to combat the Great Depression. In response to this need, the Department of Commerce commissioned Simon Kuznets of the National Bureau of Economic Research (NBER) to develop estimates of national income. . . . The estimates were presented in a report to the Senate in 1934, National Income, 1929–32.

—Bureau of Economic Analysis (BEA), *A Guide to the National Income and Product Accounts of the United States*

The system of national accounts that Simon Kuznets developed in the 1930s—now called the National Income and Product Accounts (NIPAs)—is today used by almost every country in the world. Methodologies have changed—data gathering, measurement, estimation, statistical adjustment, and reporting—but the accounts themselves, and their relationships, are largely unchanged from those that Kuznets put in place.

In 1961, Kuznets published *Capital in the American Economy: Its Formation and Financing,* an effort to discern, understand, and explain long-term trends in this essential component of the economy: fixed capital (that by his methods includes structures and equipment; software has since been added). He chose this subject because, in his words, "[Fixed] capital formation . . . represents the real savings of the nation." He gathered and regularized the best data that he could, covering the years 1869–1955.

This Appendix extends that presentation forward in time, covering the eight decades from 1930 (hence overlapping with Kuznets) to 2009. (At this writing the NIPA fixed-asset annual tables covered 1929 through 2009.)

Before presenting the data, it's worth explaining a bit about how the NIPA tables account for fixed assets.

The first thing to understand is the difference between fixed capital and financial capital (the stocks), and between savings and investment (the flows).

Financial capital is, roughly, financial assets—cash, money in bank accounts, stocks, bonds, etc. While storing your money in these things is popularly thought of as "investment," in the NIPAs this is called Saving. When you save money—no matter where you store it—you are increasing the stock of financial assets.

Investment, on the other hand, means spending money to produce—create—fixed capital: houses, factories, airports, amusement parks, machines, software, etc. (Purchases of fixed capital—equipment, for instance—at least to some extent spur its creation.) Fixed capital or fixed assets, as defined in NIPAs, consists of three things:

- Structures
- Equipment
- Software

These categories *exclude* huge categories that can reasonably be construed as being major parts of a country's assets, including:

- Knowledge, skills, ideas, and technical methodologies (developed through education, training, research, and development)
- Social capital: people's trust in each other, in businesses, and in government; their willingness to conform to the rule of law; their diligence, work ethic, and trustworthiness, etc.
- Natural resources
- Organizational capital: the whole body of business and government procedures, policies, management systems, and the ever-mysterious goodwill that constitute most of the value of many organizations—the things that make these organizations "going concerns."

Those things are all very difficult to measure (how much do people pay for trust?), which explains why fixed capital is measured based on the three fairly tangible—and purchasable—categories that are used in national accounts. While they don't present anything like a complete picture of a nation's actual capital, various measures of fixed capital are nevertheless crucial tools for judging a nation's economic condition and direction.

The NIPA tables also break out fixed capital in two other major ways:

- Private vs. government.
- Residential vs. nonresidential (almost all regarding structures, though there is a quite small category of residential equipment). Note that residential investment is money spent to build and remodel houses and apartments. Purchases of existing residences are essentially financial investments, or asset swaps, and have no direct effect on measures of fixed-investment flows.

So to speak about the U.S. business capital base (for instance) in NIPA terms, you would say "private domestic nonresidential fixed capital."

A final note: so-called domestic fixed assets are those located in the United States, with the exception of U.S. military installations, embassies, and consulates abroad, which are included in government domestic assets.

Stocks and Flows

The next key distinction is between flows and stocks. The stock of fixed assets is pretty self-explanatory. How much stuff do we have at any given time—buildings, machines, highways, etc.—and what's it worth?*

The key fixed-investment flows are (1) investment and (2) capital consumption. Investment in fixed assets—often referred to as "investment spending" to distinguish it from "consumption spending"—increases the national stock of fixed assets. Capital consumption (depreciation/obsolescence/wearing out) decreases the national stock.

---

* Note that this national stock of fixed assets is sometimes referred to as "national savings," even though it has nothing to do with the stock of financial assets. It's nevertheless a reasonable term, because unlike an individual, a nation builds or "saves" for the future by building its stock of productive assets—the stock that it will consume to create and provide future prosperity. We "spend" or "consume" that national savings to produce goods and services (business and government assets) and by living in it (residential structures).

Gross investment minus capital consumption equals net investment. In theory, net investment should equal the change in the capital stock, or "capital base":

$$\text{Year1Stock} + \text{NetInvestment} = \text{Year2Stock}.$$

But it doesn't, because of revaluation.

Businesses in particular are constantly replacing older capital stock with newer, better, more valuable and productive capital stock. (Imagine a computer-driven lathe replacing a manual one.) To account for this, the economists at the BEA reestimate the value of the existing capital stock each year. (In the course of things, they also adjust for general inflation.) The change due to net investment plus the change due to revaluation equals the total change.

The crucial fact is this: even with zero net investment (gross investment = capital consumption), the capital base can grow, and along with it the nation's productive capacity. If the consumed capital is just being replaced with better capital at the same or lower prices, both the capital stock and productive capacity increases. (Since the nation's population is growing, one would generally expect the capital base to increase at least at the same speed—probably faster, because new fixed stock is generally cheaper and/or better.)

Fixed capital stock and productive capacity can even increase when net investment is negative (gross investment < capital consumption). As Kuznets notes, this happened during the Great Depression, when business invested almost nothing, but because of technological improvements, the new equipment (in particular) they did invest in was vastly more valuable and productive.

In sum, in this Appendix we'll be looking at three different measures of fixed investment:

- Gross investment: total dollars spent on fixed assets, including replacement of consumed assets
- Net investment: investment spending above and beyond capital consumed

- Change in capital stock: the change resulting from both net investment and revaluation of the stock due to better stock being brought into service, and lesser stock being retired

Fixed Assets in America, 1930–2009

With those explanations as backdrop, what have been the major trends in fixed capital since the 1930s? We'll start with the investment flows, displayed as percentages of gross domestic product (GDP). If the economy were growing, one would expect fixed investment to grow as well. The question is, How is fixed investment changing relative to the economy? This method also obviates the need to correct for inflation (a somewhat contentious estimate, especially when trying to equate values over many decades through compounding or "chaining").

First, let's look at total national investment in fixed assets (Figure 1). In this graph and all the others, the Depression and war years, not surprisingly, display very large variations (the annual numbers often jump around quite wildly). While those variations can be illuminative, the Kuznetsian emphasis on long-term trends prompts us rather to look to the right side of the graphs, at the postwar years that are not skewed by such world-apocalyptic events—the six decades from the 1950s through the 2000s.

The most notable and consistent postwar trend is the decline in net investment, even while gross investment remained mostly flat with slight decline, and capital consumption increased slightly. Those two small trends compound to result in the quite large (35 percent) decline in net investment as a percent of GDP from the 1950s to the 2000s.

Government gross investment as a percent of GDP (not including defense) has declined or been flat since the 1950s; the decline is significantly more pronounced if you include government defense investment.

The change in defense investment as a percent of GDP has been an almost mirror image of business investment, declining 53 percent from the 1950s to the 1960s alone, and 80 percent from the 1950s to the 2000s. (Since it's so much smaller than business investment, the smaller absolute decline yielded a far more profound proportional decline.)

Also perhaps surprising given recent events in the residential real estate market, the share of gross residential investment has been mostly flat or declining since the 1960s, following a postwar surge in the 1950s.

FIGURE 1

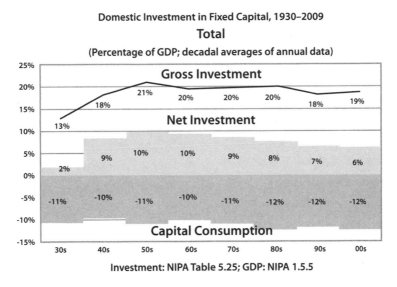

Domestic Investment in Fixed Capital, 1930–2009
Total
(Percentage of GDP; decadal averages of annual data)

Investment: NIPA Table 5.25; GDP: NIPA 1.5.5

FIGURE 2

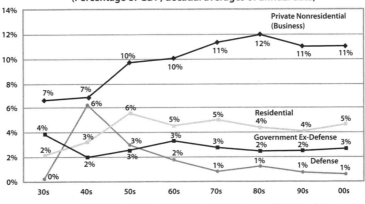

Domestic Investment in Fixed Capital, 1930–2009
Gross Investment by Sector
(Percentage of GDP; decadal averages of annual data)

Investment: NIPA Table 5.25; GDP: NIPA 1.5.5; Defense: BEA Fixed Assets 7.5

The trend for private-sector investment (residential and nonresidential, Figure 3) is similar though somewhat less pronounced than the trend in total investment: a decline in net investment, effected by both a decline in gross investment and a somewhat larger increase in capital consumption.

This brings us to the largest and arguably most important investment segment: private nonresidential, a.k.a. business investment (Figure 4). These assets are important because they're used to produce other assets and consumption goods. They are a crucial component of the national engine of production and prosperity.

FIGURE 3

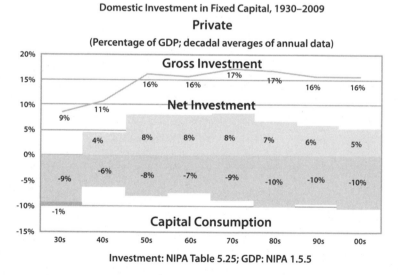

Domestic Investment in Fixed Capital, 1930–2009
Private
(Percentage of GDP; decadal averages of annual data)

Investment: NIPA Table 5.25; GDP: NIPA 1.5.5

Again we see a familiar trend, but more pronounced. Gross investment rises into the 1980s and dips slightly thereafter, but net investment, dragged down by faster capital consumption, declines significantly from the 1970s on. The net investment level in the 2000s is 40 percent below the 1970s.

It's useful here to break out gross investment in the two main components of business investment—structures and equipment/software—to see how those might have affected capital consumption in this sector

Figure 4

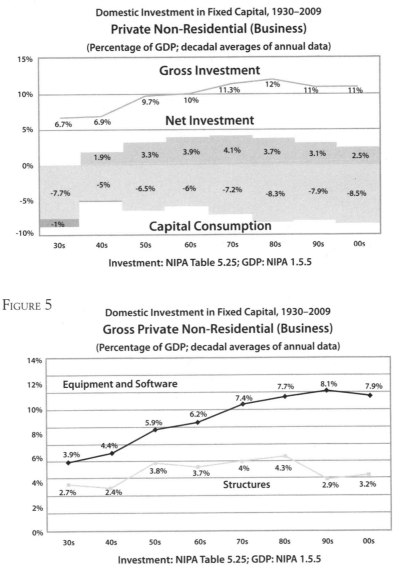

Domestic Investment in Fixed Capital, 1930–2009
Private Non-Residential (Business)
(Percentage of GDP; decadal averages of annual data)

Investment: NIPA Table 5.25; GDP: NIPA 1.5.5

Figure 5

Domestic Investment in Fixed Capital, 1930–2009
Gross Private Non-Residential (Business)
(Percentage of GDP; decadal averages of annual data)

Investment: NIPA Table 5.25; GDP: NIPA 1.5.5

(Figure 5). This graph is rather self-explanatory, and does much to explain the increase in capital consumption: equipment and software depreciate faster than structures, and an increasing share of business investment has gone into equipment and software (a 72 percent share in the 1990s/ 2000s, compared to 61 percent in the 1950s). This explains some, though not all, of the decline in net business investment.

FIGURE 6

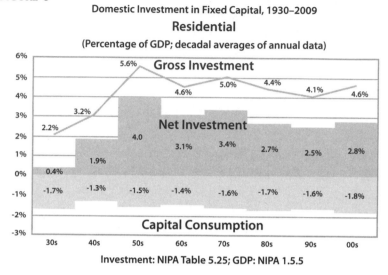

Domestic Investment in Fixed Capital, 1930–2009
Residential
(Percentage of GDP; decadal averages of annual data)

Investment: NIPA Table 5.25; GDP: NIPA 1.5.5

The residential component of private investment (Figure 6) again shows a familiar pattern: increasing capital consumption and decreasing gross investment yielding declining net investment. (The upturn in the 2000s, small as it may look here, represents a major absolute-dollar increase, and does much to explain ensuing events—especially given the amount of that investment that was generated by new credit issuance.) Note that capital consumption consistently represents a relatively small portion of gross investment compared to other sectors; this is because structures, as noted earlier, depreciate more slowly than equipment and software.

The trends in government investment are best understood by looking at three graphs, representing total government investment, government investment excluding national defense, and defense investment (Figures 7, 8, and 9).

As we saw in Figure 2, defense investment since the 1950s has constituted a moderate to (increasingly) miniscule portion of both government and total investment. But its proportional changes have been massive, so it's worth looking at first. Remember here that unlike the definition of so-called domestic assets for other sectors (only those assets located

Figure 7

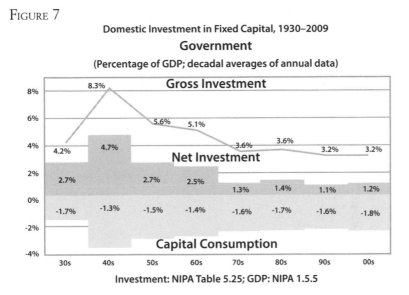

Domestic Investment in Fixed Capital, 1930–2009
Government
(Percentage of GDP; decadal averages of annual data)

Investment: NIPA Table 5.25; GDP: NIPA 1.5.5

Figure 8

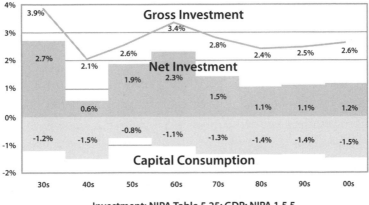

Domestic Investment in Fixed Capital, 1930–2009
Government Ex-Defense
(Percentage of GDP; decadal averages of annual data)

Investment: NIPA Table 5.25; GDP: NIPA 1.5.5

in the United States), government domestic investment/assets include U.S. military installations, embassies, and consulates abroad.

Not surprisingly, gross defense investment declined rapidly after World War II. But it continued to decline at about the same rate even into the 1970s. From the 1960s to the 1970s alone, it fell 54 percent.

FIGURE 9

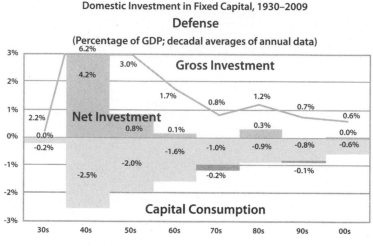

Domestic Investment in Fixed Capital, 1930–2009
Defense
(Percentage of GDP; decadal averages of annual data)

Government: NIPA Table 5.25; Defense gross (and calculated capital consumption):
BEA Fixed Asset Table 7.5; GDP: NIPA 1.5.5

Despite an uptick (quite large in absolute-dollar terms) in the 1980s, it has been largely flat since. Even with rapidly and steadily declining capital consumption, gross defense investment declined even faster, so net investment was actually negative in both the 1970s and the 1990s. Gross defense investment in the 2000s was only 1/200 of the American economy, and net investment was effectively zero.

As with business investment, it's useful to look deeper here—at structures versus equipment/software—in an attempt to discern what drove those declines (Figure 10). While the proportional declines for the two segments have been similar (an 81 percent drop from the 1950s to the 1970s for structures versus 72 percent for equipment and software), the absolute decline in structures has been far greater. This perhaps reflects the worldwide construction of military bases, embassies, and consulates in the 1950s and 1960s, which was largely complete by the 1970s.

The inclusion of the defense sector makes the decline in total government investment (both gross and net) look especially precipitous, but the net-investment trend since the 1960s for government ex-defense, after a pronounced rise from the 1950s to the 1960s (both gross: 28 per-

Figure 10

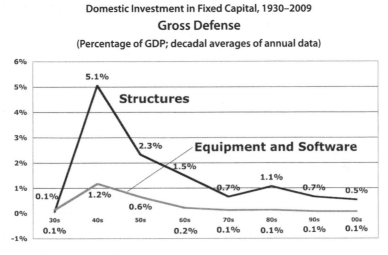

Domestic Investment in Fixed Capital, 1930–2009
Gross Defense
(Percentage of GDP; decadal averages of annual data)

Defense Investment: BEA Fixed Asset Table 7.5; GDP: NIPA 1.5.5

cent, and net: 23 percent), is similar to total government investment—a 53 percent decline in net from the 1960s to the 1980s, and generally flat thereafter. Increasing government ex-defense capital consumption (up 25 percent from the 1960s to the 1980s) was a significant contributor to that net-investment decline, but gross investment/GDP also fell by 28 percent over that two-decade period.

Turning to the stocks of fixed assets and the changes in those stocks, we will look at them in two ways: as a percentage of GDP, and in real (inflation-adjusted) dollars per capita, and per member of the workforce. GDP has grown much faster than population since 1930, and the workforce has grown faster than the population (largely as a result of women entering the workforce), so while the two methods tell somewhat similar stories, they tell it to different degrees.

In considering these graphs, remember that the changes in stock represent both the effects of net investment and the effect of newer, more valuable stock replacing older stock, and the resultant revaluation of the total capital stock. Since revaluation affects the total stock, the resultant changes are often much larger and more volatile than what we've seen from net investment.

The stock of fixed assets relative to GDP (Figure 11) has been pretty flat since the 1940s, meaning that the stock (the numerator) and production (the denominator) have grown at essentially the same pace. Both have grown much faster than the population and the workforce, however—since the 1950s/1960s, by a factor or 2.5 for the workforce, and 4.1 for the population.

The proportion of fixed assets in the major sectors (Figure 12) has also remained fairly constant since the 1940s, with the exception of defense. That sector's steady decline has been matched by increases in the other three sectors.

As a result of annual revaluation/reestimation of the value of fixed assets, changes in the stock of fixed assets (Figure 13) have been highly volatile over the decades (annual changes are even more wildly volatile, ranging up to 60 percent in some years and sectors). This volatility—especially given its basis in estimated valuations of fixed capital and its sensitivity to overall inflation levels—makes it difficult to discern any persuasive long-term trends from changes in stock.

Finally, it's worth combining flows and stocks to look at the constituents of the changes in stock (Figure 14). Net investment has contributed a notably smaller share of the changes since the 1960s, while revaluation has accounted for significantly more. The most notable

FIGURE 11

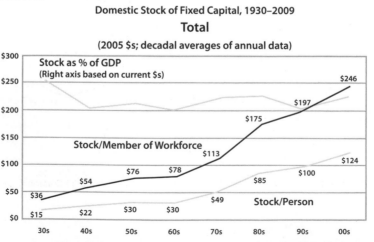

Domestic Stock of Fixed Capital, 1930–2009
Total
(2005 $s; decadal averages of annual data)

Stock: BEA Fixed Tables 2.1 and 2.2; Population: U.S. Census;
Workforce 2011 Economic Report of the President, Table B-35 Column C.

FIGURE 12

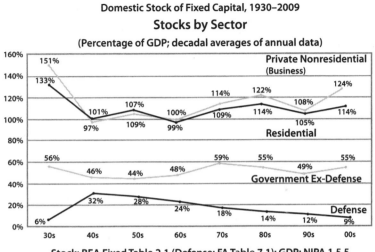

Domestic Stock of Fixed Capital, 1930–2009
Stocks by Sector
(Percentage of GDP; decadal averages of annual data)

Stock: BEA Fixed Table 2.1 (Defense: FA Table 7.1); GDP: NIPA 1.5.5

FIGURE 13

Change in Domestic Stock of Fixed Capital, 1930–2009
Total Stock
(Real stock based on 2005 $s; decadal averages of annual data)

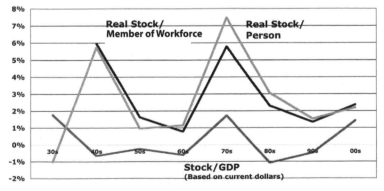

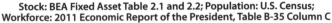

Stock: BEA Fixed Asset Table 2.1 and 2.2; Population: U.S. Census;
Workforce: 2011 Economic Report of the President, Table B-35 Column C

FIGURE 14

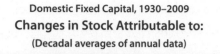

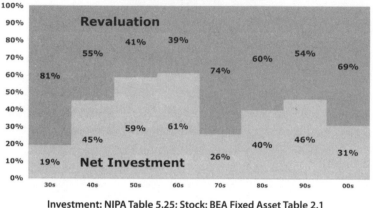

Investment: NIPA Table 5.25; Stock: BEA Fixed Asset Table 2.1

pattern is perhaps demonstrated by the 1930s, 1970s, and 2000s: troubled economic times (depression, stagflation, recession) are associated with notable lows in the net-investment share of the change in stock.

Overall, the significant postwar trends in fixed capital in the American economy are these:

- More rapid capital consumption in total, and in all sectors except defense
- Flat to declining gross investment in total, and in every sector except business, which showed a moderate increase
- As a result of the preceding two trends, a decline in net investment—total, and in every sector
- An increasing share of business and government investment devoted to equipment and software
- A relative increase in private (especially business) investment and an accompanying (quite large) decline in government investment, especially in the small and rapidly decreasing component of defense investment

- An increasing share for revaluation (based on higher value of new assets) in the changes to capital stock, relative to contributions from net investment

The Excel spreadsheet from which the figures in this appendix were generated, which includes links to the source data, is available for download at asymptosis.com

Acknowledgments

My principal debt is to my agent, Lisa Adams, who plucked me from online obscurity in October 2008 and has since become my best advocate and kindest critic. I wouldn't have written this book without her constant encouragement, fierce intelligence, and inexhaustible energy.

Many colleagues and friends have read chapters or argued with me in person on the issues I address here. At the Cullman Center for Scholars and Writers of the New York Public Library, where I wrote most of the book in 2010, Ian Frazier, Joseph O'Neill, Francois Furstenberg, John Tresch, Karen Russell, Andy Martin, and Michael Golston questioned my premises but urged me to make the argument anyway. Jean Strouse, the director of the Center, was equally encouraging, even though I arrived, thanks to Lisa Adams, with a project that departed from my original proposal. Meanwhile David Offenbach, the CEO of the Library as such, took a financial interest in the project because it intersects with his long experience in banking: he won the bets we made on the business cycle as it developed in 2010. But I'll be collecting soon on some collateral wagers.

Over the last year and a half, I have asked many people to comment on drafts of chapters. My good friends Bruce Robbins and Mike Fennell have always responded unselfishly and insightfully. So has Laura Kipnis, the real writer in our midst. I hope readers notice that I stole the book's title from her.

Meanwhile, other friends and colleagues have tried to improve the prose and the argument even while keeping their strong disagreements with me: thanks to Rachel Bowlby, Jackson Lears, Victoria de Grazia, George Prochnik, Wolfgang Schievelbusch, Benjamin Kunkel, Al-Zamar McKinney, Leonard Kipnis, Louis Ferleger, Mary Poovey, Richard Powers, Peter Maass, Martijn Konings, Christopher Fisher, James Levy, Patricia O'Toole, Rosanne Currarino, Jonathan Quann, Rick Rosenthal, Val Monroe, and David Levering Lewis.

Tim Sullivan signed the book at Perseus/Basic in January 2010, having led me through searching conversations about my purpose in writing it; he left soon after for Harvard Business Press. Lara Heimert then steered the project until Tim Bartlett came on board and took charge. His editorial direction has been invaluable: this book is a huge improvement on earlier incarnations because he just wouldn't stop demanding that I make it better. Adina Berk, Tim's assistant, and Kay Mariea, the Director of Editorial Services at Perseus, have made the strange demands of this long process a real pleasure.

When I was close to finishing, I asked Steve Roth to help me produce an Appendix that would graphically depict the trends in investment that are central to my arguments. Thanks to him, all the numbers you need are at the back of the book.

My unfortunate habit has been to dedicate books to people who are already gone or will soon disappear from my life. As my last remaining blood relative, my brother should be next on the list of people who don't outlast the print run. But I'm going to spare him this potentially lethal designation and name two people who brought me back to life in 2009. I know they'll survive.

They are Elise Salem and Laura Kipnis. They have never agreed with me—they never will—but they occasionally think my ideas have argumentative promise. Each in her own way, they have taught me how to believe in myself, as a writer and a human being. Elise did that by encouraging me to keep talking, keep writing, to see where the words took me. Laura did it by encouraging me to keep revising my self as well as my prose, to live by the law of dreams: keep moving, keep changing, or die.

This book is for both of them, for then and for always.

Bibliography

Introduction

The Freud I rely on is the author of *Three Essays on the Theory of Sexuality* (1912–1925) and *Group Psychology and the Analysis of the Ego* (1923). I rely even more on four of his most provocative, productive interpreters, each of whom revised and enlarged the master's notions of repression and sublimation: Geza Roheim, *The Origin and Function of Culture* (1944); Herbert Marcuse, *Eros and Civilization* (1955); Norman O. Brown, *Life Against Death* (1959); and Judith Butler, *Gender Trouble* (1990).

On commodity fetishism, values, money, and the "formula for capital," the place to start is Karl Marx, *Capital*, 3 vols., trans. Samuel Moore and Edward Aveling, vol. 1. On those honorable exceptions to the *Economist*'s rule, see Chapter 2 in the Bibliography, below. Keynes is quoted, not for the last time, from "The Dilemma of Modern Socialism," in the *New Republic*, April 14, 1932, and "Economic Possibilities for Our Grandchildren" (1930), reprinted in *Essays in Persuasion* (1963).

The phrase "paradigm shift" is of course taken from Thomas Kuhn's seminal work, *The Structure of Scientific Revolutions* (1962). See otherwise John Cassidy, *How Markets Fail* (2009) and the *New Yorker*, January 11, 2010.

Chapter 1

The antimonopoly tradition that culminated in the Populist Revolt of the 1890s was—and still is—deeply embedded in American culture and politics. One measure of its persistence and ubiquity is our almost uniform loathing of "big business" and the faceless bureaucracies it sponsors (whose analogue is of course "big government," another threat to the small entrepreneur, that self-made man who works for nobody but himself). The best books on Populism are historiographical antiques; they differ radically in their assessments of its democratic possibilities. See Richard Hofstadter, *The Age of Reform: From Bryan to FDR* (1955); Lawrence Goodwyn, *Democratic Promise* (1975); Bruce Palmer, *"Man Over Money": The Southern Populist Critique of American Capitalism* (1980); and Steven Hahn, *The Roots of Southern Populism* (1984). More recent scholarship amplifies the anticorporate, antimonopoly sensibility Goodwyn, Palmer, and Hahn rehabilitated: see Gretchen Ritter, *Goldbugs and Greenbacks: The Antimonopoly Tradition and the Politics of Finance in America* (1997) and Elizabeth Sanders, *Roots of Reform: Farmers, Workers, and the American State, 1877–1917* (1999). For a thorough sampling of Populist rhetoric, see Norman O. Pollack, ed., *The Populist Mind* (1967), where you can find the Omaha Platform of 1892. On the politics of antitrust jurisprudence and the Supreme Court's pro-Populist, antimonopoly majority of 1897–1911, see Martin J. Sklar, *The Corporate Reconstruction of American Capitalism* (1988).

Chapter 2

The history of the theory—or rather theories—of crisis is laid out in my *Origins of the Federal Reserve System* (1986), where the economists I mention are cited and discussed. The contemporary economists who measured the housing bubble and predicted the crash are, without exception, skeptical of self-regulating markets and "rational expectations," which, generally speaking, places them on the Left of the political spectrum, where criticism of capitalism is still commonplace. See Dean Baker, *Plunder and Blunder* (2009); Paul Krugman, *The Return of Depression Economics* (2009); Robert Shiller, *Irrational Exuberance* (2004, 2009); and Nouriel Roubini, *Crisis Economics* (2010).

Richard Posner's intellectual odyssey is announced in *A Failure of Capitalism* (2009), a very good introduction to the short-term economic history of the Great Recession. See otherwise Justin Fox, *The Myth of the Rational Market* (2009) and John Lanchester, *IOU: Why Everybody Owes Everybody and No One Can Pay* (2010). On irrational exuberance as a normal, market-driven phenomenon, see Shiller, Posner, and James Surowiecki, *The Wisdom of Crowds* (2006). On "rational expectations" and the algorithms generated by the Black-Scholes-Merton school of market analysis, both of which are ultimately indebted to Irving Fisher, the early twentieth-century Yale economist who mathematized his discipline, see Fox, *Rational Market*, Cassidy, *How Markets Fail*, and the forthcoming book by Kevin Brine and Mary Poovey, *From Facts to Explanations*, which will, I believe, revolutionize our understanding of economic theory and corporate capitalism.

The antimonopoly argument against "too big to fail" has been made most forcefully and eloquently by Matt Taibbi in *Rolling Stone* and Simon Johnson in the *Atlantic*. William Greider and Thomas Geoghegan have also made compelling contributions to the same argument in *The Nation* and *Harper's*, respectively. Annie Leonard's brilliant polemic against consumer culture is *The Story of Stuff* (2010). Arthur T. Hadley and Irving Kristol worried about the same thing in *Economics* (1896) and *Two Cheers for Capitalism* (1978). The monetarist consensus on the Great Depression, which ultimately derives from Milton Friedman and Anna Jacobson Schwartz, *A Monetary History of the United States, 1867–1960* (1963), was stated most baldly by Niall Ferguson in *Time* magazine, October 2, 2008. The more subtle variations on the theme I cite in the text are Ben Bernanke, *Essays on the Great Depression* (2000); Christina Romer, "The Great Depression," in *Encyclopedia Britannica*, entry dated December 20, 2003; and Paul Krugman in the *New York Times*, May 2, 2011. The figures on bank transactions come from Table 47 of the *75th Annual Report of the Comptroller of the Currency* (1938) covering the period 1933–1937. The best book on the big event remains Michael Bernstein, *The Great Depression* (1988)—not Bernanke, and not Friedman. The two recent bipartisan congressional documents that bear out accusations of fraud, chicanery, and idiocy in explaining the crisis are *The Financial Crisis Inquiry Report*, released January 27, 2011, and U.S. Senate, Permanent Subcommittee on Investigations, "Wall Street and the Financial Crisis: Anatomy of a Financial Collapse," April 13, 2011.

November 2009 was the moment when everyone agreed that consumer debt was the real problem facing the nation. That was when George Will's opinions on the matter were aired in his regular column for *Newsweek*, when David Brook concurred in his column for the *New York Times*, Tony Blankly started worrying in the *Washington Times*, David Leonhardt did as well in his Economic Scene columns at the *New York Times*, and Joseph Stiglitz said pretty much the same thing in an interview with National Public Radio. William Galston's findings were published at the same moment in the *American Prospect*. The other "frugalistas" I mention—talk about a bandwagon effect—are Lauren Weber, *In Cheap We Trust* (2009); Laura Miller, the cultural critic and frequent contributor to the *New York Times Book Review*, not the sociologist at Brandeis; Curtis White, *The Barbarian Heart* (2009); and Robert Samuelson in the *Wilson Quarterly* (Winter 2011).

I worry about the accusatory tone and implications of Michael Lewis's brilliant book *The Big Short* (2010), but it is by far the best single treatment of the topics related to the financial crisis. Jeff Madrick's review of it in the *New York Review of Books* (June 10, 2011) amplifies this tone and emphasizes these implications. See also Madrick's angry, funny, and indispensable new book *Age of Greed* (2011).

On Marx, Keynes, and so forth, my sources are *n + 1*, where Benjamin Kunkel is the most forceful advocate of Marxism; Robert Brenner, *The Boom and the Bubble* (2005); David Harvey, *The Enigma of Capital* (2010); and Giovanni Arrighi, *The Long Twentieth Century* (1994). I discuss the Harrod-Domar model in *Pragmatism and the Political Economy of Cultural Revolution* (1994).

Keynes's two-volume *Treatise on Money* (1930) is, to my mind, the real turning point in twentieth-century economic theory. G. L. S. Shackle almost agrees in *The Years of High Theory* (1967), but this book is required reading for anyone interested in the relevance of Keynes. See otherwise J. M. Keynes, *The General Theory of Employment, Interest, and Money* (1936) and Jacques Derrida, *Specters of Marx* (1994).

Chapter 3

The sources here are either cited in the text or can be found in two published versions of my argument: *Challenge* 52 (May–June 2009) and *Pragmatism and the Political Economy of Cultural Revolution, 1850–1940* (1994). See also the Appendix.

Chapter 4

Keynes again quoted from "Economic Possibilities for Our Grand-children." See otherwise the House Budget Committee Report, "The Path to Prosperity," April 5, 2011; and Henry James, *The American Scene* (1907).

The data on transfer payments are drawn from and cited in James Livingston, *The World Turned Inside Out: American Thought and Culture at the End of the 20th Century* (2009). *New York Times* columnists David Leonhardt and David Brooks responded to the House Budget Commit-tee Report of April 5, 2011, with essays on the moral conundrum of Medicare. Leonhardt cited a new study of the huge difference between payments and benefits on April 6; Brooks consulted his moral calendar on April 8 and pronounced this difference "immoral."

On political obligation and the difficulties of transposing consent from the key of politics to the key of society, see Carole Pateman, *The Problem of Political Obligation* (1979); Harry Jaffa, *Crisis of the House Divided* (1959); and Jane Addams, *Democracy and Social Ethics* (1902).

Chapter 5

In trying to rehabilitate Sam Gompers, my fundamental debt is to Rosanne Currarino, *The Labor Question in America* (2010). See also William B. Dick, *Labor and Socialism in America: The Gompers Era* (1972) and Stuart B. Kaufman, *Samuel Gompers and the Origins of the AFL* (1975).

The public figures I cite in the text are, of course, exemplary, but you might well ask, Of what? They crowd my narrative because they were founding fathers (and mothers) of both academic disciplines and new ways of seeing the world—disciplines and ways of seeing that are only now, in the early twenty-first century, beginning to break up. The texts I cite are Walter Lippmann, *Drift and Mastery* (1914); Thorstein Veblen, *The Theory of the Leisure Class* (1899); Pierre Bourdieu, *Distinc-tion* (1984); Wesley Mitchell, *The Backward Art of Spending Money* (1937); Charlotte Perkins Gilman, *Women and Economics* (1899); Van

Wyck Brooks, *America's Coming of Age* (1918); Walter Weyl, *The New Democracy* (1912); and William James, "The Moral Equivalent of War" (1910), in Henry James Jr., ed., *Memories and Studies* (1911).

On the Frankfurt School and its notion of "reification," see, to begin with, Georg Lukacs, "Reification and the Consciousness of the Proletariat," an essay of 1923 reprinted in *History and Class Consciousness* (1971), and then trace its echoes through the late twentieth century, which finally converge in a resounding denunciation of mass culture, a.k.a. consumer culture, in the 1960s and 1970s, the very moment of its triumph. See also Paul Gorman, *Left Intellectuals and Popular Culture in 20th-Century America* (1994).

On the 1920s and the Harlem Renaissance, the indispensable books are David Levering Lewis, *When Harlem Was in Vogue* (1981); Harold Cruse, *The Crisis of the Negro Intellectual* (1967); Houston A. Baker Jr., *Modernism and the Harlem Renaissance* (1987); George Hutchinson, *The Harlem Renaissance in Black and White* (1995); and Ann Douglas, *Terrible Honesty* (1993).

The "black aesthetic" I invoke here is a term derived from Cruse, who used it to define a culture that was the relation of the changing positions momentarily marked by the color line. The "Negro group in America," he insisted, was a weird mixture of African, European, and indigenous origins from its very beginnings in the seventeenth century, so the black aesthetic always tended toward a rethinking and renegotiation of that color line, typically by including and remixing all of the available components.

All quoted passages from Du Bois are from David Levering Lewis, ed., *W. E. B. Du Bois: A Reader* (1995) and W. E. B. Du Bois, *Dusk of Dawn: An Essay Toward an Autobiography of a Race Concept* (1940). The epochal significance of Du Bois's *Black Reconstruction* (1935) was finally validated in Eric Foner's *Reconstruction*, the prize-winning book of 1988, but the origin itself still repays study, in part because it enlarges on claims made as early as 1903, in Du Bois's *The Souls of Black Folk*.

On Antonio Gramsci and the "war of position," see my *Pragmatism, Feminism, and Democracy* (2001).

Chapter 6

The spokesmen of Black Power are Stokely Carmichael and Charles Hamilton, in *Black Power* (1967). A reading of the civil rights era that differs radically from mine—which suggests that the movement was co-opted if not entirely emptied of liberatory content by consumer culture—is Robert Weems, *Desegregating the Dollar* (2003); along very similar lines, see also James C. Davis, *Commerce in Color* (2007).

Harold Cruse borrowed from C. Wright Mills in using the notion of "cultural apparatus" to specify what was new about late twentieth-century political and intellectual possibilities. Daniel Bell and Mills—colleagues at Columbia—were meanwhile in constant debate about the role of culture in a capitalist society. All three were trying to preserve what they understood to be still useful in Marxism without submitting their claims to the dubious representatives of the received wisdom. See Cruse, *Crisis*, as cited above; Mills, *The Sociological Imagination* (1959); and Bell, *The Coming of Post-Industrial Society* (1973). On the democratic possibilities residing in the "invisible republic" of music conveyed across regional lines by radio and recording technologies, there is no better historian than Greil Marcus: see his *Invisible Republic: Bob Dylan's Basement Tapes* (1993).

Christopher Small's book *Music of the Common Tongue: Survival and Celebration in African American Music* (1987) should be read in conjunction with his brilliant introduction to the politics of Western music, *Music, Society, Education* (1971). On the blues idiom and its ambiguous colors, Albert Murray is still our best guide: see his *Stomping the Blues* (1976) and *The Hero and the Blues* (1982) to begin with, then Charles Keil, *Urban Blues* (1966); Francis Davis, *The History of the Blues* (1995); and Leroi Jones [Amiri Baraka], *Blues People* (1963).

On Russia, Eastern Europe, and the Velvet Revolution, I have relied on Timothy Garton Ash's reporting in the *New York Review of Books*, then *The Polish Revolution* (1982), and finally *The Magic Lantern* (1994), but also Bernard Wheaton and Zdenek Kavan, *The Velvet Revolution* (1992). I have also followed the intellectual evolution of market socialism for three decades now, starting with Radoslav Selucky, *Economic Reforms in*

Eastern Europe (1972) and *Marxism, Socialism, Freedom* (1978); Wlodzimierz Brus, *Economics and Politics of Socialism* (1961, 1978); and Istvan Friss, ed., *Reform of the Economic Mechanism in Hungary* (1969). The larger background is framed by Stephen Kotkin, *Armageddon Averted: The Soviet Collapse, 1970–2000* (2008) and Bell, *Post-Industrial Society* (1973), in which the author treats the intellectual innovations of the early 1960s in Czechoslovakia as incentives to rethink the possibilities of capitalism in the United States. I am quoting Vaclav Havel from Paul Wilson, ed., *Open Letters: Selected Writings, 1965–1990* (1992); note that the editor was one of the original Plastic People of the Universe.

Chapter 7

To begin with, see Neil Borden, *The Economics of Advertising* (1942). On *amour propre*, the source is Jean-Jacques Rousseau, *Discourse on the Origin and Basis of Inequality Among Men* (1755).

The cultural-intellectual revolution of the early twentieth century is traced in Donald Lowe, *History of Bourgeois Perception* (1982); Stephen Kern, *The Culture of Time and Space* (1984); John Berger, *The Success and Failure of Picasso* (1965); and Bram Dijkstra, *The Hieroglyphics of a New Speech* (1969).

On advertising and marketing as such, see T. J. Jackson Lears, *Fables of Abundance* (1994), the working title of which was "The Wand of Increase"; Rachel Bowlby, *Shopping with Freud* (1993); Thomas Frank, *The Conquest of Cool* (1996); Stuart Ewen, *Captains of Consciousness* (1976) and *All-Consuming Images* (1999); Virginia Postrel, *The Substance of Style* (2003); David Potter, *People of Plenty* (1954); Juliet Mitchell, *Woman's Estate* (1968); Daniel Bell, *The Cultural Contradictions of Capitalism* (1996); Roland Barthes, *Mythologies* (1967); and James B. Twitchell, *Adcult USA* (1976).

I quote Rob Walker from *Buying In* (2008), which to my mind is the best available book on consumer culture, although Rachel Bowlby's *Just Looking* (1985) still shapes every idea I've ever had about consumption, gender, and power. Quotations, exclamations, attitudes, and exhortations otherwise taken from Juliet Schor, *Born to Buy* (2004); Benjamin Barber, *Consumed* (2009); Kalle Lasn, *Culture Jam* (2000); Matt Mason, *The Pi-*

rate's Dilemma (2008); *Adbusters*, to which I am now a paying subscriber; and Judith Butler, *Gender Trouble* (1990).

Chapter 8

On the historiographical currents I measure here, see my *Origins of the Federal Reserve System* (1986) and *Pragmatism, Feminism, and Democracy* (2001). On Stuart Chase, the Brookings Institution, Lewis Mumford, Archibald MacLeish, and the survival of Simon Patten's idiom in the 1930s, see my *Pragmatism and the Political Economy of Cultural Revolution* (1994).

Otherwise my texts, in order, are David Potter, *People of Plenty* (1954); David Riesman, *The Lonely Crowd* (1950); Paul Goodman, *Communitas* (1947); Susan Sontag, *Against Interpretation* (1965) and *Under the Sign of Saturn* (1980); Max Horkheimer et al., *The Authoritarian Personality* (1950); Max Horkheimer, *Eclipse of Reason* (1947); Max Horkheimer and Theodor Adorno, *The Dialectic of Enlightenment* (1944); Matthew Crawford, *Shop Class as Soulcraft* (2009); N. O. Brown, *Life Against Death* (1958); Herbert Marcuse, *Eros and Civilization* (1955); Vance Packard, *The Hidden Persuaders* (1957); Herbert Marcuse, *One-Dimensional Man* (1964); *Mad Men*, the AMC TV series; and Walt Whitman, "Song for Occupations," from *Leaves of Grass* (1855).

Chapter 9

Read it and weep: Matthew B. Crawford, *Shop Class as Soulcraft: An Inquiry into the Value of Work* (2009).

My guides to the world of food, fat, nutrition, and nature are Eric Schlosser, *Fast Food Nation* (2001); Marion Nestle, *Food Politics* (2002); Warren J. Belasco, *Appetite for Change*, 2nd ed. (2007); David Kamp, *The United States of Arugula* (2007); Robert Paarlberg, *Food Politics* (2010); Raj Patel, *Stuffed and Starved* (2007); Michael Pollan, *In Defense of Food* (2008); Paul Campos, *The Obesity Myth* (2004); Suzie Orbach, *Fat Is a Feminist Issue* (1978); and Richard Klein, *Eat Fat* (1998).

The Keynes I cite here from the *New Republic*, April 14, 1932, is not the economist of the textbooks, with the exception of the theorist who appears in Lawrence R. Klein's youthful manifesto *The Keynesian Revolution* (1947).

Coda

On the Paris scene of the 1930s, see my *Pragmatism, Feminism, and Democracy* and John Heckman's Introduction to Jean Hippolyte, *Genesis and Structure of Hegel's Phenomenology of Spirit* (1974). See otherwise Georges Bataille, *Visions of Excess: Essays* (1985) and *The Accursed Share* (1962) and Jacques Derrida, *The Gift of Death* (1995).

Index